The
Most Praised Man
In The World

M. Mushfiqur Rahman

Copyright © 2025 by M. Mushfiqur Rahman

All rights reserved. No part of this publication may be reproduced, stored in a retrieval system, or transmitted in any form, or by any means, electronic, mechanical, photocopying, recording or otherwise, without the prior permission of the copyright owner.

First Edition: January, 2025 (Rajab, 1446 AH)

ISBN: 978-1-943108-15-2 (paperback)
ISBN: 978-1-943108-16-9 (hard cover)

Published by:

FITRAH PRESS
www.fitrahpress.com
info@fitrahpress.com

بِسْمِ اللَّهِ الرَّحْمَٰنِ الرَّحِيمِ

وَإِنَّكَ لَعَلَىٰ خُلُقٍ عَظِيمٍ

"And thou (standest) on an exalted standard of character." (Q. 68:4)

The Greatest

"the man who, of all men, has exercised the greatest influence upon the human race" – *John William Draper, 1861*

"Perhaps the greatest leader of all times" – *Jules Masserman, 1974*

"the most influential political leader of all time." – *Michael Hart, 1978*

"the best example that can be given of the influence of the Individual in human history." – *Winwood Reade, 1872*

"the only man in history who was supremely successful on both the religious and secular levels." – *Michael H. Hart, 1978*

"an ultra great man. The difference ... between other great men and himself was wide." – *Arthur Glyn Leonard, 1909*

"who would dare to compare humanly the greatest men of modern times to Mahomet?" – *Alphonse de Lamartine, 1854*

"the greatest of all Reformers" – *R. Bosworth Smith, 1874*

"the most influential single figure in human history." – *Michael Hart, 1978*

"he is, without doubt, one of the greatest heroes the world has ever seen." – *Thomas Patrick Hughes, 1877*

"A man not only great, but one of the greatest i.e. truest men that Humanity has ever produced." – *Arthur Glyn Leonard, 1909*

"he seems to me to stand alone, above and beyond them all [other great men]." – *R. Bosworth Smith, 1874* "if ever man devoted his life to God's service with a good and a great motive, it is certain that the Prophet of Arabia was that man." – *A. Leonard, 1909*

"one of the rarest and most transcendent geniuses the world itself ever produced." – *John Davenport, 1869*

"His whole life is one long argument for his loyalty to truth."
– *Stanley Lane-Poole, 1883*

"Unlimited was his benevolence and generosity, and so was his anxious care for the welfare of the community." – *Gustav Weil, 1866*

"So beautiful was the teaching that fell from his lips and so inspiring was his example." – *Annie Besant, 1932*

The Unique

"those who saw him were suddenly filled with reverence, those who came near him loved him, they who described him would say, 'I have never seen his like either before or after.'" – *Emanuel Deutsch, 1869*

"certainly there has never been seen on earth another man like Muhammad"
– *Rev. David Benjamin Keldani, 1904*

"no man was ever more thoroughly filled with the sense of his mission or carried out that mission more heroically." – *Stanley Lane-Poole, 1883*

"no other man has founded a [more] strong and enduring monotheistic religion." – *Marcus Dods, 1887*

"No man ever served humanity as this man did."
– *Marmaduke Pickthall, 1917*

"No man was ever more emphatically a reformer in the history of his own age and country." – *Edward Freeman, 1856*

"In the religious history of the world there is no person who has done so much to elevate the position of the fair sex as Muhammad." – *S. Leeder, 1917* "no individual figure in the history of the East is so impressive as that of Mohammed." – *Alfred von Kremer, 1873*

"No other religious leader has ever bound his creed so closely to definite political conceptions." – *Gladys M. Draycott, 1916*

"no Founder of a religion has been left on so solitary an eminence as the Muslim Apostle." – *David Geroge Hogarth, 1921*

"No other man in the whole history of the world, however mighty his enthusiasm for a cause, has served that cause so single-heartedly as did Muhammad."
– *Marmaduke Pickthall, 1920*

"Nowhere in the history of the world can we directly trace such mighty effects to the personal agency of a single mortal." – *Edward Freeman, 1856*

"Never, in fine, did man accomplish in less of time so immense and so durable a revolution in the world." – *Alphonse de Lamartine, 1854*

"A more devout man than Mohammed never lived." – *Arthur Leonard, 1909*

"Indeed there never stepped upon this earth a kinder man, nor one more sensible." – *Marmaduke Pickthall, 1917*

"He is the only conqueror and ruler in all history of whom it can be truly said that he never wronged a fellow creature in the least respect."
– *Marmaduke Pickthall, 1920*

"Never did man propose to himself voluntarily or otherwise, an end more sublime, since this end was superhuman." – *Alphonse de Lamartine, 1854*

"No emperor with his tiaras was obeyed as this man [was]" – *Carlyle, 1840*

"no man in this world has ever been more truly loved;" – *M. Pickthall, 1918*

"he never took in hand any work without bringing it to a close." – *Muir, 1861*

"we do not read of any sordid or mean incidents in his life, nor can any acts of injustice be laid to his charge." – *Lord Headley, 1914*

TRANSLITERATION TABLE

Consonants. Arabic
Initial: unexpressed medial and final:

ء	ʾ	د	d	ض	ḍ	ك	k
ب	b	ذ	dh	ط	ṭ	ل	l
ت	t	ر	r	ظ	ẓ	م	m
ث	th	ز	z	ع	ʿ	ن	n
ج	j	س	s	غ	gh	ه	h
ح	ḥ	ش	sh	ف	f	و	v
خ	kh	ص	ṣ	ق	q	ي	y

Vowels, diphthongs, etc.

short: a   ـِ   i   ـُ
long: ā   ي   ī   و
diphthongs: ـَوْ aw
            ـَيْ ay, ai

Contents

Historical Introduction

The Most Praised Man 17
Historical Europe Toward the Prophet of Islam 22
    Propaganda 22
    Post-Enlightenment Writers 28
His Life Recorded in Minute Details 34

Physical Attributes and Habits

Frame and Appearance 44
Living Quarters 46
Food 47
Meal Habits 48
Dress 49
Putting on New Clothes 50
Handshake 51
Conversation (Giving Full Attention) 51
Walking 52
Sleeping 52
Waking up 53
Laugh and Smile 53
Fun and Jest 54
Weeping 54
Speech 55
    Clarity 55
    Candid 55
    No Unnecessary Words 55
    No Coarse Language 57
    Deliberate and with Emphasis 57
    Listened To 57
Neatness in Appearance 57
Cleanliness 58
Routine and Discipline 60
Time Management 60

His Character

- Youth and Early Life (Purity Of) 62
- Accessible to All 64
- Affectionate 65
- Altruistic 67
- Ambition (Free Of) 67
- Animals (Kindness To) 68
- Arbitrator 71
- Ascetic (Detachment from Worldly Luxuries) 71
- Aura of Respect and Admiration 72
- Authority as Sacred Trust 73
- Balance and Moderation 73
- Beauty of Personality 74
- Benevolence 74
- Brotherhood (Universal) 75
- Business Ethics 76
- Calm 78
- Candor 78
- Charisma 79
- Charming 80
- Charity 80
  - Encouragement for 80
  - Charity Redefined 81
  - Gave Away All That He Owned 82
- Children (Love Of) 83
- Chores (Performed His Own Tasks) 85
- Commerce 87
  - Justice in Transactions 87
  - Monopoly and Hoarding 87
- Composure/Self-control 88
- Conscience (Freedom Of) 88
- Contentment 88
- Congruence between Interior & Exterior Character 89
- Consideration for Mankind 90
- Consistent Throughout 90

Contents

- Courage 91
- Courteous 91
- Covetousness (Free Of) 91
- Devout 92
- Dignified 92
- Down to Earth 93
- Education (Encouragement For) 93
- Eloquence 93
- Endurance 95
- Equal Treatment of People 95
- Esteemed (Even by Those Who Knew Him Intimately) 95
- Ethical Norms (Attainable) 96
- Evil (Erasing with Good) 97
- Exemplary 97
- Father 98
- Forced Conversion (Never) 98
- Foremost in Good Deeds 98
- Forgiveness 99
    - Personal Injuries 99
    - General Amnesty for His Persecutors 99
- Friendliness 102
- Friendship 103
- Frugality 104
- Funeral 104
- Generosity 105
- Genuine 106
- Gentleness 107
    - Affable with Everyone 107
    - Manners with the Young 107
- Gift (Acceptance of) 107
- God 108
    - Restored the True Concept Of 108
    - No Clergy between Man and God 109
    - Man's Relationship to God 110
    - The Ultimate Objective of All Actions 110
    - Reliance On 111

    Resignation to God's Will 112
    God-Consciousness 112
    Gratitude To 113
    Humility To 113
    Dedicated His Life For 114
Good Deeds 115
Greeting 115
Great in Prosperity as in Adversity 115
Head of State 116
Honest 116
Honoring the Status of All People 116
Hospitality 117
Humanizing 117
Humility 118
Husband 120
Impeccable Character 120
Indecency (Free Of) 121
Inspiring 122
Inspired by Him 123
    Goethe 123
    Victor Hugo 124
    Napoleon Bonaparte 124
Intellectual Capacity 127
Integrity 127
Invitations (Never Declined) 127
Judge 128
Justice 128
    Equal Application of the Law 128
    Justice by Example 129
    Balanced Justice with Mercy 129
    Balanced Justice with Humanity 130
Kind 130
Knowledge (Encouragement For) 131
Legislator 132
    Inheritance Laws 132
    Usury 133

Contents

- Gambling 134
- Alcoholic Drinks 135
- Divination (Fortune Telling) 136
- Murder 136
- Infanticide 137
- Polygamy 138
- Slavery 138
- Alleviation of Poverty 139
- Charity as Civic Duty 140
- Comprehensive Legislation 140

Leadership 141
- Trusted Leadership 141
- Clear and Decisive Judgment 141
- Led Men to the Truth 141
- Commanding Presence 142
- Treatment of Subordinates 143
- Knowledge of People 143
- Commanding in War 144

Lovable 144
Manifestation of God's Revelation in Practice 145
Marital Life 146
- A Perfect Marriage 146
- Equal Treatment of Wives 146
- Expressing Affection 148
- Loving 148
- Soft and Light-Hearted 149

Mercy 149
Military Leader 150
Mission-Driven 150
Modest 151
Modern (Ahead of His Time) 151
Money and Wealth (Perspectives On) 152
Monotheism (Absolute and Uncompromising) 153
Morality (Superior Type) 155
A Mortal (Denied Divinity) 157
Moral Perfection (A Model For) 158

Mothers (Respect and Care For) 159
Obeyed Like no Other Man Ever Was 159
Orator 160
Orphanage (Institutionalized) 160
Orphans (Treatment Of) 161
Ostentation (Free Of) 161
Patience 161
    Calm Even at Uncouth Behavior 161
    With Women 162
Patriotism-Nationalism Rejected 162
Parents (Respect and Care For) 162
Peacemaker 163
Perseverance 164
Polite 165
Political Institution (Work of a Genius) 165
Pomp of Royalty (Shunned) 166
Piety (Genuine and Sincere) 167
The Poor (Tenderness For) 167
A Practical Illustration for Human Life 168
Pragmatic 169
Preacher 170
Practiced What He Preached 171
Prisoners of War (Treatment Of) 172
Purity of Soul 172
Proactive 172
Racism (Abolished) 173
Rational 174
Realist 174
Reconcile (Ready To) 175
Refined and Cultured 175
Reformer 177
    In Moral Life 177
    Established Brotherhood 177
    Infighting Replaced with Friendship 178
    Large-Scale Reform in the Society 178
    Elevated Women 179

Contents

In Hygiene 182
    In Every Sphere of Life 183
Refused None 183
Resolve 184
Respect for People 185
    Cultural Sensitivity 185
    Valuing Others' Opinions 185
    Avoiding Disturbing People 186
    Respecting Privacy 186
Respect for All Abrahamic Faiths 187
    Disclaimed as Founder of a New Faith 187
    Previous Prophets of God 187
Revenge (Never Took) 188
Rights (Discharging Of) 188
    Giving All Things Its Due 188
    Giving Everyone His Due 189
Roles (Performed Many) 189
Role Model 191
Ruler 192
Sacrifice 192
Saintly 192
Sane 193
Selfless 193
Servants (Treatment Of) 194
Sharing 195
Sincere 195
Serving Humanity 198
Serving Others First 198
Simplicity 198
Slaves (Treatment Of) 200
Slavery 201
Social Intercourse 203
    Gave Everyone Full Attention 203
    Shared in Their Feelings 203
    Made Everyone Feel Valued 204
Social Justice and Welfare 204

State and Government 205
Struck None 207
Supernatural Powers (Denied Having) 207
Superstition (Wiped Out) 208
Talents of a Superior Order 209
Tolerance (Religious) 209
Travelling 212
Tried and Tested 212
True to All 213
Truthful 213
Trustworthy 214
    Keeping Trust 214
    Fulfilling Promise 214
    Maintaining Secrets of People 214
Uncivilized People (Treatment Of) 215
Unflinching 215
Unifier of Humanity 216
Unpretentious 217
Victor (A Most Odd) 218
Visiting the Sick 218
Warfare (Rules Of) 219
Wise and Prudent 221
Work Ethics 222
    Accomplisher of Tasks 222
    Did His Own Work 222
Women (Treatment Of) 222
Wronged None 223
Yielding to Others and Admitting Mistakes 223

The Religion He Preached

Sound and Rational Doctrines 226
Based on Reason 226
Free of Mystery 227
Free of Dogma 227
Appeals to Ignorant and Learned Alike 228

Contents

Well-Suited for Intellectual/Spiritual Development 228
Spiritually Highest 229
Simplicity 229
Purity Restored 230
Balanced 230
Peaceful 230
No Intermediaries 231
Religious Tolerance 231
Manifested in Practice 233
No Persecution 233
Social Reform 233
Democracy of the First Order 234
Freedom of Opinion 234
Liberated Man 235
Equality 235
Elevates People with Justice and Fairness 237
Cosmological Morality of the First Order 237
Civilizing Effects 238
Economic Theory of Social Responsibility 238
Ushered a New Era of Moral & Economic Prosperity 239
A Sublime Path to God 240
Promotes A Virtuous Life 240

HIS LEGACY

Transformation of People 242
Impact and Influence 243
    Upon the Human Race 243
    His Name a Mirror Image of the Religion Itself 244
    Greater than Jesus and St. Paul Combined 245
Accomplishments 245
    Most Illustrious Achievements 245
    Immense Achievement with Least Amount of Resources 246
    United Vast Swaths of Humanity Under One Religion 247
    Political Institutions 247
    Established Man's Duties to God, Man & the Lower Creation ... 248

Founder (Threefold) 248
The Greatest Human Being Ever.. 249
    A Man with a Unique Combination of Noble Qualities............... 249
    An Original Man... 251
    A Genius of the Highest Degree 252
    The Greatest Hero... 252
    The Greatest Leader.. 253
    The Best Example of One Man in History................................. 253
    The Most Influential Figure 254
    The Most Influential Political Leader 254
    An Expression of the Creative Life of God 255
    The Greatest... 255
A Prophet of God 259
    Non-Muslim Scholars on the Prophethood of Muhammad.......... 260
    Dilemma for Some When Confronted with the Truth................. 264

Appendix I: Selected Sayings of Prophet Muhammad 269
Appendix II: Supplications of Humility 291
Appendix III: Allegations of Sensuality 295
Bibliography.. 299
Suggested Resources 307

Historical Introduction

THE MOST PRAISED MAN

The reader who picks up this book might be surprised by its title and wonder about the man honored with the designation of "The Most Praised Man in the World." So allow me to introduce him through a recent incident.

In the fall of 2024, two powerful tropical hurricanes, Helene and Milton, struck the Gulf of Mexico and the southeastern United States within just five weeks of each other. These storms caused widespread destruction across Florida, Georgia, and Alabama, leaving a trail of devastation in their wake. Shortly afterward, the organization I work for—an agency that assists victims of natural disasters with government aid—was inundated with calls for help. Although we have dedicated teams of customer service representatives to handle such calls and process registrations for assistance, they were overwhelmed by the sheer volume. To address the situation, the organization called upon other employees to volunteer as temporary customer service agents, even if their regular job roles were at higher grades. Viewing this as both a call of duty and an opportunity to engage with individuals from lower socio-economic sectors of society, I decided to sign up as a volunteer.

The registration intake process was long and arduous, often lasting thirty minutes or more. It involved numerous questions and lengthy legal disclaimers, designed primarily to protect the organization from lawsuits. Many of the questions—carefully crafted to prevent fraud and abuse—were irrelevant to most applicants. Additionally, much of the legal language in the disclaimers, which applicants were required to listen to and agree to, was far beyond what many of these vulnerable individuals could reasonably understand, given their educational or socio-economic background. This highlights how a well-intentioned goal—such as providing compassionate care to devastated victims—can often be compromised by an excessive focus on procedural details rather than the overarching purpose, or on the "letter" rather than the "spirit" of the law. In any case, the registration process required significant patience from both the applicant who is calling and the customer service agent who is doing the intake.

Once I signed up, what followed was a two-month-long humbling experience which I will not detail here, except for one particular phone call. One morning, I answered a call from a very elderly woman who spoke with a frail, shaky voice. She explained that her mobile home had been damaged by the hurricane and she desperately needed help but was confused and unsure how to proceed. She lived alone, had issues with her right knee, and relied on a rollator—a four-wheeled walker with a small seat for resting—to get around. On top of that, she suffered from acute anxiety and depression.

From the moment I heard her voice, I was concerned that she might not have the endurance to complete the call and might hang up out of frustration. Determined to assist her, I kept my tone as soft and reassuring as possible, frequently encouraging her to stay with me by gently reminding her that we were "almost done."

After what felt like a very long time, we finally completed the process. Just as we were about to end the call, she asked:

"Did you say your name is Muhammad?"

All agents were required to say their first name and agent ID when answering a new call.

"Yes," I replied, surprised at her question.

"You have a blessed name," she said.

Here was something quite unexpected, yet music to my ears. I felt I

Historical Introduction

knew what she meant, but I wanted to hear more. So allowing myself a couple of moments to process what she just said, I asked:

"Why do you say so?" as if I did not understand her comment.

"You share the name of a person, the Prophet Muhammad, who was an amazing, wonderful man."

She then launched into a brief talk about what a great man he was, lamenting that, unfortunately, many in the West either know little about him or hold incorrect opinions. She also shared that she loved to read, though her failing eyesight now made it a challenge, and revealed that she had once been a teacher in New York City.

An eighty-six-year-old woman—white, Catholic, and living in the so-called Bible Belt—expressing admiration for the Prophet of Islam was, I must admit, far beyond anything I had expected on that chilly November morning.

Prophet Muhammad (ﷺ)[1] embodied an extraordinary array of qualities, inspiring countless people across time, space, and faith. During his lifetime and throughout the centuries, in his homeland and beyond, whether they believed in him or adhered to other religions, many have readily acknowledged that no one like him has been seen since his time. Though his name does not appear on either the front or back cover of this book, it proliferates all around us. Derived from the verb *ḥamada*, meaning "to praise" or "to laud," *Muhammad* translates to "one who is highly praised." Remarkably, this name perfectly encapsulated the character and conduct of the person who bore it, as well as the indelible legacy he left behind. The grandfather who bestowed this name upon this newborn of the Arabian desert would have been the happiest man alive had he known that

---

[1] The ﷺ symbol represents an Arabic phrase meaning "May peace and blessings of God be upon him." Out of love and respect for the Prophet, Muslims recite this phrase whenever they mention or write his name, or when they hear it mentioned by others.

this child would grow to become the ultimate manifestation of the name he had so carefully chosen for him.[1] It is quite astonishing that, at least in recorded history, this beautiful name had not been given to another child before him. It is as though, by divine design, this name had been reserved for the one man who would fully embody it—becoming, by word and deed, the greatest human being ever to walk on God's earth.

The story is now entirely different—the rarity of the name before his birth has long since vanished. Today, *Muhammad* is the most common name in the world given to newborn boys—a reflection of the profound love and admiration people hold for him. Remarkably, this extends even to the heart of Western civilization: the city of London, and indeed across England as a whole.[2]

Today, the number of his followers ranks second in the world, closely trailing Christianity, and is projected to surpass it by 2050.[3]

Today, not a *single moment* passes without *tens of thousands of voices* proclaiming from the minarets of mosques around the world, crying out the phrase, "I bear witness that Muhammad is the Messenger of God." This same declaration is echoed every moment by millions of Muslims in their prayers.[4]

Nor does a *single moment* pass without *millions of voices* saluting "peace be upon him," either upon uttering his name or hearing it mentioned by others.

And today, no one is more loved and revered—whether a religious figure, statesman, reformer, or otherwise. It is almost inevitable that

---

[1] Muhammad's (ﷺ) father passed away a few months before he was born, and as a result, his care was entrusted to his grandfather. However, his grandfather also passed away when he was about eight years old.

[2] Including all spelling variants. See *TheGlobal_Index*, 6/18/2023; "What's The Commonest Baby Name In Your London Borough? 2021 Stats Revealed" in *Londonist*, 10/28/2022.

[3] According to PEW Research, *The Future of World Religions: Population Growth Projections, 2010-2050*.

[4] Every Muslim recites this phrase during the five daily obligatory prayers at least nine times, and also sends peace and blessings upon Prophet Muhammad at least ten times. The number increases significantly when optional prayers are included.

anyone who objectively studies his life cannot help but develop deep admiration for him. Marmaduke Pickthall wrote about a "very learned English Orientalist" who, after a lifetime of studying the early history of Islam, confessed that he had developed such profound personal admiration and affection for the character of the Prophet that he was uncertain whether his view of the religion could be considered unbiased, given his strong affection for its founder.[1] It is out of this deep affection for him that today, any insult or act of disrespect toward his name prompts millions to take to the streets in protest across the globe. Such a reaction is unparalleled for any other religious figure, many of whom are subjects of frequent caricature and ridicule in the secular West.

It is safe to say that, in the history of the world, there has not been a second example of a man who embodied so many sterling qualities and virtues despite living a full and active life and fulfilling numerous roles. As a result, he has been lavishly praised by people across all faiths. While the founders of other religions spoke primarily in terms of theories and ideals, all that emanated from Muhammad (ﷺ) was practical, inspiring, and what he himself lived by. This was succinctly captured in Edward Gibbon's comment: "In all religions, the life of the founder supplies the silence of his written revelation: the sayings of Mahomet[2] were so many lessons of truth; his actions so many examples of virtue."[3]

Yet, Muhammad (ﷺ) never sought praise—in fact, he disliked it—and consistently reminded his followers that he was only a mortal man. The One truly deserving of all praise, he taught, is God. He was supremely successful in instilling in the hearts and minds of his followers this

---

[1] Marmaduke Pickthall, "The Prophet's Gratitude." Pickthall (d. 1936) was an English novelist, diplomat, and journal editor who is best known for the translation of the Qur'an into English. Published in 1930, it was the most faithful and unbiased translation up until that time.

[2] "Mahomet" is an archaic European rendering of the Prophet's name, often found in medieval texts. The correct transliteration from Arabic (مُحَمَّد) is "Muḥammad." Other variations include "Mohammed," "Mohamed," "Mohammad," "Muhammed," etc.

[3] Edward Gibbon, *The History of the Decline and Fall of the Roman Empire,* vol. iv, 309. Gibbon (d. 1794) was a famous British historian and politician, most known for this particular title which was published in six volumes between 1776 and 1789.

fundamental truth: their object of worship is God alone, the only Praiseworthy, while his task, as a human being, was simply to deliver the message from Him.

Over the centuries, Muslims have produced innumerable works in praise of him, including books, hymns, and songs. However, in this work, we have exclusively quoted from Western historians and authors, most of whom are non-Muslims, for a simple reason. It is taken for granted that followers of a faith will hold their founder in high esteem. When, however, notable historians and writers, even those outside of his faith tradition, offer serious praise of a historical figure, it establishes beyond any doubt that such a man is truly extraordinary and deserving of praise.

HISTORICAL EUROPE TOWARD THE PROPHET OF ISLAM

No great man or leader who made a significant impact on human lives has ever been spared criticism, and the Most Praised Man is no exception. Typically, critics of a great figure include ideological adversaries, those unable to overcome subconscious biases due to loyalty to a particular faith, or academics whose secular worldview precludes the consideration of divine agencies, leaving them to explain human behavior purely from a materialistic perspective. These critics are often ill-equipped to assess a faith-based character.

Propaganda

Enmity and hatred toward the Prophet of Islam began early in Europe. In the context of Christian lands falling under Muslim rule and the subsequent Crusades, European writers started to vilify the Prophet, creating an image of him designed to plant the seeds of antagonism and hatred in the hearts of the Christian masses, thereby preventing any favorable opinion of him or his message. Pope Innocent III (d. 1216) referred to the Prophet as the "Antichrist."[1] One of the earliest accounts of the Prophet

---

[1] Emile Dermenghem, *The Life of Mahomet*, 120. Dermenghem (d. 1971) was a French orientalist and journalist.

by a European was written by Jacobus de Voragine. He published *The Golden Legend* in 1260, where he portrayed Prophet Muhammad—whom he called "Magumeth"—as a trickster. According to de Voragine, Magumeth had a tame dove that would perch on his shoulder and eat from his ear, where he kept some grains of corn, thus deceiving people into believing that the Holy Ghost, in the form of a dove, was speaking to him. "In this way, Magumeth deluded the Saracens,"[1] wrote de Voragine. He further wrote that a Christian Nestorian heretic named Sergius joined Magumeth after being expelled from the Church. Although these stories were complete fabrications with no historical basis, they were eagerly accepted by subsequent generations of Christian writers without any need for verification. The 16th-century Dutch theologian Hugo Grotius found the story in line with his missionary zeal and included it in his proselytizing work *De Veritate Religionis Christianae*[2] to discredit Islam, despite knowing that the story had no credible sources. Calling this a "pious lie", Gibbon commented on Grotius' admission, "As this pretended miracle was brought forward by Grotius (*De Veritate Religionis Christianae*), his Arab translator, the learned Pococke, inquired of him the names of his authors, and Grotius was obliged to confess that it was unknown to the Mohammedans themselves. Lest, however, it should provoke their indignation and ridicule, the pious lie was suppressed in the Arabic version, but still maintains a conspicuous place in the numerous editions of the Latin text."[3]

Christian theologian St. Thomas Aquinas was not immune to expressing prejudicial views of the Prophet of Islam. In his *Summa Contra Gentiles*, published in 1265, Aquinas wrote that Muhammad (ﷺ) "enticed peoples with the promise of carnal pleasures," that what he taught "were mingled by him with many fables and most false doctrines," and that his followers "were not wise men" but rather "beastlike men who dwelt in the wilds." Commenting on this, Jeffrey MacCambridge observed, "Aquinas's rough, sensual characterization of Muslims relies on ethnic

---

[1] *Saracens* is a derogatory term used for Muslims in medieval Europe.

[2] Translated, "On the Truth of the Christian Religion."

[3] Gibbon, *The Decline and Fall*, vol. v, 147n154.

stereotypes... Indeed, all his representations of the Prophet Muhammad and Islam are based not on the historical person or religion, but instead on pre-Islamic Arabs or wholesale projections onto a political and theological rival of negative attributes that he opposes to Christian ideals."[1] Other Christian theologians and divines, despite their learning, used vituperative language against the Prophet of Islam, including Humphrey Prideaux[2], Abbe Marracci,[3] Johann Hottinger,[4] and Alexander Ross,[5] among others. Hottinger, for instance, wrote about Muhammad (ﷺ), "at the mention of whom the mind shudders." Ross, the first to translate the Qur'an into English in 1649—albeit from a French edition—was particularly liberal with derogatory epithets. He referred to the Prophet with terms such as "The Great Arabian Impostor," "The Little Horn in Daniel," "Arabian Swine," "Goliath," "Grand Hypocrite," "Great Thief," "Thieving Cacus," and "Mahomet the great destroyer, as his name signifies."[6]

One of the early European accounts of the Prophet of Islam was a travelogue titled *The Travels of Sir John Mandeville*, written anonymously in 1371 and first printed in 1499. This work, a fictitious travel

---

[1] Jeffrey MacCambridge, *Dante and Islam*, 49.

[2] Humphrey Prideaux (d. 1724) was an English divine and orientalist who authored *The True Nature of Imposture Fully Displayed in the Life of Mahomet,* originally published in 1697. As the title of his work amply demonstrates, Prideaux was most antagonistic toward Prophet Muhammad and he left no stone unturned in vilifying him, often resorting to things that are untrue and absurd. Much of his opinions were discarded by later post-enlightenment scholars of good repute.

[3] Abbe Marracci (d. 1700) was an Italian orientalist and chair of Arabic at the University of Rome. He wrote a Latin translation of the Qur'an in 1698 titled *Refutatio Alcorani*, the purpose of which was, in his own words, "to fight the Alcoran with the Alcoran and to slaughter Mahomet with his own sword insofar as I am able."

[4] Johann Heinrich Hottinger (d. 1667) was a Swiss philologist and a Protestant theologian. He was a bibliographer of Arabic texts and a teacher of the Arabic language.

[5] Alexander Ross (d. 1654) was a Scottish clergy. His "The Alcoran of Mahomet" was, according to S. C. Chew, "an all-pervading vulgarizing of the spirit and style of the book" (*The Crescent and the Rose*, 450-51).

[6] Henry Stubbe and Hafiz Shairani (Ed.), *An Account of the Rise and Progress of Mahometanism*, editor's Appendix, 237.

account attributed to a nonexistent "Sir John Mandeville," was deliberately crafted to discredit the Prophet. According to the account, "Mahomet" was portrayed as a camel herder who crossed the Arabian desert to Egypt. There, he supposedly entered a small Christian chapel where a hermit resided. Upon entering, the chapel's tiny, low doorway miraculously transformed into a large, grand entryway, resembling the gate of a palace. After this alleged event, the story claims Mahomet became an astronomer and eventually a governor of some province. He then married a princess named "Gadryge" but was soon afflicted with "epilepsy," causing him to fall during seizures. The account claims this led the princess to regret the marriage. To explain his episodes and "save face," Mahomet allegedly told her that during his falls, Saint Gabriel spoke to him. By 610, the story continues, Mahomet became ruler of Arabia and was often visited by the hermit he had met in Egypt and his servants. The narrative then shifts to a violent episode to explain why Muslims abstain from wine. The story claims that Mahomet often visited the hermit to hear his sermons, which angered his servants because he kept them awake at night. One night, while Mahomet was allegedly drunk on wine and asleep, his men took his sword and killed the hermit, placing the bloody weapon back in its sheath. The next morning, Mahomet found the hermit dead and was furious. When he confronted his men, they all insisted, in unison, that he had killed the hermit himself while drunk, showing him his bloodied sword as evidence. Believing their story, Mahomet is said to have cursed wine and anyone who drank it. The account concludes with the assertion that this is why devout Saracens abstain from wine.

Another bizarre story that circulated early on claimed that the Prophet's tomb was suspended in the air using lodestones after his body had been left unburied for three days. This tale appears among other gross absurdities in a late 16th-century work titled *God's Arrow Against Atheism and Irreligion* by Henry Smith.[1] Sir Walter Raleigh, a 16th-century English statesman, repeated the tale, writing: "His stinking carcasse which had lain 3 dayes on the ground unburyed, was put in an iron chest, and sent to Mecha. Hee promised his Disciples he would rise again the

---

[1] John C. Miller (ed.), *The Works of Henry Smith*, vol. ii, 407-08.

third day, but forgot it."[1] Widely circulated across Europe, particularly in England, such fabrications profoundly shaped European perceptions of Islam and its Prophet. The impact of these stories is evident in the works of German writer Hendrik van Haestens. Writing in 1627, he described the Prophet as "a transcendent Arch-heretick," "a serious professor of diabolical arts," and "a most ungodly instrument of Satan, the Viceroy of Antichrist, or his sworn forerunner." What seems to have provoked such vitriol was Muhammad's (ﷺ) rejection of Jesus as divine, instead regarding him as a human prophet. Hastens wrote: "Mahomet ... most fervently and contumeliously held that Christ was only a man and that he was only called God *secundum dici*—that is to say, according to a certain manner of speaking."[2]

Haestens also perpetuated the lodestone story, claiming: "This man when he dyed was put into an iron Tombe at *Mecca,* which by the strength of Loadstones, being as it were in the middle and centre of an arched edifice, hangs up to the astonishment of the beholders, by which means the miraculous sanctity of this Prophet is greatly celebrated."[3]

Such bizarre accounts continued to circulate among European writers before they were debunked. In 1718, John Toland referred to the dove and tomb stories, stating: "'tis but very lately that we begun to be undeceiv'd about Mahomet's pigeon, his pretending to work miracles, and his tomb's being suspended in the air: pious frauds and fables, to which the Musulmans[4] are utter strangers."[5] Edward Gibbon dismissed the tomb tale as beneath serious investigation, writing: "The Greeks and Latins have invented and propagated the vulgar and ridiculous story that Mohammed's iron tomb is suspended in the air at Mecca, by the action of equal and

---

[1] Walter Raleigh, *The History of the Worlds: The Second Part,* 110.

[2] Henrick van Haestens, *Apocalypsis or the Revelation of Notorious Advances of Heretic,* 59. Van Haestens (d. 1629) was a printer and publisher.

[3] Ibid.

[4] The words "Musulman," "Mussalman," and similar terms are Persian derivatives of the original Arabic word "Muslim."

[5] John Toland, *Nazarenus, or Jewish, Gentile, and Mahometan Christianity,* 4. Toland (d. 1722) was an Irish philosopher and historian.

potent loadstones. Without any philosophical inquiries, it may suffice, that, 1. The prophet was not buried at Mecca; and, 2. That his tomb at Medina, which has been visited by millions, is placed on the ground."[1]

Fabricating stories is one matter, but distorting the core message of the Prophet into its diabolical opposite is quite another. Muhammad (ﷺ) preached absolute and uncompromising monotheism, consistently affirming that God alone is the sole object of worship, without any association or partnership with anyone or anything. He explicitly stated that he was only a mortal man with no divine attributes. Yet, one of the greatest ironies in history is that many European writers portrayed Muslims as "pagans" who worshipped "Mahomet the idol."

In fact, "No opinion was held with greater unanimity in the Christian Churches than the belief that the Muslims were infidels and idolaters, who worshipped 'God Mahomet,'" noted Shairani.[2] This propaganda was so widely circulated and deeply entrenched that over time, the term "Mahometry"—later evolving into "Mammetry"—became synonymous with idol worship. Consequently, "Mammets" entered the English lexicon as a term for idols, dolls, or images. The lingering use of the term "Mohammedans" to refer to Muslims—even well into the 20th century—is a vestige of this historical mischaracterization. It falsely implies that Muslims revere Muhammad (ﷺ) as a deity, a stark distortion of a faith that, at its core, is dedicated to the oneness of God.

"Didn't Europeans know better?" asks John Tolan. "Didn't they know that Muslims were strict monotheists who rejected the use of images (much less idols)? Indeed, many Europeans did know better; as early as the eighth century in Constantinople, the ninth century in Spain, and the twelfth century elsewhere in Europe, Christian writers acknowledged that the 'Saracens' were monotheists, often casting them as followers of a deviant, heretical version of Christianity. But at the same time other authors, writing in Latin, French, and other Europeans languages, preferred to portray them in the familiar and despised guise of pagan

---

[1] Gibbon, *Decline and Fall*, vol. v, 145.

[2] Stubbe, *An Account of the Rise and Progress of Mahometanism*, editor's Appendix, 196.

idolaters. This caricature remains popular into the nineteenth century." These deliberate mischaracterizations of the Prophet's message served an essential purpose for Europe: rallying the crusaders. "The paganism of the Saracens is a key element in the theological justification of the crusade: the pagans killed Jesus, and the crusaders will wreak vengeance on the pagans for the murder of their 'father'," notes Tolan.[1]

Post-Enlightenment Writers

These pious frauds and fabrications were deliberately constructed to bolster Christianity against the growing influence of Islam. "Many of the events of Mohammad's life have been distorted and credited with ignoble motives by European biographers," observed Stanley Lane-Poole.[2] However, as the power of the Church over the populace waned and Europe approached the era of the Enlightenment, increased intellectual maturity of Europe could no longer justify the use of fictitious tales and blatant distortions about historical figures. This shift gave rise to a new category of writers who, while discarding the more outlandish fabrications, sought to undermine Islam and its Prophet by selectively using historical materials. These writers framed their works as objective but subtly twisted facts to discredit Muhammad (ﷺ). Among their recurring claims was the charge that he was an "impostor." Though many of these writers acknowledged his extraordinary moral character and invaluable contributions to social reform, they struggled to reconcile his role as a prophet with their Christian worldview.

How, then, to explain him? Accepting him as a genuine prophet of God was untenable within their religious framework. Instead, they resorted to labeling him a pretender or fraud. As S. C. Chew notes, "It was

---

[1] John V. Tolan, *Faces of Muhammad: Western Perceptions of the Prophet of Islam from the Middle Ages to Today*, 26. Tolan (b. 1959) is a historian of religious and cultural relations, and Professor Emeritus of History at the University of Nantes (France).

[2] Stanley Lane-Poole, *Studies In A Mosque*, 76. Lane-Poole (d. 1931) was a British orientalist and archaeologist.

difficult for Christian piety to conceive any sincere non-Christian or non-orthodox belief, and the more clearly Christians realized Islam's claim to be a separate and distinct creed, the stronger grew the belief that the Founder of Islam must have been a deliberate impostor."[1]

These writers overlooked certain fundamental flaws in their "impostor" theory. A fraud typically pretends to achieve personal gain, yet nothing in the life of the Prophet Muhammad (ﷺ) aligns with such a motive. In fact, his life demonstrates the opposite: from the moment he assumed his prophetic mission to his passing 23 years later, his journey was marked by selfless sacrifice and unwavering dedication to God. Historian Edward Freeman eloquently captured this in his analysis: "A vulgar impostor would have claimed miraculous powers or have decked himself in the pomp of earthly royalty. But Mahomet still only proclaimed himself as God's Prophet; personal honours he disclaimed; his demeanour was as courteous and equable as ever; the friends of his adversity were never forgotten. Crown and sceptre, court and palace, he had none; the lord of Arabia lived in the humblest dwelling, on the plainest fare, accessible to the meanest of believers. The master of thousands of willing slaves still patched his own shoes and milked his own cattle."[2]

Furthermore, a pretender cannot sustain his deception indefinitely, especially among his inner circles. In the case of Prophet Muhammad (ﷺ), the first to believe in his message were his own family members and dearest friends. They remained his most loyal supporters, standing by him through every trial and tribulation until their deaths. German orientalist Theodor Nöldeke, who rejected the impostor theory, posed a compelling question: "How could so many noble and sensible Muslims, particularly his close friends Abū Bakr al-Ṣiddīq and ʿUmar b. al-Khaṭṭāb, have stood by him in good days and bad if he had been nothing but an impostor? Added to the testament of such a numerous following is especially the fact that men from noted families, raised in the pedigree-arrogance of the

---

[1] Samuel C. Chew, *The Crescent and the Rose*, 398. Chew (d. 1960) was Professor of English and lectured at several universities including University of Chicago, University of Toronto, Johns Hopkins University, and Harvard University.

[2] Edward Freeman, *History and Conquests of the Saracens*, 37. Freeman (d. 1892) was an English historian and politician.

thoroughly aristocratic Arab, joined a sect consisting largely of slaves, freedmen, and individuals from the lowest strata of society, even though their countrymen considered this to be the greatest shame, solely because of their enthusiasm for the Prophet and his teaching."[1] Moreover, an impostor would not include his own mistakes in his scripture. Yet, the Qur'an contains rebukes of the Prophet, including the incident when he ignored a poor man calling for his attention while he was engaged in conversation with an aristocrat. Such inclusion is "the very last thing," wrote G. W. Leitner, "which he would have done had he been an impostor."[2]

Realities such as these made the "impostor" theory untenable for many scholars. The French orientalist Armand-Pierre de Perceval, writing around 1850, argued, "It would be an injustice to Mohammed to consider him as no more than a clever impostor, an ambitious man of genius."[3] Likewise, A. C. Benson and H. F. W. Tatham categorically dismissed it in 1892, stating, "He was not an impostor, he was not a hypocrite."[4] Well-known historian Montgomery Watt also found the impostor theory implausible. He argued that the idea of Muhammad (ﷺ) fabricating the Qur'an while presenting it as divine revelation fails to account for the immense hardships he endured, the moral uprightness of his character, and the magnitude of his achievements. In Watt's view, "These matters can only be satisfactorily explained" by accepting that "what we now

---

[1] Theodor Noldeke, *The History of the Qur'an*, 2-3. Noldeke (d. 1930) was a German orientalist who specialized in Old Testament Studies and Semitic languages including Arabic, Persian and Syriac.

[2] Gottlieb Wilhelm Leitner, "Religious Systems of the World." Leitner (d. 1899) was an eminent British orientalist and civil servant, with an extraordinary ability in languages. He started learning Arabic at the age of eight, and by the time he was ten, he had become fluent in Turkish, Arabic, and most European languages. At nineteen, he became a lecturer in Arabic, Turkish, and Modern Greek, and at twenty-one was appointed Professor of Arabic and Islamic Law at King's College London.

[3] Armand-Pierre Caussin de Perceval, *Essai sur l'histoire des Arabes,* in Snouck Hurgronje, *Mohammedanism*, 24. De Perceval (d. 1871) was Professor of Arabic in the Collège de France.

[4] A. C. Benson and H. F. W. Tatham, *Men of Might*, 34. Benson (d. 1925) was an English essayist, poet and academic.

know as the Qur'an was not the product of his own mind, but came to him from God and was true."[1]

Some proponents of the "impostor" theory openly admitted that their allegiance to the Christian faith was the primary reason for labeling Muhammad (ﷺ) as such. Thomas Patrick Hughes, for instance, despite acknowledging Muhammad's (ﷺ) numerous achievements and qualities, called him an "impostor" solely because he did not regard Jesus as divine. Hughes wrote, "When we consider his claims to supersede the mission of the Divine Jesus, we strip him of his borrowed plumes, and reduce him to the condition of an impostor!"[2]

Today, the impostor theory has been relegated to the dustbin of history. As Watt aptly put it, "To suppose Muhammad an impostor raises more problems than it solves."[3] In 1840, Thomas Carlyle condemned this theory as a "disgrace": "Our current hypothesis about Mahomet, that he was a scheming Impostor, a Falsehood incarnate, that his religion is a mere mass of quackery and fatuity, begins really to be now untenable to any one. The lies which well-meaning zeal has heaped round this man are disgraceful to ourselves only."[4] Arnold Toynbee, one of the greatest historians of the 20th century, further rejected the claim: "Was Muhammad a vulgar impostor, who posed as a prophet with his eye upon a throne from the outset? This calumny is conclusively refuted by the record of Muhammad's life..."[5]

---

[1] W. Montgomery Watt, *Muhammad At Medina*, 325. Watt (d. 2006) was a Scottish orientalist, historian, and Anglican priest. He was Professor of Arabic and Islamic Studies at University of Edinburg.

[2] Thomas Patrick Hughes, *Notes on Muhammadanism*, 5. Hughes (d. 1911) was an Anglican missionary.

[3] W. Montgomery Watt, *Muhammad At Mecca*, 52.

[4] Thomas Carlyle, *On Heroes, Hero-Worship and the Heroic in History*, 49. Carlyle (d. 1881) was a British essayist, historian and philosopher. This title is a compilation of a series of public lectures he delivered beginning on May 5, 1840.

[5] Arnold J. Toynbee, *A Study of History*, vol. iii, 468. Toynbee (d. 1975) was an English historian, a philosopher of history, and Professor of History at the London School of Economics and King's College, London. His most well-known work is the 12-volume *A Study of History* (1934–61). Toynbee was greatly influenced by Muslim

The latter half of the 19th century saw the emergence of a new group of Orientalist writers who, while acknowledging Muhammad's sincerity, still refused to recognize him as a true prophet of God. Instead, they suggested the absurd notion that Muhammad, over the course of 23 years, deluded himself into believing he was a prophet—despite the unwavering conviction of his followers, who were also supposedly caught up in this delusion. These scholars found it easier to entertain this self-deception theory than to accept Muhammad as a genuine prophet, despite the nobility of his character and the alignment of his message with previous divine revelations.

A key underlying motivation for many Orientalist writers was their collusion with the colonial project. As previously mentioned, their ideological bias—often rooted in allegiance to Christianity—shaped their work. Whether intentionally or subconsciously, these scholars contributed to the colonial mission of occupying Eastern lands, under the pretext of bringing Christianity to the "savage" populations. Edward Said, more than any other scholar, meticulously exposed the connection between Western research on Eastern peoples and the colonial project, leading to the establishment of a distinct academic discipline in Western universities called Orientalism. "Orientalist theories," wrote Al-Azami, "are born not in a vacuum, but in a world of pressing political needs which mould and colour everything about them."[1] In emphasizing the importance of Said's critique, Tolan likewise observed how scholarship is not immune to political and social pressures, and how through both deliberate distortion and unconscious bias, it can support and reinforce colonial agendas.[2] These writers—"their motives concealed behind a slender façade of

---

historian and sociologist Ibn Khaldun, and called the latter's famous work *Muqaddimah* "the greatest work of its kind."

[1] M. M. Al-Azami, *The History of the Qur'anic Text from Revelation to Compilation*, 331. Al-Azami (d. 2017) was a scholar of ḥadīth and Qur'anic history and Professor at King Saud University (Riyadh). He also taught at several other universities worldwide including Princeton University, University of Michigan, University of Colorado, and University of Wales.

[2] Tolan, *Faces of Muhammad*, 15.

sincerity'[1]— tended to accept any negative account of the Prophet Muhammad, no matter how obscure or unreliable the source, while treating any positive details with skepticism. As Watt noted, "Western writers have mostly been prone to believe the worst of Muhammad," and, whenever a negative interpretation seemed plausible, they readily accepted it as fact.[2]

And thus it is an ironic truth that the Most Praised Man in the world is also among the most maligned. Watt goes as far as to say, "Of all the world's great men, none has been so much maligned as Muhammad." His reasoning is straightforward: "It is easy to see how this has come about. For centuries, Islam was the great enemy of Christianity."[3] Western scholarship on Islam and its Prophet, according to Al-Azami, "was born from a legacy of regal ancestry, intense religious rivalry, centuries of crusades, the colonization of Muslim lands, and a colonial pride that blossomed into an overt contempt for the customs, beliefs, and history of Muslims."[4]

Yet, even the Prophet's bitterest enemies could not help but praise him. While many Western Orientalist writers are influenced by stated or subconscious ideological biases, or suffer from a lack of access to the original Arabic sources,[5] or a combination of both, and thus often attempt to find flaws in the Prophet's character, they are still compelled to acknowledge his greatness. This is not surprising: when a man's character and conduct are exemplary and supported by historical evidence, attempts to project him in a contrary light inevitably expose the writer's own bias and lack of objectivity—something few credible authors would risk. The fact is, when a vast number of non-Muslim historians and respected

---

[1] Al-Azami, *The History of the Qur'anic Text*, 342.

[2] W. Montgomery Watt, *Muhammad At Mecca*, 52.

[3] W. Montgomery Watt, *Muhammad At Medina*, 324.

[4] Al-Azami, *The History of the Qur'anic Text*, 341.

[5] According to Arthur Penrhyn Stanley (d. 1881), an English Anglican priest and a historian, "insufficient knowledge of Arabic" was responsible for much of the "gross blunders" made in the Western biographies of Muhammad (ﷺ). (See *Lectures on the History of the Eastern Church*, 246-47).

scholars praise Prophet Muhammad in the highest terms for his noble human qualities, and when criticisms by some—regardless of motive—are objectively countered by other reputable historians, the truth becomes undeniable: the Prophet of Islam was indeed an extraordinary and unparalleled figure in human history.

His Life Recorded in Minute Details

The first question that arises when assessing the character of a historical figure is the availability and reliability of information about them. In this regard, the Prophet of Islam stands out among all historical figures: he is the only figure in ancient and medieval history whose life unfolded "in the full light of history," as Ernest Renan aptly noted. He lived six centuries after Jesus, a time when methods for recording and documenting history had improved. More importantly, Arabs were renowned for their rich oral tradition, which they perfected as a scientific method to preserve the authenticity of the Prophetic details. While many early societies maintained some form of oral tradition, Muslims went a step further by developing it into a rigorous process to ensure the accuracy of Prophetic information. One crucial practice was the method of *isnād*, or chain of narrators, which traced information back to its original source. Each individual in the chain was meticulously vetted for their integrity and reliability. To support this process, a specialized field known as *asma' al-rijāl* ("Biographies of Men") was developed to document the biographies and reliability of those who transmitted knowledge about the Prophet. The details included chronology, biographical details of the person in question, and a critique of him as a reliable and trustworthy narrator. Comprehensive works, including one monumental text by al-Bukhārī, *Al-Tarikh al-Kabir*, compiled detailed information on over 42,000 individuals.[1]

The meticulous and exhaustive nature of the scientific approach to preserving and verifying historical information about the Prophet's

---

[1] Muḥammad Zubayr Ṣiddīqī, *Ḥadith Literature: Its Origin, Development & Special Features*, 95. Ṣiddīqī (d. 1976) was Professor of Islamic Culture in the University of Calcutta and specialized in Arabic and Persian medical literature.

words, actions, and biographical details has impressed many notable non-Muslim historians. German historian Aloys Sprenger (d. 1893) praised this approach, stating, "The glory of the Muhammadan literature is its literary biographies. There is no nation, nor has there been any, which, like them, narrated the life of every man of letters."[1] Similarly, D. S. Margoliouth remarked, "The biographical literature of the Arabs was exceedingly rich ... The literature consisting of collected biographies is abnormally large, making it easier for students of the history of the caliphate to find information about a person mentioned in the chronicles than in any analogous case."[2]

Another remarkable aspect of Prophet Muhammad's legacy is the vast collection of details about his life, from the way he woke up in the morning to how he slept, and everything in between. He lived under the watchful eyes of tens of thousands of followers, who saw him not just as a messenger of God, but also as their ruler, judge, teacher, brother, spiritual guide, prayer leader, counselor, and even military commander. He served as a role model for them, as they were directed by divine revelation to emulate his character and conduct (Q. 33:21). "All his actions served them as an ideal, and hence a precedent (sunna); every word which he uttered was a law to them, while his moral choices, so different from those of their age, yet so immediate in their impartial wisdom, provided them with a system of personal and social virtue that they tried to follow as faithfully as they could," wrote Ṣiddīqī.[3] Alfred von Kremer further noted, "The life of the Prophet, his discourses and utterances, his actions, his silent approval, and even his passive conduct, constituted, next to the Qur'an, the second most important source of law for the young Muslim empire."[4] What further motivated his followers to observe all the

---

[1] Ibn Ḥajar al-'Asqalānī, *al-Iṣāba fī Tamyīz al-Ṣaḥabā*, vol. i, editor's introduction, in Ṣiddīqī, *Ḥadīth Literature*, 95.

[2] D. S. Margoliouth, *Lectures on Arabic Historians*, 7-8. Margoliouth (d. 1940) was a British orientalist and Professor of Arabic at Oxford University.

[3] Ṣiddīqī, *Hadith Literature*, 3.

[4] Alfred von Kremer, *The Orient under the Caliphs*, 369. Von Kremer (d. 1889) was an Austrian orientalist and politician. He was proficient in multiple languages including Arabic, Hebrew, Persian, and Greek.

minutiae of his life was their exceptional love and respect for him. It is no exaggeration to say that no man in history has been held in such high regard and esteem as the Prophet of Islam.

When these factors are taken into account, one can better appreciate how the Prophet of Islam stands out among all historical figures, both in terms of the sheer volume of available records about his life and the exceptional reliability of those records.

In Full View of History

"[Islam was born] not amidst the mystery which cradles the origin of other religions, but rather in the full light of history."[1]

– Ernest Renan (1883)

"The development of Islam—at least, as compared with other world religions—is open to the clear light of history, and it presents us with yet another proof that the prophetic personality is the original source of the new religious creation."[2]

– Tor Andrae (1932)

"Mohammedanism or Islam is ushered into existence in the full daylight of history."[3]

– James A. Montgomery (1917)

---

[1] Soo Kim in (https://sookiwi.com/posts/class/introduction%20to%20islam/2018/04/18/midterm-paper/), accessed 11/16/2024. Renan (d. 1892) was a French orientalist, historian and biblical scholar.

[2] Tor Andrae, *Mohammed: The Man and His Faith*, 10. Andrae (d. 1946) was a scholar of religious history and bishop in the Swedish church.

[3] James A. Montgomery, *Religions of the Past and Present*, 211. Montgomery (d. 1949) was an American biblical scholar, and Professor of the Old Testament and Semitic studies at the Philadelphia Divinity School and the University of Pennsylvania.

Life History Authentically Preserved

"Of all the legislators and conquerors, there are none whose life was written with greater authenticity and in more detail by their contemporaries than was that of Mahomet."[1]
– Voltaire (c. 1756)

"It may be truly affirmed that of all known legislators and conquerors, not one can be named, the history of whose life has been written with greater authenticity and fuller detail, than that of Mohammed. In fact, strip his biography of the prodigies which Asiatic writers have ever affected, and what remains may confidently defy incredulity itself."[2]
– John Davenport (1869)

"On the whole, however, we may repeat that we have a picture of the character and work of Muhammad in Medina which is sufficiently reliable, coherent and honest."[3]
– Francesco Gabrieli (1968)

"[With regards to Muhammad] Fortunately, we are not dealing with a legendary individual, but with an historical person, whose almost every act and saying is recorded in the Hadis or collections of traditions, which, next to the Koran, form a rule of Muhammadan conduct. These 'Acts of the Apostles' are subjected

---

[1] Voltaire, *Essai sur les moeurs*, vol. i, 196, in Ziad Elmarsafy, *The Enlightenment Qur'an: The Politics of Translation and the Construction of Islam*, 97. Voltaire (d. 1778) was a French Enlightenment writer and historian.

[2] John Davenport, *An Apology for Mohammed and the Koran*, 1. As the title of his book suggests, Davenport (d. 1877), a British orientalist, was aghast by the persistent prejudices against Islam and its Prophet that had endured in Europe for centuries.

[3] Francesco Gabrieli, *Muhammad and the Conquests of Islam*, 84. Gabrieli (d. 1996) was Professor of Arabic Language and Literature at the University of Rome, and an editor of *Enciclopedia Italiana*. He was considered among the most distinguished Italian Arabists.

to the most stringent rules of criticism as to their authenticity, and unless the story of an act or saying of the Prophet can be traced to one of his own companions, it is thrown out of the order of traditions, which form the subject of critical investigation as to their actual occurrence adopted by Muhammadan commentators."[1]

"Muhammad's life is known to us from different sources. The Koran contains allusions to events in his life and the life of the young Muslim community. Furthermore, his sayings and reports about his actions were carefully preserved and collected to form, in the course of the first centuries, a large compendium, showing how his community saw him."[2]
– Annemarie Schimmel (1984)

Even Minute Details are Recorded

"From that time forth Mohammed's life, hitherto obscure and dark, stands out in its minutest details. He now is judge, lawgiver, king; even to the day of his death. We shall leave our readers to follow out the minutiae of his life in any of the biographies at their hand, which, from this period forth, no longer differ in any essential point."[3]
– Emanuel Deutsch (1869)

"I may also add, Prophet Muhammed is also a historic personality, every event of whose life has been most carefully recorded and even the minutest details preserved intact for posterity. His

---

[1] Leitner, "Religious Systems of the World."

[2] Annemarie Schimmel, *And Muhammad Is His Messenger*, 9. Schimmel (d. 2003) was a German orientalist specializing in Islamic and Persian Studies, Sufism, and poet Iqbal. She was Professor of Indo-Muslim Culture at Harvard University.

[3] Emanuel Deutsch, *Literary Remains*, 113-14. Deutsch (d. 1873) was German Jewish scholar of Semitic and Middle Eastern Studies.

life and works are not wrapt in mystery. One need not hunt for the accurate information and embark on arduous expeditions to sift the chaff and husk from the grain of truth."[1]

– K. S. Ramakrishna Rao (1989)

"Muhammad is a clear historical character, the minutest details of whose conduct and demeanour are recorded for us by his own contemporaries."[2]

– Marmaduke Pickthall (1917)

"Even the food that the Prophet liked and disliked is carefully recorded."[3]

– Annemarie Schimmel (1984)

His Life Witnessed by Thousands Who Left Records

Prophet Muhammad began his prophetic mission at the age of 40, starting with a handful of followers from his immediate family who believed in him. By the time he passed away at the age of 63, the entire Arabian Peninsula had embraced Islam. A year before his death, he performed the Farewell Pilgrimage in the presence of 40,000 believers, and by the time he left this world, an estimated 100,000 people had either seen him or heard him speak.[4]

---

[1] K. S. Ramakrishna Rao, *Muhammad: the Prophet of Islam*, 7. Rao (d. 2021) was an Indian philosopher and psychologist, and served as Chairman of GITAM school of Gandhian Studies.

[2] Pickthall, "The Prophet's Gratitude."

[3] Schimmel, *And Muhammad Is His Messenger*, 44.

[4] Al-'Asqalānī, *al-Iṣāba*, vol. i, 3, in Ṣiddīqī, *Hadith Literature*, 15.

"Few religions have been founded in plain day like Islam, which now counts its believers by more than a hundred millions, and which enlarges its domain from day to day, unaided. Most clearly and sharply does Mohammed stand out against the horizon of history. Those who knew him, not for hours, or days, or weeks, but from birth to death, almost during his whole life, count not by units, or dozens, but by thousands upon thousands, whose names and whose biographies have been collected; and his witnesses were men in the fullness and ripeness of age and wisdom, some his bitterest enemies."[1]

– Emanuel Deutsch (1869)

Comparison with Other Historical Figures

"If we knew as much of the private lives of other prophets as we know of Muḥammad, some of them would be less exalted than they now appear to be on the basis of the fragmentary surviving literature, endlessly sifted through throughout the centuries."[2]

– Theodor Noldeke (1860)

"[When compared with Muhammad] We have certainly far less authority of a secular character for the sayings and doings of our Lord Jesus Christ."[3]

– G. W. Leitner (*c.* 1914)

"We know all too little of the first and earliest labourers [i.e., historical religious figures] ... We know less of Zoroaster and Confucius than we do of Solon and Socrates; less of Moses and of Buddha than we do of Ambrose and Augustine. We know indeed some fragments of a fragment of Christ's life; but who can lift the veil of the thirty years that prepared the way for the three?

---

[1] Deutsch, *Literary Remains*, 68-69.

[2] Noldeke, *The History of the Qur'an*, 4.

[3] Leitner, "Religious Systems of the World."

... What do we know of His mother, of His home life, of His early friends, and His relation to them, of the gradual dawning, or, it may be, the sudden revelation, of His divine mission? ...

"But in Mohammedanism[1] everything is different; here instead of the shadowy and the mysterious we have history. We ... know everything of the external history of Mohammed—his youth, his appearance, his relations, his habits; the first idea and the gradual growth, intermittent though it was, of his great revelation; while for his internal history, after his mission had been proclaimed, we have a book absolutely unique in its origin, in its preservation, and in the chaos of its contents, but on the authenticity of which no one has ever been able to cast a serious doubt."[2]

– R. Bosworth Smith (1874)

"the story of Mohammed is extremely clear ... We know as much of Mohammed as we do of men who lived much closer to our epoch. His external record, his youth, his relatives, his habits are neither legendary nor hearsay."[3]

– R. V. C. Bodley (1945)

---

[1] The term "Mohammedanism" is a European mischaracterization of the word "Islam" and a legacy of the widespread propaganda in medieval Europe, which falsely depicted Muslims as worshipping Prophet Muhammad.

[2] R. Bosworth Smith, *Mohammed and Mohammedanism*, 16-17. Smith (d. 1908) was a British orientalist who taught at Trinity College (University of Oxford).

[3] R. V. C. Bodley, *The Messenger: The Life of Mohammed*, 1. Bodley (d. 1970) was a British army officer in WWII, traveler, and screen writer. He lived in the Sahara desert with a nomad Bedouin tribe for seven years.

Physical Attributes and Habits

FRAME AND APPEARANCE

"Mahomet ... was of the middle stature, square built and sinewy, with large hands and feet. In his youth he was uncommonly strong and vigorous; in the latter part of his life he inclined to corpulency. His head was capacious, well shaped, and well set on a neck which rose like a pillar from his ample chest. His forehead was high, broad at the temples, and crossed by veins extending down to the eyebrows, which swelled whenever he was angry or excited. He had an oval face, marked and expressive features, an aquiline nose, black eyes, arched eyebrows which nearly met, a mouth large and flexible, indicative of eloquence."[1]

– Washington Irving (1849)

"He was of middle height, rather thin, but broad of shoulders, wide of chest, strong of bone and muscle. His head was massive, strongly developed. Dark hair—slightly curled—flowed in a dense mass down almost to his shoulders. Even in advanced age it was sprinkled by only about twenty grey hairs—produced by the agonies of his 'Revelations.' His face was oval-shaped, slightly tawny of colour. Fine, long, arched eyebrows were divided by a vein which throbbed visibly in moments of passion. Great black restless eyes shone out from under long heavy eyelashes. His nose was large, slightly aquiline. His teeth, upon which he bestowed great care, were well set, dazzling white. A full beard framed his manly face. His skin was clear and soft, his complexion 'red and white,' his hands were as 'silk and satin'—even as those of a woman."[2]

– Emanuel Deutsch (1869)

"Slightly above the middle size, his figure, though spare, was

---

[1] Washington Irving, *Life of Mahomet*, 192. Irving (d. 1859) was an American short-story writer, essayist, biographer, historian, and diplomat.

[2] Deutsch, *Literary Remains*, 71.

handsome and commanding, the chest broad and open, the bones and framework large, the joints well knit together. His neck was long and finely moulded. The head, unusually large, gave space for a broad and noble brow. The hair, thick, jet black, and slightly curling, fell down over his ears. The eye-brows were arched and joined. The countenance thin, but ruddy. His large eyes, intensely black and piercing, received additional lustre from their long dark eyelashes. The nose was high and slightly aquiline, but fine, and at the end attenuated ... A long black bushy beard, reaching to the breast, added manliness and presence. His expression was pensive and contemplative. The face beamed with intelligence ... The skin of his body was clear and soft; the only hair that met the eye was a fine thin line which ran down from the neck toward the navel. His broad back leaned slightly forward as he walked; and his step was hasty, yet sharp and decided, like that of one rapidly descending a declivity."[1]

– William Muir (1858)

"His complexion was more ruddy than is usual with Arabs, and in his excited and enthusiastic moments there was a glow and radiance in his countenance."[2]

– Washington Irving (1849)

"His form, although little above the ordinary height, was stately and commanding. The depth of feeling in his dark black eye, and the winning expression of a face otherwise attractive, gained the confidence and love even of a stranger. His features often unbended into a smile full of grace and condescension. 'He was,' says an admiring follower, 'the handsomest and bravest, the brightest-faced and most generous of men. It was as though the

---

[1] William Muir, *The Life of Mahomet and History of Islam*, vol. ii, 28-29. Sir William Muir (d. 1905) was a Scottish orientalist, Christian missionary, and Principal of the University of Edinburg. He was also a colonial administrator, being Lieutenant Governor of the North-West provinces of British India.

[2] Irving, *Life of Mahomet*, 192.

sun-light beamed in his countenance.'"[1]
– William Muir (1861)

"Mahomet was in the full vigour of his manhood, robust, of medium height, strongly built, with broad chest and massive head; his hands and feet, although large, were fine and sensitive, his skin tanned, his cheeks clear without red in them, his hair neither very curly nor altogether straight. Although the employment of black slaves had already corrupted the purity of the Arab race in the towns, this mixture seemed scarcely perceptible in Mahomet. His hair floated freely to below his ears and his moustaches were clipped, a fashion he had adopted in order to distinguish himself from the idolaters, who wore their hair parted in the centre, and to associate himself with the *People of the Book*, both Jew and Christian. His square face with its decided aquiline nose, wide mouth, and eyebrows divided by a blue vein which sometimes swelled with anger, was framed by a tufted and very black beard overhanging his lower lip. From under a turban his countenance beamed with a majestic radiance at the same time impressive and gentle."[2]
– Emile Dermenghem (1930)

Living Quarters

"His life was simple in all its details. He lived with his wives in a row of humble cottages, separated from one another by palm branches, cemented together with mud."[3]
– R. Bosworth Smith (1874)

"Even in the height of his glory Muhammad led, as in his days of obscurity, an unpretentious life in one of those clay houses

---

[1] Muir, *Life of Mahomet*, vol. iv, 302-03.

[2] Dermenghem, *The Life of Mahomet*, 4-5.

[3] Smith, *Mohammed and Mohammedanism*, 85.

consisting, as do all old-fashioned houses of present-day Arabia and Syria, of a few rooms opening into a courtyard and accessible only therefrom."[1]

– Phillip K. Hitti (1937)

Food

"Dates and water were his usual fare, and milk and honey his luxuries. When he travelled, he divided his morsel with his servant."[2]

– Charles Mills (1817)

"He lived upon dates and the milk of his sheep, which he did not disdain to milk himself."[3]

– Alphonse de Lamartine (1854)

"His ordinary food was dates and water, or barley bread; milk and honey were luxuries of which he was fond, but which he rarely allowed himself."[4]

– R. Bosworth Smith (1874)

"Disdaining the penance and merit of a hermit, he observed, without effort or vanity, the abstemious diet of an Arab and a soldier. On solemn occasions he feasted his companions with rustic and hospitable plenty; but in his domestic life, many weeks would elapse without a fire being kindled on the hearth of the prophet ... his hunger was appeased with a sparing allowance of

---

[1] Phillip K. Hitti, *History of the Arabs*, 120. Hitti (d. 1978) was a scholar on Islam and Middle Eastern history and Semitic languages, and Professor at Princeton and Harvard Universities.

[2] Charles Mills, *An History of Muhammedanism*, 39. Mills (d. 1826) was an English historian and orientalist.

[3] Alphonse de Lamartine, *History of Turkey*, vol. i, 152. Lamartine (d. 1869) was a French author, poet, and statesman.

[4] Smith, *Mohammed and Mohammedanism*, 86.

barely-bread: he delighted in the taste of milk and honey; but his ordinary food consisted of dates and water."[1]

– Edward Gibbon (1788)

"He used to eat barley-bread, made of unsifted barley-flour, retaining all the bran. He ate the meat of sheep, camels, wild asses, hares, bustards, and fish, and sometimes also dried meat. Meat was the food he liked best, and he used to say, 'Meat strengthens the power of hearing,' yet was he not very greedy for it, nor ate too much of it."[2]

– S. W. Koelle (1888)

"Although the sources usually stress his modesty, his prolonged periods of fasting, and, at times, his starving, they still agree that he liked certain foodstuffs better than others, for instance the foreleg of lamb, milk, and dates."[3]

– Annemarie Schimmel (1984)

MEAL HABITS

"That prince ate exceedingly little. He said, 'When you have eaten, spend the strength of the food in prayer and praise, and do not sleep directly after a meal, lest your hearts should be oppressed.'"[4]

– S. W. Koelle (1888)

---

[1] Gibbon, *Decline and Fall*, vol. v, 149.

[2] Sigismund Wilhelm Koelle, *Mohammed and Mohammedanism*, 387. Koelle (d. 1902) was a German missionary and an expert in African languages.

[3] Schimmel, *And Muhammad Is His Messenger*, 44.

[4] Koelle, *Mohammed and Mohammedanism*, 387. In his work, Koelle often refers to the Prophet as "that prince," "that Excellency," or "his apostolic Excellency," etc., which perhaps indicates his deep reverence for the Prophet despite some of his prejudicial views. In any case, Prophet Muhammad was not a prince. Born an orphan, he was first cared for by his grandfather and, after his grandfather's death when he was

Physical Attributes and Habits

"He was sober and abstemious in his diet, and a rigorous observer of fasts."[1]

— Washington Irving (1849)

"Before eating he said, 'In the name of God,' and requested his friends to do the same; and if they happened to forget it, before a meal, they were to say at its conclusion, 'In the name of God, for the first and for the last.' He ate with the three fingers of his right hand. He always took what lay just before him."[2]

— S. W. Koelle (1888)

"He never reclined at meals. He ate with his fingers; and when he had finished, he would lick them before he wiped his hands."[3]

— William Muir (1861)

"He never rejected any lawful food, but ate of it, if he had an appetite, and if he had not, he did not taste it. Once, when they brought lizards to his table, and he did not taste them, his friends said, 'O Apostle of God, thou didst not eat of these: is it because they are not lawful?' He answered, 'I do not declare them unlawful, but as they are not found in our own country, I do not relish them.'"[4]

— S. W. Koelle (1888)

Dress

"He indulged in no magnificence of apparel, the ostentation of a

---

eight, by his uncle. He grew up in modest circumstances, facing semi-poverty.

[1] Irving, *Life of Mahomet*, 192.

[2] Koelle, *Mohammed and Mohammedanism*, 385. During the Prophet's time, people often ate from a shared platter, a practice still common in many indigenous cultures.

[3] Muir, *Life of Mahomet*, vol. iv, 304.

[4] Koelle, *Mohammed and Mohammedanism*, 387. The Prophet never criticized food. If he did not like a dish, he would simply avoid it without commenting on it.

petty mind; neither was his simplicity in dress affected, but the result of a real disregard to distinction from so trivial a source. His garments were sometimes of wool; sometimes of the striped cotton of Yemen; and were often patched."[1]

    – Washington Irving (1849)

"His apparel was that of the poor—the coarsest cloth of sheep's wool, the cinctures woven from camel's hair; he rejected, as an article of luxury and vanity, the white turbans of Indian cotton worn by his warriors."[2]

    – Alphonse de Lamartine (1854)

"His ordinary dress was plain, even to coarseness; yet he was fastidious in arranging it to the best advantage. He was fond of ablutions, and fonder still of perfumes."[3]

    – R. Bosworth Smith (1874)

"His ordinary dress consisted of plain white cotton stuff; but on high and festive occasions, he wore garments of fine linen, striped or dyed in red."[4]

    – William Muir (1861)

Putting on New Clothes

"When he put on new clothes (either an under-garment, a girdle, or a turban), the Prophet would offer up a prayer such as this: 'Praise be to the Lord who hath clothed me with that which shall hide my nakedness, and adorn me while I live, I pray thee for the good that is in this, and the good that hath been made for it; and I seek refuge from the evil that is in the same, and from the evil

---

[1] Irving, *Life of Mahomet*, 192.

[2] Lamartine, *History of Turkey*, vol. i, 152.

[3] Smith, *Mohammed and Mohammedanism*, 85.

[4] Muir, *Life of Mahomet*, vol. iv, 304.

that hath been made for it.'"[1]

— William Muir (1861)

HANDSHAKE

"he was never the first to withdraw his hand when he shook hands."[2]

— Winwood Reade (1872)

"he was never the first to withdraw his hand from the grasp of one who offered him his."[3]

— R. Bosworth Smith (1874)

"His handshake was as genuine as his laugh. He grasped the offered hand firmly and was never the first to withdraw."[4]

— R. V. C. Bodley (1945)

CONVERSATION (GIVING FULL ATTENTION)

"when he shook hands he would not withdraw his hand first; when he looked at a man he would wait for the other to turn away his face."[5]

— D. S. Margoliouth (1905)

"He was never the first to withdraw his hand when he greeted anyone, and he was never the first to turn his face away when conversing with another."[6]

— Tor Andrae (1932)

---

[1] Ibid., 332-33.

[2] Winwood Reade, *Martyrdom of Man*, 266. Reade (d. 1875) was a Scottish historian, novelist and philosopher.

[3] Smith, *Mohammed and Mohammedanism*, 84.

[4] Bodley, *The Messenger: The Life of Mohammed*, 39.

[5] D. S. Margoliouth, *Mohammed and the Rise of Islam*, 105.

[6] Andrae, *Mohammed: The Man and His Faith*, 262.

Walking

"His broad back leaned slightly forward as he walked; and his step was hasty, yet sharp and decided, like that of one rapidly descending a declivity."[1]

– William Muir (1858)

"His step was quick and elastic, yet firm, and as that of one 'who steps from a high to a low place.'"[2]

– Emanuel Deutsch (1869)

"The walking of that prince was a perfect motion, that is, he was not exceedingly slow, dragging his legs, like the proud and affected; nor did he show excessive haste and anxiety, like the light-minded and foolish. That prince's walk appeared so measured and grave as if he was descending from a height."[3]

– S. W. Koelle (1888)

Sleeping

"When night set in, that prince took an ablution, put off the clothes he had worn by day, and put on his night-robes. Then he blew on the palms of his blessed hands, and, after repeating a verse from the Koran, rubbed his limbs with them. He lay on his right side, putting the palm of his right hand under his right cheek, and saying, 'O God, in Thy name I die and live,' or, according to another account, 'In Thy name, O Lord, I lie down and rise again.' He sometimes lay on his night-clothes, sometimes on a carpet, sometimes on a mat, sometimes on sacking, and even on the dry earth. When he slept, he had under his head a leather

---

[1] Muir, *Life of Mahomet*, vol. ii, 29.

[2] Deutsch, *Literary Remains*, 71.

[3] Koelle, *Mohammed and Mohammedanism*, 400.

cushion, filled with date-palm fibres."[1]

– S. W. Koelle (1888)

WAKING UP

"When that prince rose from sleep, he used to say, 'Praise be to God, who has made us alive after we were dead: to Him we move and wake.' In no condition did he omit the mention of God."[2]

– S. W. Koelle (1888)

LAUGH AND SMILE

"His countenance was mild and pensive. His laugh was rarely more than a smile."[3]

– Emanuel Deutsch (1869)

"When he laughed, he laughed heartily, shaking his sides, and showing his teeth, which looked as if they were hail stones."[4]

– R. Bosworth Smith (1874)

"his chief charm was in his smile. The muscles of the mouth and cheeks had a way of contracting which made the most hostile pause when a quarrel was on the way."[5]

– R. V. C. Bodley (1945)

"when they [his companions] laughed, he either was silent or smiled. He would laugh so that his teeth could be seen."[6]

– S. W. Koelle (1888)

---

[1] Ibid., 401.

[2] Ibid.

[3] Deutsch, *Literary Remains*, 71.

[4] Smith, *Mohammed and Mohammedanism*, 84.

[5] Bodley, *The Messenger: The Life of Mohammed*, 39.

[6] Koelle, *Mohammed and Mohammedanism*, 393.

"All reports speak of Muhammad's friendly, kindly but serious attitude and point out that he did not often laugh. (One famous Prophetic tradition, frequently quoted by the early ascetics, says: 'If you knew what I know you would cry much and laugh little.') However, he is also said to have had a most winning smile that never failed to enchant his followers..."[1]

– Annemarie Schimmel (1984)

Fun and Jest

"That prince made also fun and jests with his friends. Abd Allah Ibn Harith relates: ... his jests were always just and true. When once his companions said to him, 'O Apostle of God, thou tellest us jokes and jests, which does not become thy position,' he replied, 'I say nothing but what is true;' and Aisha[2] the faithful declared, 'The Prophet made many jests, and said that God does not punish just jokes made in fun.'"[3]

– S. W. Koelle (1888)

Weeping

"That prince's weeping also was most moderate: his tears flowed; and from his bosom, void of rancour, a sound was heard like the seething of a pot. His weeping was either on account of a dead person, or from tender affection for his people, or from the fear of God."[4]

– S. W. Koelle (1888)

---

[1] Schimmel, *And Muhammad Is His Messenger*, 46.

[2] 'Ā'isha, variously spelled by different authors as 'Aisha, Aisha, Ayesha, etc., was the third wife of Prophet Muhammad.

[3] Koelle, *Mohammed and Mohammedanism*, 394. The Prophet was not known for being a humorous person. His jokes or light-hearted comments were always modest and based on truth. He never told a lie or made fun of anyone, even in jest.

[4] Ibid., 393.

Physical Attributes and Habits

"He wept like a child over the death of his faithful servant Zeid.[1] He visited his mother s tomb some fifty years after her death, and he wept there because he believed that God had forbidden him to pray for her."[2]

– R. Bosworth Smith (1874)

SPEECH

Clarity

"He did not speak rapidly, running his words into one another, but enunciated each syllable distinctly, so that what he said was imprinted in the memory of every one who heard him."[3]

– William Muir (1861)

Candid

"[He] speaks plainly to all manner of Persian Kings, Greek Emperors, what it is they are bound to do ... A candid ferocity, if the case call for it, is in him; he does not mince matters!"[4]

– Thomas Carlyle (1840)

No Unnecessary Words

"They noted that he always meant something. A man rather taciturn in speech; silent when there was nothing to be said; but pertinent, wise, sincere, when he did speak; always throwing light

---

[1] Zayd, also spelled as Zaid or Zeid by different authors, was a former slave of the Prophet who he freed. Some details about him are given on page 130.

[2] Smith, *Mohammed and Mohammedanism*, 84-85.

[3] Muir, *Life of Mahomet*, vol. iv, 326.

[4] Carlyle, *On Heroes*, 81.

on the matter. This is the only sort of speech worth speaking!"[1]
  – Thomas Carlyle (1840)

"In his intercourse with others, he would sit silent among his companions for a long time together, but truly his silence was more eloquent than other men's speech, for the moment speech was called for, it was forthcoming in the shape of some weighty apothegm or proverb, such as the Arabs love to hear."[2]
  – R. Bosworth Smith (1874)

"He spoke considerately and slowly, so that it would have been possible for any one so minded to count his words and sounds. But mostly he chose to be silent, and only spoke when necessary. Avoiding redundancy, prolixity, wearisomeness and confusion, he spoke to his friends concise, useful words,—all wisdom and prudence. Sometimes he would repeat the same words thrice, so that those present might well remember and understand them."[3]
  – S. W. Koelle (1888)

"Mohammed was not much of a talker. That is to say, he had that admirable Arab gift of speaking only when he had something which he thought was worth while making a basis for conversation. 'The beauty of man's Islam,' he declared, 'is that he shuns discussing unnecessary things.'"[4]
  – R. V. C. Bodley (1945)

"He never spoke unnecessarily. What he said was always to the point and sufficient to make his meaning clear, but there was no padding."[5]
  – W. Montgomery Watt (1955)

---

[1] Ibid., 59.

[2] Smith, *Mohammed and Mohammedanism*, 84.

[3] Koelle, *Mohammed and Mohammedanism*, 393.

[4] Bodley, *The Messenger: The Life of Mohammed*, 40.

[5] Watt, *Muhammad At Medina*, 321.

No Coarse Language

"Anas, his servant during ten years, praised his patience and said that he never spoke crossly. He was gentle with everyone, even in his rebukes; he never used coarse language and while he was easy of access, he protected his solitude against intrusion."[1]

– Emile Dermenghem (1930)

Deliberate and with Emphasis

"He was of great taciturnity, but when he spoke it was with emphasis and deliberation, and no one could ever forget what he said."[2]

– Emanuel Deutsch (1869)

Listened To

"When that Excellency spoke in an assembly, those present would keep silence, and lean forwards with their heads."[3]

– S. W. Koelle (1888)

NEATNESS IN APPEARANCE

"He combed his beard with care ... He used for a glass or mirror a bucket full of water, in which he used to look to adjust, decently, the folds of his turban."[4]

– Alphonse de Lamartine (1854)

---

[1] Dermenghem, *The Life of Mahomet*, 167.

[2] Deutsch, *Literary Remains*, 73.

[3] Koelle, *Mohammed and Mohammedanism*, 393.

[4] Lamartine, *History of Turkey*, vol. i, 152.

"When sovereign he found fault with[1] those whose hair was untidy, or whose clothes were dirty, being himself particular as to his appearance. He disliked yellow teeth, and almost made the use of the toothpick a religious ordinance."[2]

— D. S. Margoliouth (1905)

"He was fond of ablutions, and fonder still of perfumes; and he prided himself on the neatness of his hair, and the pearly whiteness of his teeth."[3]

— R. Bosworth Smith (1874)

"Scrupulous care was bestowed by him on his person."[4]

— D. S. Margoliouth (1905)

"Scrupulously neat in his personal habits, and ever ready to condemn untidiness (yellow teeth, in particular) in his companions … When he donned freshly laundered clothes, he was accustomed to remark: 'Praise be to the Lord, who hath clothed me with that which shall hide my nakedness and adorn me while I live.'"[5]

— R. F. Dibble (1926)

Cleanliness

"Frequent ablutions [prescribed in Islam] are essential to the

---

[1] The expression "found fault with" does not quite represent the gentle demeanor of the Prophet who did not have a critical personality and often preferred silence over criticism. If he was displeased with something, his companions would typically notice it in his expression rather than hearing it in his words.

[2] Margoliouth, *Mohammed and the Rise of Islam*, 64.

[3] Smith, *Mohammed and Mohammedanism*, 85.

[4] Margoliouth, *Mohammed and the Rise of Islam*, 105.

[5] R. F. Dibble, *Mohammed*, 181. Dibble (d. 1929) was an American orientalist and Professor of English at Columbia University.

health, and grateful to the senses of men in the heat of an Oriental clime; and to the mind of an Asiatic, external purification presents a lively image of the internal purity of the heart. The cleansing of the body is pronounced by Muhammed to be the key of prayer, without which it cannot be acceptable to God."[1]

– Charles Mills (1817)

"Ayesha tells us that Mahomet never lay down, by night or by day, but on waking he applied the toothpick[2] to his teeth before he performed ablution ... The toothpick was always placed conveniently for him at night, so that when he got up in the night to pray, he might use it before his lustrations ... He never travelled without one."[3]

– William Muir (1861)

"Before going to bed he cleaned his teeth with a particular kind of wood. He slept upon a carpet or a mattress of leather stuffed with fibres of the palm-tree, which he shook very thoroughly in order to drive out the vermin, for Mahomet was meticulously clean."[4]

– Emile Dermenghem (1930)

"He was scrupulous as to personal cleanliness, and observed frequent ablutions."[5]

– Washington Irving (1849)

"Cleanliness of body, which he made in his Koran the image of

---

[1] Mills, *An History of Muhammedanism*, 308.

[2] Translating the original Arabic word *miswāk* as "toothpick" is not entirely accurate. A few inches long, thin twig with one end chewed into bristle-like fibers, it would be more appropriate to refer to it as a small "toothbrush."

[3] Muir, *Life of Mahomet*, vol. iv, 334.

[4] Dermenghem, *The Life of Mahomet*, 164.

[5] Irving, *Life of Mahomet*, 193.

purity of soul, was his sole delicacy."[1]
> – Alphonse de Lamartine (1854)

"He used to wash his pure hands, both before and after meals, and then stroked his blessed face and arms, saying, 'The blessing of a meal consists in the washing of the hands before and after it.'"[2]
> – S. W. Koelle (1888)

ROUTINE AND DISCIPLINE

"Amongst all the habits of the Prophet there was also this, that he combed his hair and beard ... and that he anointed his blessed head and beard. His moustache he clipped, and commanded also his companions to do the same. Every Friday, before going to mosque, he attended to his moustache and cut his nails. He made use of his right hand for making ablutions, for eating, combing his hair and beard, for cleaning his teeth, snuffing up water and the like; but his left for removing what is unpleasant and for cleaning impurities. When he had to take anything from any one or to give something, he did so with his right hand."[3]
> – S. W. Koelle (1888)

TIME MANAGEMENT

"He used to divide his time into three parts: one was given to God, the second allotted to his family, the third to himself. When public business began to press upon him he gave up one half of the latter portion to the service of others."[4]
> – William Muir (1861)

---

[1] Lamartine, *History of Turkey*, vol. i, 152.

[2] Koelle, *Mohammed and Mohammedanism*, 386.

[3] Ibid., 396.

[4] Muir, *Life of Mahomet*, vol. iv, 330.

His Character

Youth and Early Life (Purity Of)

"The character of Mahomet, according to Eastern historians, had been hitherto preserved unblemished: his moral qualities, no less than his other accomplishments, had contributed to raise him in the esteem of his fellow citizens; and his integrity in particular had been honoured with the most flattering and distinguished testimony of their approbation."[1]

– Joseph White (1784)

"In his youthful days he was decent in his morals, pious, contemplative, and retired in disposition. From the age of twenty-five to forty he industriously pursued his occupation of a merchant, and nursed his genius in solitude."[2]

– Charles Mills (1817)

"All the authorities agree in ascribing to the youth of Mahomet a correctness of deportment and purity of manners, rare among the people of Mecca ... it is quite in keeping with the character of Mahomet that he should have shrunk from the coarse and licentious practices of his youthful friends. Endowed with a refined mind and a delicate taste, reserved and meditative, he lived much within himself, and the ponderings of his heart supplied occupation for the leisure hours spent by men of a lower stamp in rude sports and riotous living. The fair character and honourable bearing of the unobtrusive youth won, if not the approbation, at least the respect, of his fellow citizens; and he received the title, by common consent, of AL AMÎN, 'the Faithful.'"[3]

– William Muir (1858)

---

[1] Joseph White, *Sermons Preached Before the University of Oxford*, 97. White (d. 1814) was an English orientalist and theologian, and Professor of Arabic and Hebrew.

[2] Mills, *An History of Muhammedanism*, 36-37.

[3] Muir, *The Life of Mahomet*, vol. ii, 14-15.

His Character

"His youth had been always remarkable for a serious deportment, and strict attention to devotional exercises; and so general was the reputation of his piety, that on the finding in the well Zemzem of the black stone, which, it is said, the angel Gabriel brought to Abraham when he built the Caaba,[1] the people unanimously deferred to the grandson of Abdol-Motalleb[2] the honour of replacing it in its station."[3]
– Charles Mills (1817)

"His early life appears to have been absolutely blameless."[4]
– Edward Freeman (1856)

"He never frequented the wine-shop, or looked at the dancing-girls, or talked abroad in the bazaars."[5]
– Winwood Reade (1872)

"In his youth he is said to have lived a virtuous life."[6]
– William Muir (1861)

"his unmarried youth had been exceptionally pure."[7]
– Marcus Dods (1887)

"Up to the age of forty his unpretending modest way of life had attracted but little notice from his townspeople. He was only

---

[1] "Ka'bah" (كعبة) is the correct spelling. It is the cube-shaped stone building in Mecca toward which Muslims face during their daily prayers. It was built by Prophet Abraham as the first mosque for mankind to worship God.

[2] Grandfather of Prophet Muhammad.

[3] Mills, *An History of Muhammedanism*, 11.

[4] Freeman, *History and Conquests of the Saracens*, 40.

[5] Reade, *Martyrdom of Man*, 266.

[6] Muir, *Life of Mahomet*, vol. iv, 309.

[7] Dods, *Mohammed, Buddha, and Christ*, 23. Dods (d. 1909) was a Scottish theologian and minister, and Principal of New College in Edinburgh.

known as a simple, upright man, whose life was severely pure and refined, and whose true desert sense of honour and faith-keeping had won him the high title of El-Amin, 'the Trusty.'"[1]
— Stanley Lane-Poole (1883)

Accessible to All

"He was accessible to all, and at all times."[2]
— Gustav Weil (1866)

"He was easy of approach to all who wished to see him…"[3]
— R. Bosworth Smith (1874)

"He was accessible to small and great, was hospitable, charitable, generous—within the limit of his means, for he was never rich."[4]
— Marmaduke Pickthall (1917)

"He was the most accessible of men."[5]
— Marcus Dods (1887)

"He … was at all times within the reach of his people."[6]
— Phillip K. Hitti (1937)

"Mahomet, with his wives, lived in a row of low and homely cottages built of unbaked brick; the apartments were separated by walls of palm branches rudely daubed with mud; curtains of

---

[1] Lane-Poole, *Studies In A Mosque*, 37.

[2] Gustav Weil, *A History of Islamic Peoples*, 28. Weil (d. 1889) was a German orientalist and a pioneering Jewish scholar in the subject of Qur'anic studies. He knew Hebrew, Persian, Turkish, and Arabic, and translated several Arabic texts.

[3] Smith, *Mohammed and Mohammedanism*, 84.

[4] Marmaduke Pickthall, "Address on the Prophet's Birthday."

[5] Marcus Dods, *Mohammed, Buddha, and Christ*, 90.

[6] Hitti, *History of the Arabs*, 120.

leather, or of black hair-cloth, supplied the place of doors and window. His abode was to all easy of access, 'even as the river's bank to him that draweth water therefrom.'"[1]

– William Muir (1861)

Affectionate

"He was affected even to tear when the sword of the enemy sundered the bands of friendship; and his feelings of gratitude to Kadijah,[2] neither time nor the death of his benefactress could eradicate."[3]

– Charles Mills (1817)

"Mohammed was at all times of an affectionate disposition, and even demonstratively so; he expressed disgust at a man who having ten children declared that he had never kissed one of them: and he remained demonstratively affectionate to the end towards the slave Zaid, whom he adopted as a son ... Affectionate treatment of step children is [also] attested for a later period of his life."[4]

– D. S. Margoliouth (1905)

"He was very affectionate towards his family. One of his boys died on his breast, in the smoky house of the nurse, a blacksmith's wife."[5]

– Emanuel Deutsch (1869)

---

[1] Muir, *Life of Mahomet*, vol. iv, 304.

[2] Khadīja, a widow of 40, and variously spelled by different Western authors as Khadijah, Khadija, Kadijah, Cadijah, etc., was the first wife of Prophet Muhammad.

[3] Mills, *An History of Muhammedanism*, 39-40.

[4] D. S. Margoliouth, *Mohammed and the Rise of Islam*, 70-71.

[5] Deutsch, *Literary Remains*, 72. The name of this boy was Ibrahim who was wet-nursed by the wife of a blacksmith named Abu Saif in the outskirts of Medina. The Prophet used to visit his boy, and did so on the day he died when he heard that he was

"To men and for the Faith a strong hard man, to the weak and helpless he was tender and affectionate. As he was strong, so he was merciful and full of human sympathies."[1]

– Arthur Glyn Leonard (1909)

"There are many stories illustrating his gentleness and tenderness of feeling ... [One example is] the story of how he broke the news of the death of Ja'far b. Abī Ṭalib to his widow Asma' bint 'Umays; the story is said to have been told by Asma' herself to her grand-daughter. She had been busy one morning with her household duties, which had included tanning forty hides and kneading dough, when Muhammad called. She collected her children—she had three sons by Ja'far—washed their faces and anointed them. When Muhammad entered, he asked for the sons of Ja'far. She brought them, and Muhammad put his arms round them and smelt them (as a mother would a baby). Then his eyes filled with tears and he burst out weeping. 'Have you heard something about Ja'far?', she asked, and he told her that he had been killed. Later he instructed some of his people to prepare food for Ja'far's household, 'for they are too busy today to think about themselves'. About the same time the little daughter of Zayd b. Ḥārithah (who had been killed along with Ja'far) came to him in tears to be comforted, and he wept along with her; afterwards, when questioned about this, he said it was because of

---

sick. "We went with Allah's Messenger (ﷺ)," narrates Anas, one of his Companions, "to the blacksmith Abu Saif ... Allah's Messenger (ﷺ) took Ibrahim and kissed him and smelled him. And later we entered Abu Saif's [inner] house, and at that time Ibrahim was in his last breaths, and the eyes of Allah's Messenger (ﷺ) started shedding tears." Seeing this, another of his Companions named 'Abdur Rahman bin 'Auf remarked, "O Allah's Apostle, even you are weeping!"—apparently under the impression that shedding tears was a sign of weakness. The Prophet replied, "O Ibn 'Auf, this is mercy." Then he wept more and said, "The eyes are shedding tears and the heart is grieved, and we will not say anything except what pleases our Lord. O Ibrahim! Indeed we are grieved by your separation." (paraphrased from a report by al-Bukhārī)

[1] Arthur Glyn Leonard, *Islam: Her Moral and Spiritual Value*, 79. Major Leonard was a British colonial army officer and anthropologist.

the great love between Zayd and himself. The memory of his first wife Khadīja could also soften his heart. After [the battle of] Badr the husband of his daughter Zaynab was among the prisoners taken by the Muslims, and Zaynab sent a necklace of Khadīja's to Muhammad for a ransom, but he was so moved at the sight of it that he set the man free without payment."[1]

– W. Montgomery Watt (1955)

ALTRUISTIC

"Personal ambition and aggrandizement never for a moment entered his head, or formed part of it. The national good, to be attained only by a national or universal God—the one and only God of the universe—was the one great ambition that inspired and impelled him."[2]

– Arthur Glyn Leonard (1909)

AMBITION (FREE OF)

"That Mohammed was wholly free from the vice of ambition is proved by almost every circumstance of his life, but more especially by the indisputable fact that, after living to see his religion fully established, and himself in possession of unlimited power, he never availed himself of it for the purposes of self-aggrandizement, but retained to the very last his original simplicity of manners."[3]

– John Davenport (1869)

---

[1] Watt, *Muhammad At Medina*, 322.

[2] Leonard, *Islam: Her Moral and Spiritual Value*, 28.

[3] Davenport, *An Apology for Mohammed and the Koran*, 127-28.

ANIMALS (KINDNESS TO)

"The charity of the Mahometans[1] descends to the animal creation; and the Koran repeatedly inculcates, not as a merit, but as a strict and indispensable duty, the relief of the indigent and unfortunate."[2]

– Edward Gibbon (1788)

"[According to Mahomet] Man's love should extend to all creatures; for when even the humblest bird unfolds its wings, it praises the Lord ... 'There will be a reward for whoever quenches the thirst of any creature endowed with a living heart. He who has caused a well to be dug will be rewarded for every camel which comes to drink of the water.' ... Mahomet cursed anyone who mutilated an animal and forbade the killing of animals in cold blood when not necessary. Ibn 'Omar, remembering the Prophet's words, rescued a hen from some ragamuffins who wanted to use her as a target. The animals will be present at the Last Judgment to testify against cruel masters. A woman who had let a cat die of hunger shall suffer for ever in hell as the cat claws at her. But, on the other hand, a prostitute shall enter the kingdom of heaven because one day having seen a dog dying of thirst beside a well she attached her shoe to her veil and drew water for it to drink."[3]

– Emile Dermenghem (1930)

"Mohammed's acutely sensitive nature now led him to proscribe anything that savored of torture inflicted on animals: living birds might not be used as targets in shooting contests; camels were not to be tied up and left to die on their owners' graves; cattle were not to be blinded to avert the evil eye; droughts were not to

---

[1] Similar to "Mohammedans", a European mischaracterization of the word "Muslims."

[2] Gibbon, *Decline and Fall*, vol. v, 116.

[3] Dermenghem, *The Life of Mahomet*, 259-60.

be broken by the common process of affixing flaming torches to the tails of cattle; horses were not to lose their manes and tails, and asses were no longer to be branded or hit in the face. So scrupulously fastidious was the Prophet that he once ordered some Moslems to stop burning an anthill, and he also strongly disapproved the ubiquitous practice of cursing camels and cocks."[1]

– R. F. Dibble (1926)

"He was fond of animals, and they, as is often the case, were fond of him."[2]

– R. Bosworth Smith (1874)

"[Once the Prophet saw a donkey being branded on the face to prevent theft, and said:] 'An animal's face is the most sensitive part of its body. If you must brand, then do it on the flanks, where the flesh is thicker.' And the custom spread."[3]

– James A. Michener (1955)

"He used to … lie on his back on the floor of the mosque, get up to let in a cat, look after a sick cockerel, wipe the sweat from his horse with his sleeve…"[4]

– Emile Dermenghem (1930)

"The prophet once passed by a camel whose belly clave to its back. 'Fear God', said he, 'in these dumb animals, and ride them when they are fit to be ridden, and let them go free when it is meet they should rest.' The following [report] of kindness to birds: We were on a journey with the apostle of God, who left us

---

[1] Dibble, *Mohammed*, 242.

[2] Smith, *Mohammed and Mohammedanism*, 84.

[3] James A. Michener, "Islam: The Misunderstood Religion." Michener (d. 1997) was a famed American writer and a recipient of the Pulitzer Prize and US Presidential Medal of Freedom awards.

[4] Dermenghem, *The Life of Mahomet*, 165-66.

for a short space. We saw a hummara with its two young, and took the young birds. The hummara hovered with fluttering wings, and the prophet returned, saying, 'Who has injured this bird by taking its young? Return them to her.' Again: 'Do not clip the forelocks of your horses, nor their manes, nor their tails; for the tail is their fly-whisk; the mane is their covering; and the forelock has good fortune bound within it.'

"Animals are not to be ridden unnecessarily. By precept and example the prophet showed consideration for beasts of burden. Thus Abu Huraira reports that he said: 'Do not use the backs of your beasts as pulpits, for God has only made them subject to you in order that He may bring you to a town only otherwise reach by fatigue of body.' . . . While Anas writing of his custom says: 'When we stopped at a halt we did not say our prayers until we had unburdened the camels.'"[1]

– Alfred Guillaume (1924)

"His kindness extended even to animals, and this is something remarkable for Muhammad's century and part of the world. As his men marched towards Mecca just before the conquest they passed a bitch with puppies, and Muhammad not merely gave orders that they were not to be disturbed, but posted a man to see that the orders were carried out."[2]

– W. Montgomery Watt (1955)

"His humanity even extended itself to the lower creation. He forbade the employment of living birds as targets for marksmen; and remonstrated with those who ill-treated their camels. When some of his followers had set fire to an anthill he compelled them to extinguish it. Foolish acts of cruelty which were connected with old superstitions were swept away by him with other

---

[1] Alfred Guillaume, *The Traditions of Islam*, 106-7. Guillaume (d. 1965) specialized in Arabic and hadith, and was Professor of Hebrew and oriental languages.

[2] Watt, *Muhammad At Medina*, 323.

institutions of paganism. No more was a dead man's camel to be tied to his tomb to perish of thirst and hunger. No more was the evil eye to be propitiated by the blinding of a certain proportion of the herd. No more was the rain to be conjured by tying burning torches to the tails of oxen and letting them loose among the cattle. Horses were not to be hit on the cheek; and their manes and tails were not to be cut, the former being meant by nature for their warmth, and the latter as a protection against flies. Asses were not to be branded or hit on the face. Even the cursing of cocks and camels was discouraged. When a woman vowed to sacrifice her camel if it brought her safely to her destination, the Prophet ridiculed this mode of rewarding the beast's services, and released her from her vow."[1]

– D. S. Margoliouth (1905)

ARBITRATOR

"Historical records show that all contemporaries of Muhammed, both friends and foes, acknowledged the sterling qualities, the spotless honesty, the noble virtues, the absolute sincerity and the absolute trustworthiness of the apostle of Islam in all walks of life and in every sphere of human activity. Even the Jews and those who did not believe in his message accepted him as arbitrator in their personal disputes on account of his scrupulous impartiality."[2]

– K. S. Ramakrishna Rao (1989)

ASCETIC (DETACHMENT FROM WORLDLY LUXURIES)

"his life was sober, austere, even ascetic, spent in meditation, in prayer, abstinence, fear of God, self-restraint, attendance at the temple, painful ablutions, prostrations in the dust, preachings to

---

[1] Margoliouth, *Mohammed and the Rise of Islam*, 458-59.

[2] Rao, *Muhammad: the Prophet of Islam*, 17.

the people; he affected in his intercourse with the people no other superiority than that of the prophetic sanctity."[1]

– Alphonse de Lamartine (1854)

AURA OF RESPECT AND ADMIRATION

"those who saw him were suddenly filled with reverence, those who came near him loved him, they who described him would say, 'I have never seen his like either before or after.'"[2]

– Emanuel Deutsch (1869)

"It is a hard thing to form a calm estimate of the Dreamer of the Desert. There is something so tender and womanly, and withal so heroic, about the man, that one is in peril of finding the judgement unconsciously blinded by the feeling of reverence and well-nigh love that such a nature inspires. He who, standing alone, braved for years the hatred of his people, is the same who was never the first to withdraw his hands from another's clasp, the beloved of children, who never passed a group of little ones without a smile from his wonderful eyes and a kind word for them, sounding all the kinder in that sweet toned voice. The frank friendship, the noble generosity, the dauntless courage and hope of the man, all tend to melt criticism into admiration."[3]

– Stanley Lane-Poole (1883)

"It is impossible for anyone who studies the life and character of the great Prophet of Arabia, who knows how he taught and how he lived, to feel anything but reverence for that mighty Prophet, one of the great messengers of the Supreme. And although in what I now put to you I shall say things which may be familiar to many, yet I myself feel, whenever reread them, a new way of

---

[1] Lamartine, *History of Turkey*, vol. i, 151.

[2] Deutsch, *Literary Remains*, 73.

[3] Lane-Poole, *Studies In A Mosque*, 75-76.

admiration, a new sense of reverence to that mighty Arabian Teacher."[1]

– Annie Besant (1932)

"The most noteworthy of his external characteristics was a sweet gravity and a quiet dignity, which drew involuntary respect…"[2]

– R. Bosworth Smith (1874)

AUTHORITY AS SACRED TRUST

"The public income he expended for the public good. Authority he held not as a weapon of ambition, but a sacred trust to benefit mankind."[3]

– Marmaduke Pickthall (1917)

BALANCE AND MODERATION

"[The] Prophet was a gentle and forbearing man, averse to passionate excess of every kind."[4]

– Marmaduke Pickthall (1918)

"He insisted that men should be neither lavish nor niggardly, neither too liberal (17:31) nor wasteful (17:28), but rather observant of a proper mean in the expenditure of their substance (25:67). He emphasized sanity in social obligations. He ruled that out of justice to their heirs men might not give away the whole of their property. Once having heard of the zealous asceticism of Abdullah, son of 'Amr ibn al-'Asi, who, for example, would impose

---

[1] Annie Besant, *The Life and Teachings of Muhammad*, 4. Besant (d. 1932) was an English theosophist and women's rights advocate.

[2] Smith, *Mohammed and Mohammedanism*, 85.

[3] Pickthall, "Address on the Prophet's Birthday."

[4] Pickthall, "The Prophet's Character."

upon himself continuous fasts and spend whole nights sleepless in reading the Koran, Mohammed exhorted him to be reasonable, out of consideration for himself, his family, and his guests."[1]
– John Clark Archer (1924)

BEAUTY OF PERSONALITY

"Mahomet was distinguished by the beauty of his person, an outward gift which is seldom despised, except by those to whom it has been refused."[2]
– Edward Gibbon (1788)

BENEVOLENCE

"it will be readily admitted by all unprejudiced minds, that Mohammed's religion,—by which prayers and alms were substituted for the blood of human victims, and which, instead of hostility and perpetual feuds, breathed a spirit of benevolence and of the social virtues, and must, therefore, have had an important influence upon civilization;—was a real blessing to the Eastern world..."[3]
– John Davenport (1869)

"The sincerity of his exhortations to benevolence, was testified at his death by the exhausted state of his coffers."[4]
– Charles Mills (1817)

"Besides these specific regulations for moral conduct, the exhortations to virtue are numerous in the Koran and Sonna ... The

---

[1] Archer, *The Mystical Elements of Mohammed*, 55.
[2] Gibbon, *Decline and Fall*, vol. v, 101-02.
[3] Davenport, *An Apology for Mohammed and the Koran*, 84-85.
[4] Mills, *An History of Muhammedanism*, 39.

golden rule of reciprocal benevolence is repeated in both."[1]

— Charles Mills (1817)

"Unlimited was his benevolence and generosity, and so was his anxious care for the welfare of the community."[2]

— Gustav Weil (1866)

"The benefit of active benevolence [in the Prophet's teachings] is inculcated, by the promise of 'a reward for him who directs to good, as great as for him who is the doer of good.'"[3]

— Charles Mills (1817)

BROTHERHOOD (UNIVERSAL)

"His ideal was a brotherhood of the whole of humanity, binding man to man and nation to nation. The doctrine that each man will be judged by *his works* was a decided advance on the early doctrines that gods could be propitiated by sacrifice or by mere belief in the efficacy of a sacrifice, either animal, human, or divine. His salvation depended on his labours, on his acts and thoughts."[4]

— John Parkinson (1917)

"The brotherhood of believers ... is a truth on which no little stress is laid in the teaching of Mohammed ... 'Take tight hold of God's rope altogether, and do not part in sects; but remember the favour of God towards you, when ye were enemies and He made friendship between your hearts, and on the morrow ye were, by His favour, brothers.' 'The believers are but brothers, so make

---

[1] Ibid., 329.

[2] Weil, *A History of Islamic Peoples*, 28.

[3] Mills, *An History of Muhammedanism*, 331.

[4] John Parkinson, "Muhammad As Social Reformer." Parkinson (d. 1918) was a Scottish poet, essayist and critic. He authored several books of poetry and works on Islamic philosophy.

peace between your two brethren and fear God, haply ye may obtain mercy'; so runs the injunction of the Quran in what are, so far as I know, the two clearest and most emphatic utterances on the subject. And to a considerable degree the injunction has been obeyed in practice ... And there can be no doubt whatever that the institution of the Hajj[1] ... has done a great deal to maintain and deepen this sense of brotherhood in a common faith."[2]

– G. A. Lefroy (1907)

"The principle of universal brotherhood and the doctrine of the equality of mankind which he proclaimed represent very great contribution of Muhammed to the social uplift of humanity. All great religions have also preached the same doctrine, but the Prophet of Islam had put this theory into actual practice and its value will be fully recognized, perhaps, sometime hence, when international consciousness being awakened, racial prejudices would disappear and a stronger concept of the brotherhood of humanity comes into existence."[3]

– K. S. Ramakrishna Rao (1989)

BUSINESS ETHICS

"Mohammed commands men to be honest in business and conduct, loyal, true to their word, humble, and peace-loving: 'And the servants of the God of mercy are they who walk upon the earth softly; and when the ignorant address them, they reply; Peace!'" (25:64).[4]

– Tor Andrae (1932)

---

[1] The pilgrimage to Mecca, which is incumbent upon those who are financially able.

[2] G. A. Lefroy, *Mankind and the Church*, 299. Lefroy (d. 1919) was an Anglican priest and served as the Bishop of Lahore and Calcutta during British colonial rule in India.

[3] Rao, *Muhammad: the Prophet of Islam*, 10-11.

[4] Andrae, *Mohammed: The Man and His Faith*, 107.

"A chapter [in the compiled volumes of the Prophet's sayings] bearing the title *Gentleness in social relations* contains the prayer that God may deal kindly with the man who sells and buys and claims his debts in a kindly spirit. 'The place of the faithful merchant who speaks the truth is with the prophets, the veracious, and the martyrs.' The prophet expressly forbade buying from a person in distress; the purchase of any thing to which a risk or hazard attaches; and of fruit before it has ripened. 'He who sells a thing without notifying the buyer of a defect in it will abide in the hate of God, and the angels will curse him unceasingly!' Muhammad is said to have related the following story [of] ... A man of the people who were before you bought a plot of land, and found in it a jar containing gold. Whereupon he said to the seller, 'Take your gold for I only bought your plot.' The latter replied, 'But I sold you the ground and whatever it contained.' So they went to an arbitrator, who instructed them to marry the one's son to the other's daughter and endow them with the proceeds, giving something in alms."[1]

– Alfred Guillaume (1924)

"The golden rule is implicitly taught in the following [saying of the Prophet]: 'Let no one milk a man's cattle without his permission. Would any one of you like to have his upper chamber broken into, his treasury ransacked, and his food taken away? Now the udders of their cattle are the treasury of their food.' Again: 'There was a man who used to lend money and to say to his servant, "If you come to a man who is unable to pay, pass him over; peradventure God will pass over our shortcomings." And when he stood before God He did so pass him over.'"[2]

– Alfred Guillaume (1924)

---

[1] Guillaume, *The Traditions of Islam*, 99-100.

[2] Ibid., 100-01.

Calm

"Nothing was more mild and gentle than his speech, nothing more courteous and obliging then his Carriage;[1] he could dexterously accommodate himself to all Ages, Humours, and Degrees."[2]

– Henry Stubbe (1671)

"His deportment, in general, was calm and equable; he sometimes indulged in pleasantry, but more commonly was grave and dignified; though he is said to have possessed a smile of captivating sweetness."[3]

– Washington Irving (1849)

"Mohammed was a calm, yet by no means an unprogressive agent of Providence."[4]

– Arthur Glyn Leonard (1909)

Candor

"Look at the candour of the man. When his follower said that he was infallible, he calmly and frankly replied: 'I am such a man like yourself.' Only one instance of his frank self-condemnation whenever a mistake was committed by him, will suffice. One day as he was talking to a rich man whom he desired to win to his cause—for to win the rich and powerful man meant life for those who followed him—a blind man came along and cried aloud: 'O

---

[1] "Carriage" is one's bearing or deportment in Old English.

[2] Henry Stubbe, *An Account of the Rise and Progress of Mahometanism*, 141. Stubbe (d. 1676) was an English physician and historian. He was perhaps the first English writer who, with remarkable courage for his time, conducted a complete reassessment of Prophet Muhammad's life and mission despite the prevailing prejudices against him and Islam.

[3] Irving, *Life of Mahomet*, 192.

[4] Leonard, *Islam: Her Moral and Spiritual Value*, 43.

Prophet of God, teach me the way of salvation;' but he did not listen. He was talking to the high-born and the well-to-do, and the blind beggar, why should he interrupt! And the blind beggar knowing not that he was engaged, cried aloud again: 'O Prophet of God, show me the way.' The Prophet frowned and turned aside. The next day there came a message[1] that forever remains written in Al Quran, 'The Prophet frowned and turned aside because the blind man came to him: and how dost thou know whether he shall peradventure be cleansed from his sins, or whether he shall be admonished and the admonition will profit him? The man who is wealthy thou receivest respectfully; whereas, it is not to be charged on thee, that he is not cleansed; but him who cometh unto thee earnestly seeking his salvation, and who feareth God, dost thou reject. By no means shouldst thou act thus.'[2] Ever after, when the Prophet saw the blind man he treated him with great respect, saying: 'This man is welcome, on whose account my Lord hath reprimanded me.'"[3]

– Annie Besant (1932)

CHARISMA

"It is evident that Mohammed had a remarkable gift for winning people. Often, as with a magic stroke, he succeeded in transforming dissatisfaction into surrender and dislike into attraction."[4]

– Tor Andrae (1932)

"it would be unthinkable that such a tradition [of the Prophet's example being intimately followed by his followers] could have developed if Muhammad had not been blessed by an unusual charisma. As Johann Fück aptly says, 'Still today we see in true

---

[1] A Revelation came to the Prophet correcting his mistake.

[2] Q. 80:1-11.

[3] Besant, *The Life and Teachings of Muhammad*, 31-32.

[4] Andrae, *Mohammed: The Man and His Faith*, 262.

Muslim piety a reflection of that *Gotteserlebnis* [experience of the divine] which forced—1,300 years ago—Muhammad son of Abdallah to come forward and to preach of God and the Last Judgment.' ... And we certainly agree with Tor Andrae, who in 1917 wrote in his study of the role of the Prophet in Muslim doctrine and piety: 'We have all reason to believe that Muhammad indeed knew the art of winning hearts to a rare degree.'"[1]

– Annemarie Schimmel (1984)

Charming

"All who came in contact with him felt his charm of personality, a charm diffusing happiness and peace of mind. One word from him sufficed to silence angry disputants, to cheer the sorrowful, and heal the sick at heart. Even those who, in his absence, worked against him were vanquished by his presence and made willing slaves."[2]

– Marmaduke Pickthall (1918)

Charity

Encouragement for

"His charity, his frugality, procured for him universal respect, and these periodical retreats exalted the feelings of the Arabians into veneration."[3]

– Charles Mills (1817)

"A whole series of aphorisms is probably with justice ascribed to him, in which he recommended economy, and warned against

---

[1] Schimmel, *And Muhammad Is His Messenger*, 55.

[2] Pickthall, "The Prophet's Character."

[3] Mills, *An History of Muhammedanism*, 11.

lavish generosity. The upper hand is better than the lower (i. e., giving is better than receiving). Waste of money is to be avoided no less than idle loquacity. Charity begins at home. The best alms are such as leave wealth behind."[1]

– D. S. Margoliouth (1905)

"[According to his teachings] God's curse was upon those who refused to give alms, for charity is the only possible purification of wealth."[2]

– Emile Dermenghem (1930)

Charity Redefined

"His definition of charity embraced the wide circle of kindness. Every good act, he would say, is charity. Your smiling in your brother's face is charity; an exhortation of your fellow man to virtuous deeds is equal to alms-giving; your putting a wanderer in the right road is charity; your assisting the blind is charity; your removing stones and thorns and other obstructions from the road is charity; your giving water to the thirsty is charity."[3]

– Washington Irving (1849)

"the Prophet says ... 'Charity is a duty for every Muslim. He who has not the means for it, let him do a good act or abstain from a bad one: that is his charity.'"[4]

– Marmaduke Pickthall (1917)

"Charity is more fully enjoined in Al Quran than in any of the other Scriptures: 'Be not niggardly, but give in charity for the religion; for he who is niggardly, is niggardly to his own soul.

---

[1] Margoliouth, *Mohammed and the Rise of Islam*, **465**.

[2] Dermenghem, *The Life of Mahomet*, **264**.

[3] Irving, *Life of Mahomet*, **87-88**.

[4] Pickthall, "Islam and Progress."

God wants nothing; but thy own soul wants. God is high above all needs, but you profit.' 'Charity enlarges the mind and expands the sympathies.'"[1]

— Annie Besant (1932)

Gave Away All That He Owned

"He laid up no treasure; he distributed the whole produce of the tithe, which he established upon general property and the spoils of war, between his soldiers and the poor. He had made, for his own part, a vow of poverty. He gave all that he received to the hands and hearts of the poor, to keep for him, as depositories, charged to give all back in heaven."[2]

— Alphonse de Lamartine (1854)

"He gave away so much of his worldly belongings that he hardly ever had quite enough to live on."[3]

— Lord Headley (1914)

"The little he left he regarded as state property."[4]

— Phillip K. Hitti (1937)

"His herd of camels, and his flock of sheep, his sole heritage, became, at his death, the common property, subject only to a pension on the public treasury for the support of his widows and his

---

[1] Besant, *The Life and Teachings of Muhammad*, 33.

[2] Lamartine, *History of Turkey*, vol. i, 152.

[3] Lord Headley, *A Western Awakening to Islam*, 12. Rowland Allanson-Winn, 5th Baron Headley (d. 1935), was an English nobleman, author, poet, newspaper editor, traveler, civil engineer, lieutenant colonel in the British army, and an amateur boxer. He made headlines in 1913 when he openly declared his conversion to Islam, defying public criticism. A graduate of Cambridge University, he authored several books on poetry, Islam, religion, and boxing.

[4] Hitti, *History of the Arabs*, 120.

servants. 'A prophet,' said he, 'should leave no inheritance to his family upon the earth. His goods belong to his nation.'"[1]

– Alphonse de Lamartine (1854)

CHILDREN (LOVE OF)

"Gentle and unbending towards little children, he would not disdain to accost a group of them at play with the salutation of peace."[2]

– William Muir (1861)

"When he met children he would stop and pat their cheeks."[3]

– Winwood Reade (1872)

"He seldom passed a group of children playing together without a few kind words to them."[4]

– R. Bosworth Smith (1874)

"Loving children as he did, it must have been a cause of great regret that he had no son. He allowed his grandchildren to climb about his shoulders during prayers and to play about in the pulpit while he was being consulted by the faithful. One day a little girl, dressed in a yellow tunic which was so pretty that Mahomet congratulated her on it, began to play with the hairy growth on his back—the 'Seal of Prophecy'. Her mother scolded her, but Mahomet said: 'No, no, let her play.'"[5]

– Emile Dermenghem (1930)

---

[1] Lamartine, *History of Turkey*, vol. i, 153.

[2] Muir, *Life of Mahomet*, vol. iv, 305.

[3] Reade, *Martyrdom of Man*, 266.

[4] Smith, *Mohammed and Mohammedanism*, 84.

[5] Dermenghem, *The Life of Mahomet*, 166-67.

"In his prayers he would at times hold a child in his arms when he stood up, putting it down when he prostrated himself. At Medinah he would let a little girl take his hand and lead him where she chose. Affectionate treatment of step children is attested for a later period of his life."[1]

– D. S. Margoliouth (1905)

"Mahomet loved to play with his grandchildren, to kiss them on the navel, to have them pass between his legs, to suck their tongues, to make them jump upon his knees. He allowed them to climb upon his back while he knelt in prayer, and he prolonged his prostration so as not to disturb their play. If they made water on his clothes, he would not allow them to be scolded, but would pour a few drops of clean water over his tunic. Should they arrive at the mosque dressed in pretty, red robes, Mahomet would interrupt his sermon, descend from the pulpit and take them by the hand, excusing himself by saying: Allah has indeed said, 'Your children shall be a temptation unto you.'"[2]

– Emile Dermenghem (1930)

"He was sincerely fond of animals and children. Little boys and girls always crowded round him when he walked. He would not allow his followers to ill-treat dumb creatures."[3]

– R. V. C. Bodley (1945)

"Muhammad seems to have felt especial tenderness towards children ... Among the stories showing his affection for children are some about his granddaughter, Umāmah bint Abī 'l-'Ās (the daughter of Zaynab). He sometimes carried her on his shoulder during the Worship, setting her down when he bowed or prostrated, then picking her up again. On one occasion he teased his

---

[1] Margoliouth, *Mohammed and the Rise of Islam*, 71.

[2] Dermenghem, *The Life of Mahomet*, 206.

[3] Bodley, *The Messenger: The Life of Mohammed*, 39.

wives by showing them a necklace and saying he would give it to the one who was dearest to him; when he thought their feelings were sufficiently agitated, he presented it not to any of them but to Umāmah."[1]

    – W. Montgomery Watt (1955)

"He had fun with the children who came back from Abyssinia[2] and spoke Abyssinian. We hear of a house in Medina where there was a small boy with whom he was accustomed to have jokes, for it is recorded that once he found the small boy looking very sad; when he asked what was the matter, he was told that his pet nightingale had died, and he did what he could to comfort him ... A baby was once brought to Muhammad; he took it in his arms, and in due course it wet him. When the mother slapped it, he reproached her saying 'You have hurt my son,' and ... refused to change his clothes to have them washed."[3]

    – W. Montgomery Watt (1955)

CHORES (PERFORMED HIS OWN TASKS)

"the apostle of God submitted to the menial offices of the family; he kindled the fire, swept the floor, milked the ewes, and mended with his own hands his shoes and his woolen garments."[4]

    – Edward Gibbon (1788)

"he waited always on himself, mending his own clothes, milking his own goats."[5]

    – Winwood Reade (1872)

---

[1] Watt, *Muhammad At Medina*, 322-23.

[2] Modern day Ethiopia.

[3] Watt, *Muhammad At Medina*, 323.

[4] Gibbon, *Decline and Fall*, vol. v, 148-49.

[5] Reade, *Martyrdom of Man*, 266.

"He would kindle the fire, sweep the floor, and milk the goats himself. Ayesha tells us that he slept upon a leathern mat, and that he mended his clothes, and even clouted his shoes, with his own hand. For months together, Ayesha is also our authority for saying that he did not get a sufficient meal."[1]

– R. Bosworth Smith (1874)

"Often and often indeed was he seen in the market purchasing provisions; often and often was he seen mending his clothes in his room, or milking a goat in his courtyard."[2]

– Gustav Weil (1866)

"Mahomet was ... very simple in his habits. He used to sweep his bed-chamber, mend his clothes and his sandals, milk the ewes, lie on his back on the floor of the mosque, get up to let in a cat, look after a sick cockerel, wipe the sweat from his horse with his sleeve..."[3]

– Emile Dermenghem (1930)

"In the possession of the kind and generous affections of the heart, and in the performance of most of the social and domestic duties, he disgraced not his assumed title of an apostle of God. With that simplicity which is so natural to a great mind, he performed the humblest offices, offices whose homeliness it would be idle to conceal in the pomp of diction; even while lord of Arabia, he mended his own shoes and coarse woolen garment, milked the ewes, swept the hearth, and kindled his fire."[4]

– Charles Mills (1817)

---

[1] Smith, *Mohammed and Mohammedanism*, 85.

[2] Weil, *A History of Islamic Peoples*, 28.

[3] Dermenghem, *The Life of Mahomet*, 165-66.

[4] Mills, *An History of Muhammedanism*, 39.

His Character

COMMERCE

Justice in Transactions

"[The Prophet taught that] Contracts should be made in writing in the presence of witnesses. All deceit in selling is forbidden, and the vendor must announce any defect in his goods. Each party should submit to a trifling loss rather than occasion it to the other. Ali[1] said, 'the Prophet has forbidden bargaining with a person whose poverty compels him to sell his goods at a low rate: humanity dictates the relief of him.' An option for the performance of a contract exists with both parties till either of them has left the place of commerce. The purchaser having ultimately concluded his contract, should repeat his profession of faith, and glorify God. The traditions insist on the propriety of liberality and mutual mild dealing. Merchants of honesty and veracity will be raised 'at the last day with the prophets.'"[2]

– Charles Mills (1817)

Monopoly and Hoarding

"[In the Prophet's teachings] Monopoly is a practice highly disapproved, and pronounced abominable. The articles to which this prohibition extends are wheat, barley, dates, raisins, oil, and, according to some authorities, salt; all which being of necessary consumption, the hoarding them in order to enhance their value is followed by most prejudicial effects to mankind, and should be discouraged by law."[3]

– Charles Mills (1817)

---

[1] 'Alī was the Prophet's son-in-law.

[2] Mills, *An History of Muhammedanism*, 348-49.

[3] Ibid., 349.

Composure/Self-control

"He was the subject of strong passions, but they were so absolutely under the control of reason or of discretion, that they rarely appeared upon the surface."[1]

– William Muir (1858)

Conscience (Freedom Of)

"He claims no temporal power, no spiritual domination; he asks but for simple toleration, for free permission to win men by persuasion into the way of truth. He is sent neither to compel conviction by miracles, nor to constrain outward profession by the sword."[2]

– Edward Freeman (1856)

"Conscious of his reason and of his weakness, he asserted the liberty of conscience, and disclaimed the use of religious violence; but he called the Arabs to repentance, and conjured them to remember the ancient idolaters of Ad and Thamud, whom the divine justice had swept away from the face of the earth."[3]

– Edward Gibbon (1788)

Contentment

"His bread, it is said, was made from unsifted barley, and some reports describe how he and his family, especially his beloved daughter Fatima, suffered from hunger many a night ... 'Umar

---

[1] Muir, *Life of Mahomet*, vol. ii, 30. Regarding Muir's assessment of "strong passions," see Appendix III on page 295.

[2] Freeman, *History and Conquests of the Saracens*, 35.

[3] Gibbon, *Decline and Fall*, vol. v, 122. Gibbon adds this footnote in his text: "The passage of the Koran in behalf of toleration are strong and numerous."

ibn al-Khattab, destined to become Muhammad's second successor, once wept when looking at the Prophet's miserable household; upon being asked the reason for his tears, he ['Umar] replied that he could not bear the idea that Khosroes and Caesar, the rulers of Iran and Byzantium, lived in luxury while the Prophet of God was near starvation in his poverty. 'They have this world, and we the next one,' answered the Prophet, consoling him. Had not God offered him the keys of all treasures on earth? Yet he had refused them because he wanted to stay with his Lord, 'Who feeds me and gives me to drink.' Did not God want to make him a king-prophet like David and Solomon, though he preferred to be a servant-prophet? 'I eat as a slave eats, and sit as a slave sits, for I am a slave [of God].' His prayer, which became a favorite with mystics and ascetics, was: 'Oh Lord, keep me hungry one day and satiated one day. When I am hungry I pray to you, and when I am full I sing your praise.' And the sufferings inflicted upon him by the unfeeling Meccans resulted in his remark that 'those most afflicted are the prophets, then the saints, and then the others according to their position.'"[1]

– Annemarie Schimmel (1984)

CONGRUENCE BETWEEN INTERIOR & EXTERIOR CHARACTER

"But this external beauty was but a mirror of his interior beauty, for God had created him perfect in nature and moral qualities, *khalqan wa khulqan*. When 'A'isha, his favorite young wife, was once asked about his character she simply stated: "His character was the Koran—he liked what the Koran liked, and grew angry when the Koran was angry."[2]

– Annemarie Schimmel (1984)

---

[1] Schimmel, *And Muhammad Is His Messenger*, 47-48.

[2] Ibid., 45-46.

Consideration for Mankind

"The moral grandeur and beauty of many of the sayings attributed to Muhammad in the hadith[1] is not the least of the causes of the veneration and affection in which he is held throughout the Muhammadan world. And any estimate of his living influence must necessarily be one-sided unless it allows not only for the all-pervading authority and example of the prophet applied as it is to every single detail of human life, but also for the constant expression of a loving and affectionate consideration for mankind. It is this aspect of Islam and of its founder which has not obtained in the West the generous recognition it has earned."[2]

– Alfred Guillaume (1924)

Consistent Throughout

"Muhammad ... was as sane and practical in the last days of his life as he had been when he first received his mission; the burden of his teaching, the burden of his message was the same; his simplicity of life, his piety, remained unaltered. And this becomes the more noteworthy when we consider that in the last years of his life he was a mighty potentate, whose will was law, well able, if he wished, to gratify his every whim. To the last he was a pious Muslim, simple in his habits, regular in prayer, vigorous and far-seeing in affairs of state, gentle and forgiving in his private intercourse with men, a loyal friend, a noble enemy, faithful in all things that he undertook."[3]

– Marmaduke Pickthall (1917)

---

[1] Ḥadīth, or tradition, refers to the recorded statements and actions of Prophet Muhammad. These were collected, authenticated, and preserved in various volumes by early Muslim scholars.

[2] Guillaume, *The Traditions of Islam*, 98-99.

[3] Pickthall, "The Prophet's Gratitude."

"Circumstances changed, but the Prophet of God did not. In victory or in defeat, in power or in adversity, in affluence or in indigence, he was the same man, disclosed the same character. Like all the ways and laws of God, Prophets of God are unchangeable."[1]

– K. S. Ramakrishna Rao (1989)

COURAGE

"he had a great Strength and Agility of body, an indefatigable Industry and an undaunted Courage such as never forsook him in the greatest Dangers."[2]

– Henry Stubbe (1671)

"The courage of Mohammed, which is one of the outstanding traits throughout his career, points in the same direction. The opposition which his rebellious utterances aroused and which in time became threatening did not swerve him from his path."[3]

– James A. Montgomery (1917)

COURTEOUS

"his demeanour was as courteous and equable as ever."[4]

– Edward Freeman (1856)

COVETOUSNESS (FREE OF)

"Mahomet was never covetous of wealth, or at any period of his

---

[1] Rao, *Muhammad: the Prophet of Islam*, 24.

[2] Stubbe, *An Account of the Rise and Progress of Mahometanism*, 142.

[3] Montgomery, *Religions of the Past and Present*, 221.

[4] Freeman, *History and Conquests of the Saracens*, 37.

career energetic in the pursuit of riches for their own sake."[1]
– William Muir (1858)

"Mahomet was neither vain, covetous nor corrupted by ambition and fanaticism."[2]
– Emile Dermenghem (1930)

Devout

"A more devout man than Mohammed never lived ... and he proved his devoutness by putting his beliefs to the infallible test of stern and rigid practice."[3]
– Arthur Glyn Leonard (1909)

Dignified

"His simple eloquence was rendered impressive by a manner of mixed dignity and elegance, by the expression of a countenance wherein the awfulness of majesty was so tempered by an amiable sweetness, that it excited emotions of veneration and love..."[4]
– Charles Mills (1817)

"His whole gait and presence were dignified and imposing."[5]
– Emanuel Deutsch (1869)

"certainly there has never been seen on earth another man like Muhammad, who has rendered more material and moral service to his own nation in particular and to the world in general. It is

---

[1] Muir, *Life of Mahomet*, vol. ii, 16.

[2] Dermenghem, *The Life of Mahomet*, 165.

[3] Leonard, *Islam: Her Moral and Spiritual Value*, 43.

[4] Mills, *An History of Muhammedanism*, 38-39.

[5] Deutsch, *Literary Remains*, 71.

impossible to imagine another human being so dignified and so worthy as Muhammad for such a magnificent glory and honour as depicted in the prophetical vision."[1]

– 'Abdul-Ahad Dawud (c. 1904)

DOWN TO EARTH

"No man who had not the common touch could have inspired such sincere friendship or love of Khadija and Aisha[2] and probably of his other ladies. He could not have drawn children to him. Often, in the mosque, he had a child in his arms while he spoke. He was often seen walking in the oasis holding a child by each hand."[3]

– R. V. C. Bodley (1945)

EDUCATION (ENCOURAGEMENT FOR)

"The ... spirit of Muhammed was liberal. In a noble admiration of science, he could exclaim, that 'a mind without erudition was like a body without a soul,' and that 'glory consists not in wealth but in knowledge.'"[4]

– Charles Mills (1817)

ELOQUENCE

"His ordinary discourse was grave and sententious, abounding

---

[1] 'Abdul-Ahad Dawud, *Muhammad in the Bible*, 77. He was formerly Rev. David Benjamin Keldani, an ordained Catholic priest who specialized in early Biblical texts. He converted to Islam in 1904 after realizing that the original teachings of Jesus were essentially the same as the teachings of Islam, and that Prophet Muhammad was foretold in the Bible according to his textual analysis.

[2] Khadīja and 'Ā'isha were wives of Prophet Muhammad.

[3] Bodley, *The Messenger: The Life of Mohammed*, 342.

[4] Mills, *An History of Muhammedanism*, 380-81.

with those aphorisms and apologues so popular among the Arabs; at times he was excited and eloquent, and his eloquence was aided by a voice musical and sonorous."[1]

– Washington Irving (1849)

"He had ... such an Elocution as no Arabian before or since hath ever equaled;"[2]

– Henry Stubbe (1671)

"His natural eloquence was enhanced by the use of the purest dialect of Arabia, and adorned by the charm of a graceful elocution."[3]

– John Davenport (1869)

"He had a lively and forcible eloquence."[4]

– Voltaire (1759)

"Being also a master in eloquence, his language was cast in the purest and most persuasive style of Arabian oratory. His fine poetical genius exhausted the imagery of nature in the illustration of spiritual truths; and a vivid imagination enabled him to bring before his auditory the Resurrection and the Day of Judgment, the joys of believers in Paradise, and the agonies of lost spirits in hell, as close and impending realities."[5]

– William Muir (1861)

"He had not studied philosophy in the school of Athens or Rome, Persia, India or China, yet he could proclaim the highest truths

---

[1] Irving, *Life of Mahomet*, 192.

[2] Stubbe, *An Account of the Rise and Progress of Mahometanism*, 141.

[3] Davenport, *An Apology for Mohammed and the Koran*, 11.

[4] Voltaire, *An Essay on Universal History, the Manners, and Spirit of the Nations*, vol. i, 42.

[5] Muir, *Life of Mahomet*, vol. iv, 316.

of eternal value to mankind. Unlettered himself, he could yet speak with an eloquence and fervour which moved men to tears of ecstasy."[1]

– K. S. Ramakrishna Rao (1989)

Endurance

"… his patient endurance, cannot but extort the admiration of all."[2]

– John Davenport (1869)

"For the first twelve years of his mission he endured such cruel persecution and distress as would have killed or driven mad a man of slighter faith."[3]

– Marmaduke Pickthall (1920)

Equal Treatment of People

"He treated friends and strangers, the rich and poor, the powerful and the weak, with equity, and was beloved by the common people for the affability with which he received them, and listened to their complaints."[4]

– Washington Irving (1849)

Esteemed (Even by Those Who Knew Him Intimately)

"those who knew him best, trusted him the most. No man, they tell us, is a hero to his valet-de-chambre. The simple life of the Arab admitted of no one in that exact capacity; but in the nearest approach to it, in his noble freedman Zeyd, Mahomet found one

---

[1] Rao, *Muhammad: the Prophet of Islam*, 20.

[2] Davenport, *An Apology for Mohammed and the Koran*, 11.

[3] Marmaduke Pickthall, "A Sermon."

[4] Irving, *Life of Mahomet*, 193.

in whose eyes he was emphatically a hero. The confidence and affection of a wife to whom he owed his position, and one fifteen years older than himself; the constant confidence and affection of men of the noblest and at the same time the most opposite characters—the calm Abu-Bekr, the chivalrous Ali, the fiery Omar—certainly tend to show that the personal character of Mahomet in no way gave the lie to his lofty pretensions."[1]

– Edward Freeman (1856)

Ethical Norms (Attainable)

"The ethical norms that are handed down from him breathe the same spirit as those taught by all great religious leaders. Asked 'What is virtue?' he answered: 'Ask your heart for a *fatwa* [legal decision]. Virtue is when the soul feels peace and the heart feels peace, and sin is what creates restlessness in the soul and rumbles in the bosom.' And when asked 'What is the best Islam?' he replied: 'The best Islam is that you feed the hungry and spread peace among people you know and those you do not know.'"[2]

– Annemarie Schimmel (1984)

"The great strength [in the message of the Prophet] of Islam lies in its simplicity, its adaptability, its high yet perfectly attainable ethical standard ... The ideal Muslim state is conceivable and was actually realized, or very nearly so, by Muhammad's immediate successors..."[3]

– Edward G. Browne (1902)

---

[1] Freeman, *History and Conquests of the Saracens*, 40.

[2] Schimmel, *And Muhammad Is His Messenger*, 55.

[3] Edward G. Browne, *A Literary History of Persia*, 188. Browne (d. 1926) specialized in Persian Studies and was Professor of Arabic and Persian at the University of Cambridge.

EVIL (ERASING WITH GOOD)

"The prophet is said to have declared that 'A Muslim is he from whose tongue and hands [other] Muslims are safe', and that 'it is required of the best of men that they should love God and his apostle above all others and their fellowmen for God's sake'. The prophetic view of honesty as a principle of life is well expressed in the hadith, 'A servant of God shall not acquire property unlawfully and give alms thereof which shall be accepted. Nor shall he spend thereof and be blessed. And he shall not leave it behind him as it will bring him to hell. God does not blot out evil by evil, but God blots out evil by good.'"[1]

– Alfred Guillaume (1924)

EXEMPLARY

"He is but a preacher sent to warn men that there is one God and that there is none other but He, that all that He requires is that men should do justice and love mercy, and walk humbly with their God, and, as the sanction of all, that there will be a resurrection of the dead, as well of the just as of the unjust. Such was the teaching of one who in his own person fulfilled the duties which he taught, a thoroughly good and righteous man according to his light."[2]

– Edward Freeman (1856)

"His own treatment of his bitterest enemies was the noblest example for his followers."[3]

– K. S. Ramakrishna Rao (1989)

"The authenticated story for the Prophet's earthly life affords the most complete example to humanity, for he experienced both

---

[1] Guillaume, *The Traditions of Islam*, 99.

[2] Freeman, *History and Conquests of the Saracens*, 35.

[3] Rao, *Muhammad: the Prophet of Islam*, 10.

poverty and wealth, persecution and prosperity, helplessness and the extreme of power; and in every circumstance he was exemplary."[1]

– Marmaduke Pickthall (1917)

Father

"As a father he was loving and tender."[2]

– William Muir (1861)

Forced Conversion (Never)

"but even its most hostile critics have absolutely failed to lay their finger even on one instance where war resulted in individual or tribal conversion to Islam ... He never tried to exercise his power to convert his prisoners, for he followed his instructions: 'Let there be no compulsion (no violence) in Religion.'"[3]

– Lord Headley (1914)

Foremost in Good Deeds

"Most times it was impossible to anticipate that Excellency in saluting;[4] but if any one saluted him first, he would return the salutation in the same or in a still better way. He returned the salutation anon, without any delay, except for some special reason. He saluted in an audible voice, and did not content himself

---

[1] Pickthall, "The Holly Prophet As An Example."

[2] Muir, *Life of Mahomet*, vol. iv, 309.

[3] Headley, *A Western Awakening to Islam*, 80-81; quoting Q. 2:256.

[4] Meaning he was usually the first to perform any good deed, even in greeting a person.

with a mere sign with his finger. In returning a salutation, he said, 'And upon thee be peace!'"[1]

– S. W. Koelle (1888)

Forgiveness

Personal Injuries

"The higher law of forgiveness is clearly propounded [in the teachings of the Prophet]. Abu Darda says: I heard the prophet say, 'There is no man who receives a bodily injury and forgives the offender but God will exalt his rank and diminish his sin.'"[2]

– Alfred Guillaume (1924)

"Innumerable are the instances of his forgiveness. He forgave the Jewess who prepared for him a poisoned meal, from which one of his companions died and he himself derived a painful illness which eventually caused his death. He forgave the man who, by an act of brutal rudeness, killed his daughter. He forgave Hind, the wife of Abu Sufian, who devoured the flesh of true believers on the field of Ohod like a ghoul, when she declared repentance. He forgave, so far as I know, every one who ever wronged him personally."[3]

– Marmaduke Pickthall (1917)

General Amnesty for His Persecutors

"The chiefs of the Koreish were prostrate at his feet. [He asked] 'What mercy can you expect from the man whom you have wronged?' [They replied] 'We confide in the generosity of our

---

[1] Koelle, *Mohammed and Mohammedanism*, 399.

[2] Guillaume, *The Traditions of Islam*, 101.

[3] Pickthall, "Address on the Prophet's Birthday."

kinsman.' 'And you shall not confide in vain: begone! you are safe, you are free.'"[1]

– Edward Gibbon (1788)

"Facts are hard things; and it is a fact that the day of Mohammad's greatest triumph over his enemies was also the day of his grandest victory over himself. He freely forgave the Kureysh all the years of sorrow and cruel scorn they had inflicted on him: he gave an amnesty to the whole population of Mekka. Four criminals, whom justice condemned, made up Mohammad's proscription list when he entered as a conqueror the city of his bitterest enemies. The army followed his example, and entered quietly and peaceably; no house was robbed, no woman insulted. One thing alone suffered destruction. Going to the Kaaba, Mohammad stood before each of the three hundred and sixty idols and pointed to it with his staff, saying, "Truth is come and falsehood is fled away," and at these words his attendants hewed it down; and all the idols and household gods of Mekka and round about were destroyed.

"It was thus that Mohammad entered again his native city. Through all the annals of conquest, there is no triumphal entry like this."[2]

– Stanley Lane-Poole (1883)

---

[1] Gibbon, *Decline and Fall*, vol. v, 137. In these two lines of text, Gibbon seeks to capture the dramatic conversation that took place between the Prophet and the people of Mecca following his re-entry into his native city. For context, the ruling aristocrats and polytheists of Mecca rejected the Prophet's message of worshipping One God, and persecuted him and his followers for years, with many perishing at their hands, including some who were painfully tortured to death. As the persecution intensified, his followers began to flee the city, some under the cover of night. Ultimately, the Prophet followed them, leaving his native city on the very night a plot was devised to kill him. Twelve years later, he returned to the city with an army of 10,000. Overpowered, the Meccans surrendered without resistance but feared imminent revenge by their victim who was now victorious over them.

[2] Lane-Poole, *Studies In A Mosque*, 73-74.

"The long and obstinate ... [persecutions of him] by the inhabitants of his native city, might have induced a haughty tyrant to mark his indignation in indelible traces of fire and blood. But Mahomet, excepting a few criminals, granted an universal pardon; and, nobly casting into oblivion the memory of the past, with all its mockings, its affronts, and persecutions, he treated even the foremost of his opponents with a gracious and even friendly consideration. Not less marked was the forbearance shewn to Abdallah[1] and the disaffected party at Medîna, who for so many years persistently thwarted his schemes and resisted his authority; nor the clemency with which he received the submissive advances of the most hostile tribes, even in the hour of victory."[2]

– William Muir (1861)

"All the qualities of patience and steadfastness of purpose were shown during that thirteen years of suffering which marked the early portion of his struggles in Mecca ... It is, however, later on in is life and during the prosperous days at Medina that our feelings of admiration are perhaps more deeply aroused. When he had the power of retaliation, and could have had his revenge, we find that he forgave his enemies."[3]

– Lord Headley (1914)

---

[1] 'Abdullah bin 'Ubay was a chieftain in Medina where the Prophet took refuge after fleeing from Mecca. 'Ubay was known as the leader of the hypocrites who outwardly presented themselves as Muslims but were in fact enemies. 'Ubay's hope of becoming the ruler of Medina—an outcome that was widely expected—was dashed when the people of Medina accepted the Prophet as their undisputed leader and ruler. This failed aspiration fueled his enmity. Although the Prophet was aware of 'Ubay's intentions and, along with the Muslims, was often vexed by his actions, he never exposed him or took any action against him.

[2] Muir, *Life of Mahomet*, vol. iv, 306-7.

[3] Headley, *A Western Awakening to Islam*, 70.

"His own treatment of his bitterest enemies was the noblest example for his followers. At the conquest of Mecca, he stood at the zenith of his power. The city which had tortured him and his followers, which had driven him and his people into exile and which had unrelentingly persecuted and boycotted him even when he had taken refuge in a place more than 200 miles away, that city now lay at his feet. By the laws of war he could have justly avenged all the cruelties inflicted on him and his people. But what treatment did he meet out to them? Muhammed's heart overflowed with the milk of love and kindness as he declared, 'This day, there is no reproof against you and you are all free.'"[1]

– K. S. Ramakrishna Rao (1989)

"Meccah was now the Prophet's ... All Meccah was now to be an inviolable sanctuary: no blood was to be shed within its precincts ... Like Motley's cardinal preaching religious toleration, Mohammed took the earliest opportunity of impressing on his townsmen the abhorrence with which bloodshed should be regarded. And indeed though at the first he had drawn up a short proscription list, for one reason or another he reduced it to the modest number of two. Therein we can see ... an example of the Prophet's clemency ... All old injuries were forgotten on that day of final triumph. The Refugees were not even allowed to reclaim their houses which had been seized or sold by the Meccans: they had to be satisfied with the promise of houses in Paradise instead—Mohammed setting the example with Khadijah's former dwelling."[2]

– D. S. Margoliouth (1905)

FRIENDLINESS

"The Prophet's friendliness and largesse encompassed everyone;

---

[1] Rao, *Muhammad: the Prophet of Islam*, 10.

[2] Margoliouth, *Mohammed and the Rise of Islam*, 387-88.

His Character

he was like a father for his companions.'"¹

– Annemarie Schimmel (1984)

FRIENDSHIP

"Mahomet was also a faithful friend. He loved Abu Bakr with the romantic affection of a brother; Ali, with the fond partiality of a father. Zeid, the Christian slave of Khadija, was so strongly attached by the kindness of Mahomet, who adopted him, that he preferred to remain at Mecca rather than return to his home with his own father ... The friendship of Mahomet survived the death of Zeid, whose son, Osâma, was treated by him with distinguished favour for his father's sake. Othmân and Omar were also the objects of a special attachment; and the enthusiasm with which the Prophet, at Hodeibia, entered into 'the Pledge of the Tree' and swore that he would defend his beleaguered son-in-law with his last breath, was a signal proof of faithful friendship. Numerous other instances of Mahomet's ardent and unwavering regard might be adduced. And his affections were in no instance misplaced; they were ever reciprocated by a warm and self sacrificing love."[2]

– William Muir (1861)

"the friends of his adversity were never forgotten."[3]

– Edward Freeman (1856)

"The good manners of that prince were such that he never grieved any one of his friends and servants."[4]

– S. W. Koelle (1888)

---

[1] Schimmel, *And Muhammad Is His Messenger*, 47.

[2] Muir, *Life of Mahomet*, vol. iv, 306.

[3] Freeman, *History and Conquests of the Saracens*, 37.

[4] Koelle, *Mohammed and Mohammedanism*, 377-78.

"If the warmth of his attachment may be measured, as in fact it may, by the depth of his friends devotion to him, no truer friend than Mohammed ever lived. Around him, in quite early days, gathered what was best and noblest in Mecca; and in no single instance, through all the vicissitudes of his chequered life, was the friendship then formed, ever broken."[1]
—R. Bosworth Smith (1874)

"Hosein Ibn Ali[2] narrates: When I asked my father how the Prophet lived in public, he answered, '... He never neglected good manners, duly saluted his companions, and inquired after their state."[3]
– S. W. Koelle (1888)

"Throughout the whole of his life, he never changed his allegiance to a friend."[4]
– R. V. C. Bodley (1945)

Frugality

"He believed in frugality, and that the stomach need only be half-filled ... the Prophet's wardrobe was no richer than his table."[5]
– Emile Dermenghem (1930)

Funeral

"[Once] A bier passed by with the corpse lying on it and someone said to him that it was the body of a Jew. 'Whether it be the body

---

[1] Smith, *Mohammed and Mohammedanism*, 84.

[2] "Ḥussain," son of Ali, was a grandson of the Prophet. He was six years old when the Prophet died.

[3] Koelle, *Mohammed and Mohammedanism*, 378.

[4] Bodley, *The Messenger: The Life of Mohammed*, 39.

[5] Dermenghem, *The Life of Mahomet*, 163.

of a Jew or Christian or Mussalman,' answered the Prophet, 'You should stand up as the bier passes by.' And so it is that when studying his teachings you cannot help avoiding a deep reverence and even a respectful love for the man."[1]

– Annie Besant (1932)

"At funerals he never rode: he would remain silent on such occasions, as if conversing with himself, so that the people used to think he was holding communication with the dead."[2]

– William Muir (1861)

"he followed the bier that passed him in the street; he visited the sick."[3]

– Winwood Reade (1872)

GENEROSITY

"Unlimited was his benevolence and generosity, and so was his anxious care for the welfare of the community. Despite innumerable presents which from all quarters unceasingly poured in for him; despite rich booty which streamed in—he left very little behind, and even that he regarded as State property. After his death his property passed to the State and not to Fatima, his only daughter, the wife of Ali."[4]

– Gustav Weil (1866)

"It is creditably narrated that once some one came to his Excellency to ask for something, and that he gave this reply, 'At the present moment nothing remains in my hand: but buy whatever thou desirest and put it to my account; and as soon as anything

---

[1] Besant, *The Life and Teachings of Muhammad*, 10.

[2] Muir, *Life of Mahomet*, vol. iv, 327.

[3] Reade, *Martyrdom of Man*, 266.

[4] Weil, *A History of Islamic Peoples*, 28.

comes to my hand I will defray the debt.' On another occasion, when 100,000 dirhems[1] were brought to that Excellency, he had them all forthwith poured out on a mat and divided amongst the people, so that, on rising up, not a single dirhem remained in his hand."[2]

– S. W. Koelle (1888)

"He used to ... give alms to the poor when he had anything to give..."[3]

– Emile Dermenghem (1930)

GENUINE

"Through life we find him to have been regarded as an altogether solid, brotherly, genuine man."[4]

– Thomas Carlyle (1840)

"there shines out [in the character of the Prophet] unmistakably a largeness of humanity—sympathy for the weak, a gentleness that seldom turned to anger save when dishonour seemed to be done to God, something even of shyness in personal intercourse, and a glint of humour all of which contrasts so strangely with the prevailing temper and spirit of his age and of his followers that it cannot be other than a reflection of the real man."[5]

– Hamilton A. R. Gibb (1948)

---

[1] *Dirham* is a silver coin.

[2] Koelle, *Mohammed and Mohammedanism*, 381.

[3] Dermenghem, *The Life of Mahomet*, 166.

[4] Carlyle, *On Heroes,* 59.

[5] Hamilton A. R. Gibb, *Mohammedanism: An Historical Survey*, 31-32. Scottish born Sir Gibb (d. 1971) was a Professor of Arabic and Oriental Studies and taught at Edinburg University, St. John's College (Oxford), and Harvard University.

His Character

GENTLENESS

Affable with Everyone

"He was mostly gentle, sensitive, and humane, even irresolute at the moments when he felt himself uninspired; he was affable with everyone."[1]

— Emile Dermenghem (1930)

Manners with the Young

"Many of the hadith already cited will have shown the good sense, amiability, and liberality of the prophet; and the following further examples of the qualities which have ever endeared him to his followers must suffice. Rafi' b. 'Amr al Ghaffari: When I was a boy I threw stones at the Anṣār's[2] date-palms, and so they brought me before the prophet of God. 'Boy,' said he, 'why did you throw stones at the date-palms?' 'So that I might eat dates,' I said. 'Don't throw stones,' said he, 'but eat the fallings.' Then he touched his head and prayed: 'O God, satisfy him with food.'"[3]

— Alfred Guillaume (1924)

GIFT (ACCEPTANCE OF)

"No one, whether a red man or a black (that is, an Arab or a negro) ever spoke to him without receiving a reply, and he often picked up discarded dates and put them into his mouth because

---

[1] Dermenghem, *The Life of Mahomet*, 165.

[2] The people of Medina who welcomed and provided refuge to the Prophet and his companions after their persecution and expulsion from Mecca were given the honorific title "Anṣār," meaning "Helpers."

[3] Guillaume, *The Traditions of Islam*, 150-51.

he thought that they might be a gift and did not wish to offend the giver."[1]

— Tor Andrae (1932)

GOD

Restored the True Concept Of

"His definition of God is expressed in a manner still more sublime: on being asked who was that Allah whom he preached, he replied: 'It is he who holds his being of himself, and from whom all other beings are derived; who begetteth not, neither is begotten; and who has no likeness throughout the whole extent of being.'"[2]

— Voltaire (1759)

"For Mohammed the essential element of true belief was an uncompromising monotheism ... True belief demands *ikhlās*, the giving of one's whole and unmixed allegiance to God, and its opposite is *shirk*, the ascribing of partners to God and the worship of any creature ... God exists from all eternity to all eternity. He is the only reality ... 'To Him belongeth the rule and to Him shall ye be brought back for judgement' (28:88). All else from the Seven Heavens downwards comes into existence by His Will and at His creative Word 'Be!' He alone gives life and death, His Decree is inescapable, and all things are determined and disposed by His foreknowledge ... [Besides the] majestic aspects of God as Creator, Supreme Power, Judge, and Avenger, the Koran stresses also His bounty and loving-kindness. He is not only 'the Compassionate One, the Merciful', but also the Protector, the Provider, the Pardoner, the Clement, ever ready to turn to the repentant sinner. He is the Subtle, Who is 'closer to man than his

---

[1] Andrae, *Mohammed: The Man and His Faith*, 262.

[2] Voltaire, *An Essay on Universal History*, vol. i, 45.

own neck-vein' (50:15), 'the First and the Last, the Manifest and the Hidden.'" (57:3).[1]

– Hamilton A. R. Gibb (1948)

"It is true indeed that the rigid Monotheism of the creed, the truth that God is ONE, has been often represented, as the very kernel of its doctrine and system ... vitally important as this truth obviously is, and all-essential as a condition of any larger view, I cannot for a moment doubt myself that there is an even larger, deeper, more vital principle which lies behind it, and which is, indeed, the secret alike of the extraordinary power for conquest and advance which Islam has in its best ages evinced, and of all that still remains of true life and health in the system. Not so much that God is one as that God IS—that His existence is the ultimate fact of the universe—that His will is supreme—His sovereignty absolute—His power limitless; —this is beyond question the truth which sank into the soul of Mohammed..."[2]

– G. A. Lefroy (1907)

No Clergy between Man and God

"Islam [preached by Prophet Muhammad] swept away the secrecy with which others had shrouded the study of sacred scriptures, reproaching those who were only able to recite the words and comparing those who claimed to be the repositories of the Pentateuch to a donkey loaded with books. It invited any man of religious sentiments to acquire the knowledge that was necessary for understanding God's word. Among the Muslims, there was no duly authorized exegesis of the holy book on which they were required to base their beliefs. Nor were there councils or synods which, after discussion, presumed to lay down the precise

---

[1] Gibb, *Mohammedanism: An Historical Survey*, 54-56.

[2] Lefroy, *Mankind and the Church*, 283.

formula which was to be considered as the living symbol of orthodoxy."[1]

– Laura Vaglieri (1925)

Man's Relationship to God

"There is a great deal of truth in what the Muhammadan Religion teaches with reference to Man's relations to God. Man as a creature is absolutely dependent upon his Creator in every thing. His first duty is to believe in, worship and confess his Lord and Maker, and that too precisely in the way which God has laid down for his guidance. He must submit himself to His will and pleasure and be perfectly resigned to Him in everything, submitting himself humbly as a slave to his master."[2]

– James A. Montgomery (1917)

The Ultimate Objective of All Actions

"to him personally Islam was something more than a mere creed or belief. It was God's own religion sealed and delivered to him by God... But with him God always came first. His duty to his country was subordinate to his duty to his Maker. His duty to Him, therefore, was his duty to his country."[3]

– Arthur Glyn Leonard (1909)

"Like all noble characters, Mohammed certainly felt a real and sincere concern for the poor and neglected. But we find in him no real indignation concerning their hard lot, and still less did it occur to him to attempt to abolish poverty. Pious gifts are not

---

[1] Laura Vaglieri, *An Interpretation Of Islam*, 34. Vaglieri (d. 1989) was an Italian orientalist and scholar of Arabic and Islamic Studies. She was a professor at the University of Naples (Italy).

[2] Montgomery, *Religions of the Past and Present*, 21.

[3] Leonard, *Islam: Her Moral and Spiritual Value*, 98.

made for this purpose. Alms are given for Allah's sake because they are pleasing to Him, or they are given for one's own benefit, for the 'cleansing' of the soul, to eradicate the effects of sin committed, or to prevent accumulated wealth from becoming a damning burden on the Day of Judgment, or to store up good works with which to earn Paradise."[1]

— Tor Andrae (1932)

"The difference (as it appears to me) between other great men and himself was wide. The ordinary type of great man—a John Knox for example—is a patriot essentially. He is for his country first, then for God and humanity. As I have shown, with Mohammed it was just the reverse. An Arab by accident of birth, he put God and nature before everything. It was this that made him a humanist; this that placed him before his age."[2]

— Arthur Glyn Leonard (1909)

Reliance On

"Without God he felt himself alone and weak. 'O God,' he prayed in the night, 'do not let me fall again. Do not abandon me for a single moment.' 'Why do you speak so?' asked his wife, Omm Selma, 'when God has forgiven you your sins past and future?' 'O Omm Selma, how can I be safe when God once abandoned the Prophet Jonah? O my God, pardon me my sins, past and present, great and small, secret or known. Every day I repent seventy times. Wash me of my sins in snow and ice, wash my heart as one washes a garment, place between me and my faults the distance between the East and the West.'"[3]

— Emile Dermenghem (1930)

---

[1] Andrae, *Mohammed: The Man and His Faith*, 103.

[2] Leonard, *Islam: Her Moral and Spiritual Value*, 109.

[3] Dermenghem, *The Life of Mahomet*, 250-51.

Resignation to God's Will

"From being in most humble circumstance, and starting life as an orphan, he passed through the different stages of life allotted to him with beautiful resignation to God's will."[1]

– Lord Headley (1914)

God-Consciousness

"He sometimes swore, in important matters. His most frequent oath was, 'By Him in whose hands my soul is,' or, 'By Allah.'[2] When he arose from an assembly, he would say, by way of atonement for the assembly, 'Praise be to God, and for Thy honour I testify that there is no God but Thou: I ask pardon of Thee, and repent towards Thee.'"[3]

– S. W. Koelle (1888)

"This conviction [of all pervading providence of God] moulded his thoughts … He never entered a company 'but he sat down and rose up with the mention of the Lord.' When the first fruits of the season were brought to him, he would kiss them, place them upon his eyes and say, 'Lord as thou hast shown us the first, show unto us likewise the last.' In trouble and affliction, as well as in joy and prosperity, he ever saw and humbly acknowledged the hand of God."[4]

– William Muir (1861)

---

[1] Headley, "Self-Control."

[2] The Prophet's swearing, which usually preceded important statements, was limited to invoking God, typically with phrases like "By Allah" or "By the One in Whose hand is my soul." The latter phrase implied that God could take his soul at any moment if what he was about to say did not represent the truth or was displeasing to God.

[3] Koelle, *Mohammed and Mohammedanism*, 393.

[4] Muir, *Life of Mahomet* vol. iv, 311.

Gratitude To

"He used to stand for such a length of time at prayer that his legs would swell. When remonstrated with, he said 'What! Shall I not behave as a thankful servant should?'"[1]

– William Muir (1861)

"After a meal he would thank God for it. It is said that whoever, on eating, recites the words, 'Praise be to Him who has fed us with this food, and provided us with it, without our own efforts and strength,' he will have his sins forgiven. When he ate with other people, as their guest, he prayed for them."[2]

– S. W. Koelle (1888)

"the duty of being grateful to God is a theme which he never tires of elaborating. He constantly returns to the benevolence which Allah bestows upon man. He marvelously created him in his mother's womb, He sends rain from heaven and gives life to the dead earth so that it may sustain grass and seed; He has enriched man with cattle and has taught him metal working, navigation, and commerce. And Allah expects man to be thankful for everything that He has given to him, and show his gratitude by believing and by passing on some of these gifts to the poor."[3]

– Tor Andrae (1932)

Humility To

"[In his recorded] prayers, the Messenger's humility and trust in God is especially evident. He always appears aware of his own need for forgiveness: 'I ask forgiveness from God seventy [sometimes, one hundred] times a day.' Even though such an

---

[1] Ibid., 327.

[2] Koelle, *Mohammed and Mohammedanism*, 386.

[3] Andrae, *Mohammed: The Man and His Faith*, 98-99.

expression seems to contradict the long-standing doctrine of his prophetic *'isma*, that is, freedom from sins and defects, it is usually interpreted as his effort, whatever his own excellence, to provide an example for his sinful community so that they might pray in awareness of their human weakness. Here his role as teacher of his followers comes to the fore. He is, after all, quoted as saying: 'I have come to perfect the noble habits.'"[1]

– Annemarie Schimmel (1984)

Dedicated His Life For

"If ever man on this earth found God, if ever man devoted his life to God's service with a good and a great motive, it is certain that the Prophet of Arabia was that man."[2]

– Arthur Glyn Leonard (1909)

"Truly 'My prayers and my worship and my life and my death are unto God, Lord of the Worlds. He hath no associate. This am I commanded, and I am the first of the Muslims.'[3] (Sura 6:163) *The first of the Muslims!* Mohammed is absolutely justified in so designating himself ... Even to-day, after a period of development of thirteen centuries, one may clearly discern in genuine Islamic piety the uniqueness which is ultimately derived from its founder's personal experience of God."[4]

– Tor Andrae (1932)

See Appendix II on page 291 for some of Muhammad's (ﷺ) supplications to God showing his utmost humility before Him.

---

[1] Schimmel, *And Muhammad Is His Messenger*, 54-55.

[2] Leonard, *Islam: Her Moral and Spiritual Value*, 18-19.

[3] The literal meaning of the word "Muslim" is "one who submits to the will of God." It is in this sense that the word is used in verse Q. 6:163.

[4] Andrae, *Mohammed: The Man and His Faith*, 11-12.

GOOD DEEDS

"Islam [as preached by Prophet Muhammad] stresses the value of good deeds, which are the consequences of human pity toward one's neighbor, just as it stresses God's pity. The orphan, the poor, the humble, the unfortunate are protected by the most concerned promptness. Islam declares that brotherhood and charity are the two cornerstones of Muslim society."[1]

– Laura Vaglieri (1925)

GREETING

"He greeted everyone, slaves and little children as well. When 'Ayesha was questioned as to the conduct of the Prophet in private life, she replied: 'The most gentle and noble of men. Otherwise he was like other men, except that he loved to laugh and smile.'"[2]

– Tor Andrae (1932)

GREAT IN PROSPERITY AS IN ADVERSITY

"A character so lofty should be better understood ... He was as great in prosperity as in adversity. At the first battle fought by the Prophet, his followers said: 'We are too few to go against our enemies.' The Prophet replied: 'God is with us, and that is enough'; so they marched against overwhelming odds and conquered."[3]

– Annie Besant (1932)

---

[1] Vaglieri, *An Interpretation Of Islam*, 53.

[2] Andrae, *Mohammed: The Man and His Faith*, 262.

[3] Besant, *The Life and Teachings of Muhammad*, 30.

Head of State

"Head of the State as well as of the Church, he was Caesar and Pope in one; but he was Pope without the Pope's pretensions, and Caesar without the legions of Caesar. Without a standing army, without a bodyguard, without a palace, without a fixed revenue, if ever any man had the right to say that he ruled by a right Divine, it was Mohammed; for he had all the power without its instruments and without its supports."[1]

– R. Bosworth Smith (1874)

Honest

"Muhammed was more than honest."[2]

– K. S. Ramakrishna Rao (1989)

Honoring the Status of All People

"He knew how to pay his submissions to the great without servility, and to be complacent to the meaner sort without abasing himself."[3]

– Henry Stubbe (1671)

"In the familiar offices of life he scrupulously adhered to the grave and ceremonious politeness of his country: his respectful attention to the rich and powerful was dignified by his condescension and affability to the poorest citizens of Mecca … and the habits of courtesy were imputed to personal friendship, or universal benevolence."[4]

– Edward Gibbon (1788)

---

[1] Smith, *Mohammed and Mohammedanism*, 235.

[2] Rao, *Muhammad: the Prophet of Islam*, 25.

[3] Stubbe, *An Account of the Rise and Progress of Mahometanism*, 141.

[4] Gibbon, *Decline and Fall*, vol. v, 102.

His Character

Hospitality

"Hospitality, for which the Arabs have ever been justly praised, is in hadith a mark of the true believer. Thus, Abu Huraira tells us that the prophet said: 'Whoever believes in God and the last day, let him honour his guest, let him not injure his neighbour, and if he has nothing good to say let him remain silent.' A more precise definition of the hospitality incumbent on a Muslim [are these words of the Prophet]: 'Whosoever believes in God and the last day let him entertain his guest bountifully for a day and a night. Hospitality (should be given) for three days. What is done over and above that is in the nature of almsgiving. It is not right for a guest to stay in a man's house so long as to embarrass him.'"[1]

— Alfred Guillaume (1924)

"He used to converse during the meal, and repeatedly offered food to the guests, saying, 'Eat!'"[2]

— S. W. Koelle (1888)

"he was ... a lover of hospitality, benevolent, wise, assiduous in the cause of God..."[3]

— S. W. Koelle (1888)

Humanizing

"He was human to the marrow of his bones. Human sympathy, human love was the music of his soul. To serve man, to elevate man, to purify man, to educate man, in a word, to humanize man—this was the object of his mission, the be-all and end-all of

---

[1] Guillaume, *The Traditions of Islam*, 104-5.

[2] Koelle, *Mohammed and Mohammedanism*, 386.

[3] Ibid., 383.

his life. In thought, in word, in action he had the good of humanity as his sole inspiration, his sole guiding principle."[1]

– K. S. Ramakrishna Rao (1989)

Humility

While Muslims believe in and respect all the previous prophets of God and make no distinctions between one and another of them, they consider Prophet Muhammad as being the leader and the most important of all the prophets due the facts that he was the final messenger of God, that his message was for all of humanity[2] rather than to a specific people, and that he left a complete and best example and guidance for all areas of human life, having himself lived a full life and filled virtually all roles. Muslim scholars cite additional references in support of this viewpoint from the Prophet's authenticated statements, including his leading all other prophets in prayer during his miraculous night journey and him being the leader of the "sons of Adam" on the Day of Judgement as well as the first to intercede to God on their behalf.

All good and sound arguments; however, the humble Prophet himself never made a statement about him being the greatest of all the prophets. Quite the contrary, he would rebuke anyone who would make such suggestions in his presence. He would say, "No one should say that I am better than Yūnus bin Mattā [Prophet Jonah]"[3] or "Do not give me superiority over the other prophets"[4] or "Do not exaggerate in praising me as the Christians praised the son of Mary, for I am only a slave. So call me the *slave of Allāh and His Messenger*."[5] Once a man said to the Prophet, "O best of creatures!" He corrected him saying, "That is Abraham."[6]

---

[1] Rao, *Muhammad: the Prophet of Islam*, 25.

[2] Q. 21:107.

[3] Authenticated by al-Bukhārī.

[4] Ibid.

[5] Ibid.

[6] Authenticated by al-Tirmidhī (paraphrased).

His Character

"That Excellency's humility was so great that, when he was sitting in an assembly, he would not extend his blessed knees beyond the knees of those who sat by him; that he greeted those he met and was first in shaking hands; and that he never stretched out his legs before his companions, or made the place narrow for any one ... He never interrupted another in speaking; and if any one in need came to him, whilst he was at prayer, he would shorten his prayers, help the person, and afterwards complete his prayers."[1]
– S. W. Koelle (1888)

"He restrained the people from regarding him with too great reverence, and frequently rebuked their superstition. On the day when little Ibrahim, the son of his old age, died, an occasion of great grief to all the Muslims, there happened to be an eclipse of the sun. What an opportunity for an impostor or for one puffed up with spiritual pride! The people were all saying, "It is for the death of Ibrahim." Muhammad chid them for their foolishness. He said: 'The sun and the moon are two signs of the signs of Allah. They are not eclipsed on account of the life or death of any one.'"[2]
– Marmaduke Pickthall (1917)

"The Western reader, raised in a centuries-old tradition of aversion to Muhammad, will probably be surprised to learn that in all

---

[1] Koelle, *Mohammed and Mohammedanism*, 380.

[2] Pickthall, "Address on the Prophet's Birthday." This eclipse, coinciding with the death of a son of any man pretending to be a prophet, would have been a golden opportunity to substantiate his claim to prophethood. Citing this incident, Pickthall posed elsewhere, "Are those the words of an impostor? The symptoms of imposture are well known, and they are altogether absent from the records of the Prophet's life." (See Pickthall, "The Prophet's Gratitude")

reports the quality that is particularly emphasized in the Prophet is his humility and kindness."[1]
     – Annemarie Schimmel (1984)

Husband

"Mahomet, being married, seemed to give himself up totally to the satisfaction of his spouse; never was [a] husband more tender or more obliging than he shewed himself to Cadijah."[2]
     – Henry Stubbe (1671)

"As a husband his fondness and devotion were entire, bordering, however, at times, upon jealousy ... At the age of twenty five he married a widow forty years old; and for five and twenty years he was a faithful husband to her alone. Yet it is remarkable that during this period were composed most of those passages of the Coran in which the black-eyed Houris, reserved for believers in Paradise, are depicted in such glowing colours."[3]
     – William Muir (1861)

Impeccable Character

"we do not read of any sordid or mean incidents in his life, nor can any acts of injustice be laid to his charge."[4]
     – Lord Headley (1914)

"As yet nothing can be alleged against his life which even a

---

[1] Schimmel, *And Muhammad Is His Messenger*, 46.

[2] Stubbe, *An Account of the Rise and Progress of Mahometanism*, 227.

[3] Muir, *Life of Mahomet*, vol. iv, 309. Here, a brief digression is needed to address the obsession some orientalists have with criticizing the Prophet and Islam in relation to sexuality. See Appendix III on page 295.

[4] Headley, "Self-Control."

higher morality than that of the Koran could condemn ... have we a right to assert this of any man, above all of one whose every action creates a presumption in his favour?"[1]

– Edward Freeman (1856)

INDECENCY (FREE OF)

"Among many excellencies of which the Koran [as preached by Prophet Muhammad] may justly boast are two [that are] eminently conspicuous; the one being the tone of awe and reverence which it always observes when speaking of or referring to the Deity, to whom it never attributes human frailties and passions; the other the total absence throughout it of all impure, immoral and indecent ideas, expressions, narratives, &c., blemishes, which, it is much to be regretted, are of too frequent occurrence in the Jewish Scriptures. So exempt, indeed, is the Koran from these undeniable defects, that it needs not the slightest castration, and may be read, from beginning to end, without causing a blush to suffuse the cheek of modesty itself."[2]

– John Davenport (1869)

---

[1] Freeman, *History and Conquests of the Saracens*, 35.

[2] Davenport, *An Apology for Mohammed and the Koran*, 78. Davenport seems to be referring to the incestuous and vulgar sexual conducts depicted in the Bible, such as instances involving two girls and their father (Genesis 19:31-36), a woman and her father-in-law (Genesis 13:15-18), a man and his half-sister (Genesis 20:12-13), a man and two women who are full sisters (Genesis 29:16-28), a man and his paternal aunt (Exodus 6:19-20), a boy and his full sister (II Samuel 13:8-12, 14), and a man and his brother's daughter (Genesis 11:26-29), etc. It would disturb anyone to see that some of these stories involve prophets and their family members, which could not be true and only point to textual corruptions of the original scriptures by human hands. In contrast, the Qur'an is completely free from such immodest stories, let alone those involving prophets. It presents all prophets with the highest levels of character and moral uprightness, portraying them as models for humanity.

It would not be surprising if there is a correlation between the promiscuity and significant cases of incest seen in the modern West and such sexually provocative stories

Inspiring

"he lived up to what he taught, when you find that he never revenged himself on an enemy, when you find that in the days when he was at war instead of killing the prisoners of war, as was the brutal habit of this time, he not only gave them life, but his followers gave them all the bread they had and only kept the dates for themselves. So much were they inspired by the teaching of the Prophet that they began to realize that they were face to face with one of the mighty Ones of history, a man whom all men should reverence, whether they be followers of his special teachings or not."[1]

– Annie Besant (1932)

"So beautiful was the teaching that fell from his lips and so inspiring was his example."[2]

– Annie Besant (1932)

"His commanding mien inspired the stranger with an undefined and indescribable awe; but on closer intimacy, apprehension and fear gave place to confidence and love."[3]

– William Muir (1858)

---

found in the Bible. Until recently, nearly every child in the West grew up reading the Bible, and therefore would have encountered these stories. A person reading these accounts might find justifications for their own sexual misconduct, thinking, 'If individuals considered spiritual guides can fall prey to their carnal desires and engage in illicit activities, then certainly I cannot be expected to have greater control over mine.' Over time, such justifications might have led to a diminishing moral guilt associated with illicit sexual acts in the minds of many.

[1] Besant, *The Life and Teachings of Muhammad*, 7.

[2] Ibid., 10.

[3] Muir, *Life of Mahomet*, vol. ii, 30-31.

His Character

INSPIRED BY HIM

Numerous people throughout history have been inspired by Prophet Muhammad, including leaders, philosophers, historians, reformists, politicians, and even clerics from other faiths. In this section, we briefly discuss three such figures, whose inclusion in this category may surprise the reader.

Goethe

Goethe, the greatest of German poets, was a life-long admirer of Prophet Muhammad and the Qur'an. Stanford University professor Katharina Mommsen who specialized in Goethe's connection to the Prophet wrote, "[Goethe] was only 23 years old when he wrote a wonderful hymn in praise of Prophet Muhammad. But even when he was 70 years old, the poet declared quite publicly that he was considering 'devoutly celebrating that holy night in which the Koran in its entirety was revealed to the prophet from on high.'"[1] Impressed with the Qur'an's message and its unique composition, Goethe wrote, "The style of the Qur'an, in keeping with its content and purpose, is stern, majestic, terrifying, and at times truly sublime."[2] Muslims often find the Qur'an extraordinary in the sense that no matter how frequently they read it—many do so as part of their daily routine—they never tire of it. While such an appreciation might be unexpected from a non-Muslim, Goethe felt the same: "as often as we approach it, it always proves repulsive anew; gradually, however, it attracts, it astonishes, and, in the end, forces into admiration."[3] A verse from one of his poems reads:

"If Islam means submission to God
We all live and die in Islam's dominion."[4]

---

[1] Katharina Mommsen, "Goethe's Relationship to Islam."

[2] Katharina Mommsen, *Goethe and the Poets of Arabia*.

[3] In Deutsch, *Literary Remains*, 121.

[4] Goethe, *Poems of the West and the East*.

Goethe was writing in the mid-18th century, a time when Europe had yet to fully free itself from the Islamophobic narrative that had persisted for centuries. Yet, he was foresighted enough to recognize the role the Qur'an would play in shaping mankind. "This book," he wrote, "will go on exercising through all ages a most potent influence."[1]

In 1772, Goethe began work on a new drama in which he intended to depict the life of Prophet Muhammad. Regrettably, he never completed the work.

Victor Hugo

Few people know that Victor Hugo was a defender of Islam and Prophet Muhammad, whom he regarded as "a brilliant general and a charismatic leader."[2] Hugo wrote two poems on Islam: *L'an IX de l'Hégire* and *Le Cèdre*. The former, written in 1858, served as a funeral eulogy for Prophet Muhammad, in which he "presents Mahomet as a figure of modesty and asceticism, who milks his own ewes and sews his own clothing, a pillar of sagacity and justice."[3] According to Tristan Semiond, the poem "perfectly illustrates Victor Hugo's knowledge of Islam—both of the Sunna, the Islamic tradition that narrates the sayings and actions of the Prophet, and of the Qur'an—as well as the respect he had for Muslim culture."[4]

Hugo's immersion in the Qur'an prompted Théophile Gautier, the French poet and dramatist, to comment that Hugo might just pass for a Muslim: "To describe Muhammad, [Hugo] imbibes the Qur'an to such an extent that he could be taken for a son of Islam."[5]

Napoleon Bonaparte

In May of 1798, Napoleon began his Egyptian campaign with a naval fleet

---

[1] In Rao, *Muhammad: the Prophet of Islam*, 14.

[2] Tolan, *Faces of Muhammad*, 184.

[3] Ibid., 207.

[4] Tristan Semiond, *Victor Hugo and his poetry against Islamophobia*.

[5] Semiond, *Victor Hugo and his poetry against Islamophobia*.

of 55,000 men. He had with him a copy of Savary's 1783 translation of the Qur'an, which he had read. Prior to landing at Alexandria, he wrote a letter on July 1, 1798, to the Egyptian people, starting with the well-known Islamic formula: "In the name of God, the Beneficent, the Merciful. There is no other God than God; He has neither son nor associate to His rule."[1] Subsequently, after his conquest of Egypt, Napoleon funded and supported the celebration of Prophet Muhammad's birth day. According to Jean-Louis Detroye, a French officer who served in Napoleon's army, he even ordered an imposing parade of French troops at the celebration in honor of the Prophet, as well as a procession by a French marching band, whose martial strains intermingled with the chants of the Muslims. Detroye further adds, "The French artillery saluted Muhammad."[2] For the occasion, wrote one Captain Say in the army, Napoleon "dressed in oriental costume and declared himself protector of all the religions. The enthusiasm was universal, and he was unanimously given the name of the son-in-law of the Prophet. Everyone called him Ali Bonaparte."[3]

This may come as a surprise to many, but Napoleon is on record for having considered converting to Islam when invited by the Egyptian mufti, Sheikh Abdullah al-Sharqawi. It is unclear whether his interest was genuine or simply a political strategy to garner the support of the Egyptian. Regardless of his motive, Napoleon identified two obstacles that prevented such a consideration: circumcision and the giving up of wine. "There are two great difficulties," he said, "preventing my army and me from becoming Muslims. The first is circumcision, the second is wine. My soldiers have the habit from their infancy, and I will never be able to persuade them to renounce it."[4] In any case, "Bonaparte's admiration for the Prophet Muhammad," wrote Juan Cole, "was genuine."[5]

---

[1] Henri Laurens, *L'Exp'edition d'Egypte*, in Tolan, *Faces of Muhammad*, 186.

[2] Juan Cole, *Napoleons's Egypt: Invading the Middle East*, 125.

[3] Jean-Honoré Say and Louis de Boissy, *Bonaparte au Caire*, 126, in Cole, *Napoleons's Egypt: Invading the Middle East*, 126.

[4] Cole, *Napoleons's Egypt: Invading the Middle East*, 128.

[5] Ibid., 129.

Napoleon later wrote in his memoirs, "Arabia was idolatrous when Muhammad, seven centuries after Jesus Christ, introduced to it the religion of the God of Abraham, Ishmael, Moses, and Jesus Christ ... Muhammad declared that there was only one God, who had neither father nor son and that the Trinity imported an idea from paganism ... He rescued more souls from false gods, overturned more idols, and pulled down more pagan temples in fifteen years than the adherents of Moses and Jesus Christ had in fifteen centuries."[1]

Confined in the Island of Saint Helena, Napoleon had ample time to carry on his reading of Prophet Muhammad. "It is here," wrote Tolan, "he develops his portrait of Mahomet as a model lawmaker and conqueror." The Prophet also eradicated idolatry in Arabia and "introduced the cult of God of Abraham, Ishmael, Moses and Jesus Christ," wrote Napoleon. While Christian theologians were arguing about how to explain the Trinity, "Mahomet declared that there was one unique God who had neither father nor son; that the Trinity implied idolatry." He even wrote on the frontpiece of his copy of the Qur'an: "There is no other god than God," a literal translation of the Islamic creed in Arabic: *lā ilāha illā Allāh*.[2]

Being a general himself, Napoleon was inspired by the Prophet's military leadership and saw "Mahomet above all as a brilliant general who knew how to motivate his people, the Arabs, to accomplish great things—something of a role model for the emperor himself," wrote Tolan. Napoleon was impressed that the "prophet's eloquence, his gift of persuasion, allowed him to change the course of history,"[3] something perhaps he himself desired to do but ultimately was unsuccessful.

Napoleon correctly recognized another spectacular achievement of Prophet Muhammad, one that the Western world has long struggled with: the problem of racism. He observed that "the particularly Western vice of racism was eradicated in the Orient through the sage legislation of the Muslim prophet."[4]

---

[1] Ibid., 129-30.

[2] Tolan, *Faces of Muhammad*, 194.

[3] Ibid., 185.

[4] Ibid., 195.

His Character

In short, Napoleon was deeply inspired by Prophet Muhammad, to the extent that "Not a cloud darkens the radiant image that the fallen emperor paints of the prophet of Islam."[1]

INTELLECTUAL CAPACITY

"His intellectual qualities were undoubtedly of an extraordinary kind. He had a quick apprehension, a retentive memory, a vivid imagination, and an inventive genius."[2]

– Washington Irving (1849)

INTEGRITY

"His readiness to undergo persecution for his beliefs, the high moral character of the men who believed in him and looked up to him as leader, and the greatness of his ultimate achievement— all argue his fundamental integrity."[3]

– W. Montgomery Watt (1952)

INVITATIONS (NEVER DECLINED)

"he would accept the invitation of a slave to dinner."[4]

– Winwood Reade (1872)

"he never declined the invitation or small offering even of the meanest of the people."[5]

– Marcus Dods (1887)

---

[1] Ibid., 195.

[2] Irving, *Life of Mahomet*, 192.

[3] Watt, *Muhammad At Mecca*, 52.

[4] Reade, *Martyrdom of Man*, 266.

[5] Dods, *Mohammed, Buddha, and Christ*, 90.

"He was not known ever to refuse an invitation to the house even of the meanest, nor to decline a proffered present however small. When seated by a friend, 'he did not haughtily advance his knees towards him.'"[1]

– William Muir (1861)

"On account of his exceeding great humility and unceremoniousness, he would sit down, lie, and sleep on the dry earth, would accept an invitation from a slave, even to dry barley-bread."[2]

– S. W. Koelle (1888)

JUDGE

"the testimony even of his enemies is that he administered wisely. The wisdom he displayed in judging intricate cases became the basis for the religious law that governs Islam today. In his final years he was invited to become a dictator or a saint, but he rejected both temptations, insisting that he was an average man to whom God had sent another of His periodic messages to the world."[3]

– James A. Michener (1955)

JUSTICE

Equal Application of the Law

"In his private dealings he was just. He treated friends and strangers, the rich and poor, the powerful and the weak, with equity, and was beloved by the common people for the affability

---

[1] Muir, *Life of Mahomet*, vol. iv, 305.

[2] Koelle, *Mohammed and Mohammedanism*, 380.

[3] Michener, "Islam: The Misunderstood Religion."

with which he received them, and listened to their complaints."[1]
   – Washington Irving (1849)

"Mahomet was indignant at the cupidity of his people; he thundered against hoarding, usury, the extortions of the merchants, the partiality of the law towards the rich."[2]
   – Emile Dermenghem (1930)

Justice by Example

"he preached this gospel of fraternity and human justice, not by words alone, but by his personal example."[3]
   – Marmaduke Pickthall (1918)

Balanced Justice with Mercy

"He was just but merciful; stern but kind ... Like a wise governor, he was kind enough to forgive, but strong enough to punish, when sternness was required."[4]
   – Annie Besant (1932)

"Muhammad, Head of a State, defender of the life and freedom of his people, in the exercise of justice punished severely individuals guilty of crimes, and this attitude of his has to be considered in the light of his times and also in the light of the wild and barbarian society in which he lived. Muhammad, as a preacher of the religion of God, was gentle and merciful even towards his personal enemies. In him were blended justice and mercy, two of

---

[1] Irving, *Life of Mahomet*, 193.

[2] Dermenghem, *The Life of Mahomet*, 264.

[3] Pickthall, "The Prophet's Character."

[4] Besant, *The Life and Teachings of Muhammad*, 32.

the noblest qualities which the human mind can conceive."[1]

– Laura Vaglieri (1925)

Balanced Justice with Humanity

"In regulating the pecuniary transactions of his followers, Muhammed endeavoured to reconcile the virtues of humanity and justice. Creditors are exhorted to forbearance and even forgiveness of obligations, but debtors are threatened with future punishment who wantonly violate their faith, and Muhammed refused to pray over those who had died without leaving means of paying their debts."[2]

– Charles Mills (1817)

KIND

"he was humble, gentle, and kind."[3]

– Winwood Reade (1872)

"Zeid, the Christian slave of Khadija, was so strongly attached by the kindness of Mahomet, who adopted him, that he preferred to remain at Mecca rather than return to his home with his own father: 'I will not leave thee,' said he, clinging to his patron, 'for thou hast been a father and a mother to me.'"[4]

– William Muir (1861)

---

[1] Vaglieri, *An Interpretation of Islam*, 28.

[2] Mills, *An History of Muhammedanism*, 347-48.

[3] Reade, *Martyrdom of Man*, 266.

[4] Muir, *Life of Mahomet*, vol. iv, 306. Zayd ibn Ḥāritha was not born a slave but belonged to the prominent Kalb tribe in the north. While traveling with his mother as a boy, he was kidnapped in a tribal raid and sold into slavery. He eventually ended up in the household of Khadīja in Mecca, nearly a thousand miles from his home in Najd. Later, she presented him as a gift to Muhammad (ﷺ) upon their marriage. Years later,

"he was of a kindly disposition and noble acts ... he was amicable, meek, affectionate, and tender..."[1]

– S. W. Koelle (1888)

"A long section of the hadith literature is full of sayings [of Prophet Muhammad] inculcating the necessity of kindliness and love, of which the following may serve as examples: 'God will not have compassion on him who hath not compassion on mankind.' 'The Compassionate has compassion on those who show compassion. Show compassion to those on earth, and He who is in Heaven will have compassion on you.' 'For every young man who honours an old man on account of his age will God ordain one who will honour him in his old age.' 'The best house amid the Muslim community is that which contains an orphan who is well treated; and the worst is that wherein an orphan is wronged.' 'He who is destitute of gentleness is destitute of goodness.'"[2]

– Alfred Guillaume (1924)

"Indeed there never stepped upon this earth a kinder man, nor one more sensible."[3]

– Marmaduke Pickthall (1917)

KNOWLEDGE (ENCOURAGEMENT FOR)

"'Acquire knowledge,' the Prophet says in one of his sermons, 'because he who acquires it in the way of the Lord performs an

---

Zayd's father and uncle tracked him down and arrived in Mecca to secure his release, offering any price his master demanded. Muhammad (ﷺ) left the decision to stay or leave up to Zayd, adding that he would not require any payment for his release. Zayd chose to remain with him, while his father and uncle returned home, pleased and unconcerned. All of this occurred before Muhammad's (ﷺ) initiation of prophethood.

[1] Koelle, *Mohammed and Mohammedanism*, 383.

[2] Guillaume, *The Traditions of Islam*, 104.

[3] Pickthall, "Address on the Prophet's Birthday."

act of piety; who speaks of it praises the Lord; who seeks it adores God; who dispenses instruction in it, bestows alms; and who imparts it to its fitting objects, performs an act of devotion to God. Knowledge enables its possessor to distinguish what is forbidden from what is not; it lights the way to Heaven; it is our friend in the desert; our society in solitude, our companion when bereft of friends; it guides us to happiness; it sustains us in misery; it is our ornament in the company of friends; it serves as an armour against our enemies. With knowledge, the servant of God rises to the height of goodness and to a noble position, associates with sovereigns in this world, and attains to the perfection of happiness in the next.' Again: 'The ink of the scholar is more valuable than the blood of the martyr.' The result of this preaching was an outburst of learning which led to the foundation of a great philosophy and of a great University."[1]

– Annie Besant (1932)

Legislator

"the great Arabian legislator, who was destined so completely to change the face of the world in his own age, and to exercise so important an influence upon it for all time. And in dealing with the character of this mighty man, I rejoice that justice can now be dealt to it without fear of misconception or misrepresentation."[2]

– Edward Freeman (1856)

Inheritance Laws

"Before the days of Muhammed, the property succession of a deceased Arabian was divided between such of his relations as were

---

[1] Besant, *The Life and Teachings of Muhammad*, 34-35.

[2] Freeman, *History and Conquests of the Saracens*, 31.

able to bear arms; and the equitable share of the widow and orphan was, unjustly taken from them by their ferocious, brethren. The dowry of a woman was also frequently seized. Muhammed vindicated the rights of the female sex, and appeared in this instance a wise and humane legislator. The laws relating to infancy, succession, and dowry, are stated in the following terms, in the fourth chapter of the Koran: 'Give women their dowry freely and give not unto those who are weak of understanding the substance which God has appointed you to preserve for them; but maintain them thereout, and clothe them, and speak kindly unto them. And examine the religious state of the orphans, and their capacity for the management of their affairs, until they attain the age of marriage and maturity; but if ye perceive they are able to manage their affairs well, deliver their substance unto them, and waste it not extravagantly or hastily, because they will soon be of age. Let him who is rich abstain entirely from the orphan's estate and let him who is poor take thereout for the trouble of their education what shall be reasonable."[1]

– Charles Mills (1817)

"To his elaborate regulations on inheritance some tribute is still paid by those who in India administer the law according to them: he has left out no member of the family who can have any equitable claims, and, so far as his arithmetical knowledge went, endeavoured to settle those claims fairly."[2]

– D. S. Margoliouth (1905)

Usury

"By this Law of Mahomet it is prohibited [for] any Musulman to practise Usury not only with a Musulman, but with any Christian living under the protection of their Monarchy, or any other

---

[1] Mills, *An History of Muhammedanism*, 342-44.

[2] Margoliouth, *Mohammed and the Rise of Islam*, 463.

stranger coming to inhabit among them. Any one that considers the Civil Constitutions of Mahomet will find perpetual Reasons to admire his sagacity and Wisdom. It was a secret of Moses that no Israelite should practise Usury with an Israelite, and this was very well considering that Moses did not designe to enlarge the Jewish Empire, but to preserve his people intire and unanimous in their narrow Precincts. But Mahomet proposing vaster designes, prohibits it to all Strangers living under the protection of the Musulman."[1]

– Henry Stubbe (1671)

Gambling

"From this Law [of prohibiting gambling] it appears how prudently Mahomet weighed the least & most remote Consequences; and would not allow of those Distinctions betwixt use and abuse, or those Sophisms by which the Christians delude themselves into practises that terminate at last in the Ruine of their Comon Wealth ... He foresaw that such as were given to gaming, and engaged by the hopes of winning or sense of losing, would be apt to forget their Sallah or daily prayers, and so lapse into irreligion. He foresaw that gaming and the profit arising therefrom would induce Men to cheat each other, and that the first principle of cheating was a Contempt of God, a disregard of other Men and an inordinate desire of Wealth ... He knew that private Quarrels often occasion publick damages, and involve Families, Town, and Kingdoms in an Universal Ruine. Nor did the inconveniences seem less which follow private losses, which not only include the small Detriment of a few but many, and excite the desperate & needy to the highest and most pernicious Attempts, in which the publick suffers. He knew that the Example of some Gamesters might infect others, that Men are naturally more prone to hope then fear, to be idle then to work, to neglect

---

[1] Stubbe, *An Account of the Rise and Progress of Mahometanism*, 175-76.

then to attend the Service of God, to desire trials of enriching themselves suddenly (tho' with great Hazards) rather then stay the tedious procedure which Industry and Wisdom puts them upon. And therefore made this severe prohibition, the strictness whereof is such that it doth not permitt them so much as to draw Lotts, who shall pay a Reckoning ?"[1]

– Henry Stubbe (1671)

Alcoholic Drinks

"The limitations upon the enjoyment of life which Islam has imposed on its followers are but few, are equal for all, and show great wisdom. Today when a severe battle is being fought in the Western world against alcoholism and when the West tries to limit gambling by means of prohibitions and limitations, can anybody blame Islam for having banged shut these two 'doors of danger', these causes of corruption both of the spirit and of wealth? Thrift is a virtue in the words of the Quran, but this is not enough. We read in the holy book of prohibition of gambling and of making money through charging interest on loans. Would you not say that God's wisdom shines in this repression of illegal earnings?"[2]

– Laura Vaglieri (1925)

---

[1] Ibid., 177-78. Stubbe's 17th-century English with unconventional spelling and grammar—judged by modern standards—may be difficult to read. However, these words, when one takes the time to reflect upon them, reveal the man's deep insights, as he correctly understood some of the underlying wisdom behind the prohibition of gambling and divination.

[2] Laura Vaglieri, *An Interpretation Of Islam*, 61-62. Vaglieri was writing at a time when the United States attempted to ban the production, import, sale, and transportation of alcoholic beverages, known as "The Prohibition." Though the ban went into effect in 1920, the long-lasting effort to enforce it, which spanned over a decade, ultimately failed, and the ban was repealed in 1933. Much has been written about why it failed, but the underlying reason is a simple fact: people simply were not willing to give up drinking. (*continued to next page*)

Divination (Fortune Telling)

"Whether it were his great Prudence, or Care for the Worship of the true God, I shall not determine, but certainly his Legislative Care extended farr when he prohibited all Observation of Omens and all divination by Lotts, as Debates to do or forbear an Action, by opening the Alcoran (as the Romans did Virgil), or shooting an Arrow into the Air, or drawing an Arrow out of the Sheaf, whereon should be written it is not the pleasure of God. This great Prophet would not suffer his Moslemin[1] to employ anything but Reason in their Debates. He imprinted in their minds that there is not any such thing as Chance, no Mistakes in Providence whereby that befalls one which God intended for another, and that it was a folly to imagine that God would reveal that by the flight or cry of a Bird, which he would conceal from human Prudence, or to conceive that a Man's hand could discover more then his Judgement, or that a wise Conduct, and the directions of the Alcoran, were not more to be relied upon then the blind drawing out or shooting up of an Arrow."[2]

– Henry Stubbe (1671)

Murder

"The laws of Muhammed respecting murder deserve

There can hardly be a greater contrast to this unsuccessful attempt than what happened in Medina during the Prophet's time. When the final revelation came down, prohibiting consumption of alcoholic drinks and describing it as "an abomination of Satan's handiwork" (Q. 5:90), the alleys of Medina were filled with wine as people—no less inclined to drinking than their Western counterparts—emptied their jars outside their doors. It is reported that upon hearing the announcer's cry that alcoholic beverages had just been made forbidden by divine revelation, those who had cups in hand, ready to drink, emptied them onto the sands instead. Since then, the Muslim world has largely remained free of alcohol and its associated evils.

[1] i.e., Muslims.

[2] Stubbe, *An Account of the Rise and Progress of Mahometanism*, 178.

consideration. In the infancy of society, when the civil magistrate has but little authority, private retaliation is necessary ... Among the Arabs, whose national spirit may be said to dwell in their poems, the finest and most sublime pieces of sacred verse are devoted to the praises of the blood avenger ... artifice, treachery, and even assassination were lawful in avenging blood. The Arabian legislator endeavoured to mitigate this horrible custom. He acknowledges the right of retaliation, but recommends the blood avenger to be satisfied with a moderate compensation in money."[1]

– Charles Mills (1817)

Infanticide

"Infanticide has been correctly termed the prevailing and stubborn vice of antiquity ... Before the days of Muhammed, the birth of a female child was accounted by the Arabs a misfortune, and the feelings of the father were not shocked by inhuming his daughter alive. Muhammed is eloquent and energetic against this barbarous practice, and with all the collected authority of a divine, a moralist, and a legislator, he commands the preservation of all children that may be born."[2]

– Charles Mills (1817)

"One other inhuman custom—the ancient practice of female infanticide—was summarily abolished by him; and a tale survives that well-illustrates the horror he felt concerning such deeds."[3]

– R. F. Dibble (1926)

"To the same genuine humanity we may ascribe the one innovation of [the Prophet of] Islam which ordinarily receives praise

---

[1] Mills, *An History of Muhammedanism*, 350-51.

[2] Ibid., 352-53.

[3] Dibble, *Mohammed*, 244.

even from its enemies: the abolition of the practice of burying girls alive. The tradition records the thrill of horror with which the Prophet heard the recital of a man who had covered with earth a girl whom her mother, owing to the father's absence, had ventured to save and bring up."[1]

– D. S. Margoliouth (1905)

Polygamy

"I cannot in this place avoid taking Notice of some of the Political Institutions of Mahomet, because they seem to evince his great wisdom as a Legislator. One is the permission of Polygamy. The Alcoran gives liberty to each Musulman to take to himself wives two, three, or four, as he pleaseth, except he fear he is not able to render them all due benevolence. Wherein the doctrine of Mahomet doth exactly agree with the Law of Nature, except that he puts a positive restraint in his Law to a determinate Number, as Grotius, Saint Austin, and all the Jewish Rabbis even to Maimonides (whose saying exactly agrees with Mahomet's as to the Law of Nature), do averr, as you may see in Selden. But what the Law of Nature doth so indefinitely permitt, the Mosaical Law hath somewhat moderated."[2]

– Henry Stubbe (1671)

Slavery

"whatever laws he made respecting women and slaves were made with the view of improving their condition."[3]

– Winwood Reade (1872)

---

[1] Margoliouth, *Mohammed and the Rise of Islam*, 459-60.

[2] Stubbe, *An Account of the Rise and Progress of Mahometanism*, 172.

[3] Reade, *Martyrdom of Man*, 268.

"Some of his regulations in the matter [of slavery] were humane: the parting of a captive mother from her child was forbidden, and threatened with an appropriate punishment in the next world ... At the Farewell Pilgrimage he is said to have ordered his followers to feed and clothe their slaves as they fed and clothed themselves, and if the slaves offended, to sell them rather than punish them. The scourging of slaves was made by him characteristic of the worst of men; manumission was also declared by him to be an act of piety, and many an offence might be expiated by the setting free of a neck. A Himyari chief is said to have freed four thousand slaves at the Prophet s request. A system was further encouraged by which slaves might contract for their own manumission, and assistance of such persons with presents was regarded by the code with favour. When a man died without heirs, but leaving a slave, the slave was manumitted by the Prophet, and received the inheritance ... A man who shared one slave with seven brothers, and had cuffed the slave, was made to manumit him; and murder or maiming of slaves was to be punished by retaliation."[1]

– D. S. Margoliouth (1905)

Alleviation of Poverty

"Another Prudent Law of Mahomet was that whereby he prohibited usury to his Musulmin.[2] ... This prudent Legislator knowing of what importance it was to an Empire that was to be great and lasting, that the subjects be not too poor and needy lest that incline them to rebellion and Revolt against their Prince, nor exasperated against each other by reason of some growing too great by their oppressions and extortions on the rest, amended this former Law. Besides his general Obligations to Deeds of Charity, as an addition or means thereto, he strictly forbid all manner of

---

[1] Margoliouth, *Mohammed and the Rise of Islam*, 461-62.

[2] i.e., Muslims.

Usury, so that they might more readily releive their necessitous brethren either by giving or lending frankly, when they had not that way of making advantages of their Money."[1]

– Henry Stubbe (1671)

Charity as Civic Duty

"Mahomet, perhaps, is the only law-giver who has defined the precise measure of charity: the standard may vary with the degree and nature of property, as it consists either in money, in corn or cattle, in fruits or merchandise"[2]

– Edward Gibbon (1788)

Comprehensive Legislation

"If [the Prophet of] Islam succeeded in creating a united and strong nation based on moral principles in an Arabia where the most complete anarchy then reigned, where the idea of government as an independent social institution was completely unknown, where any form of human authority was considered unbearable, where cruelty was the rule, and where killing and stealing were not punishable crimes but only acts which invited reprisals by the family or tribe of the dead or injured person, this could only be achieved because Islam was both a law and a religion. The Sharia, the canon law of Islam, is not confined to ritual. All aspects of public and private life are subject to its rulings and it has the purpose of relating every act of the individual with his religious duties."[3]

– Laura Vaglieri (1925)

---

[1] Stubbe, *An Account of the Rise and Progress of Mahometanism*, 174-75.

[2] Gibbon, *Decline and Fall*, vol. v, 116.

[3] Vaglieri, *An Interpretation Of Islam*, 63-64.

His Character

LEADERSHIP

Trusted Leadership

"It is a notable feature in the history of the Prophet of Islam that his nearest relation, his beloved cousin and his bosom friends, who knew him most intimately, were thoroughly imbued with the truth of his mission and convinced of the genuineness of his divine inspiration ... the devotion of his followers was such that he was voluntarily acknowledged leader of their lives. They braved for his sake, persecutions and danger; they believed, trusted, obeyed and honoured him even in the most excruciating torture and severest mental agony caused by excommunication; even unto death. Would this have been so had they noticed the slightest backsliding in their leader?"[1]

– K. S. Ramakrishna Rao (1989)

Clear and Decisive Judgment

"He had a ready Wit, a penetrating Judgement..."[2]
– Henry Stubbe (1671)

"His memory was capacious and retentive, his wit easy and social, his imagination sublime, his judgment clear, rapid, and decisive. He possessed the courage both of thought and action."[3]
– Edward Gibbon (1788)

Led Men to the Truth

"[In the 41st year of Mahomet's life] we ... behold the

---

[1] Rao, *Muhammad: the Prophet of Islam*, 18.
[2] Stubbe, *An Account of the Rise and Progress of Mahometanism*, 141.
[3] Gibbon, *Decline and Fall*, vol. v, 102.

metamorphosis of a private man into a Prophet; illumin'd with revelations ... its chief design is to lead men to the knowledge of truth, and the practice of good works, that is, those that are relative to justice and the general good of society."[1]

– Henri de Boulainvilliers (1730)

Commanding Presence

"He had ... an air of authority and insinuation, animated by piercing eyes, and a happy disposition of features."[2]

– Voltaire (1759)

"His talents were equally fitted for persuasion, or command. Deeply read in the volume of nature, though entirely ignorant of letters, his mind could expand into controversy with the wisest of his enemies or contract itself to the apprehension of the meanest of his disciples ... and he was gifted with that authoritative air of genius, which alike influences the learned, and commands the illiterate."[3]

– Charles Mills (1817)

"People felt that this inspired man was born to command and they obeyed him blindly."[4]

– Emile Dermenghem (1930)

---

[1] Henri de Boulainvilliers, *Life of Mohammed*, 245. Boulainvilliers (d. 1722) was a French writer and historian. He wrote this book to clarify allegations and misconceptions about Prophet Muhammad, which were prevalent in Europe at the time, and argued that he was a divinely inspired messenger from God. Not surprisingly, Boulainvilliers' book was banned in Catholic France but was later published in 1730, after his death, in Protestant Amsterdam and London.

[2] Voltaire, *An Essay on Universal History*, vol. i, 42.

[3] Mills, *An History of Muhammedanism*, 39.

[4] Dermenghem, *The Life of Mahomet*, 5. More accurately, they willingly obeyed him out of love, respect, and full conviction in his benevolent and liberating teachings as

His Character

"[His audience felt] his commanding presence, his majestic aspect, his piercing eye, his gracious smile, his flowing beard, his countenance that painted every sensation of the soul, and his gestures that enforced each expression of the tongue."[1]

– Edward Gibbon (1788)

Treatment of Subordinates

"He was most indulgent to his inferiors, and would never allow his awkward little page[2] to be scolded, whatever he did. 'Ten years,' said Anas, his servant, 'was I about the prophet, and he never said as much as *uff* to me.'"[3]

– Emanuel Deutsch (1869)

"he was kind` to his inferiors."[4]

– Winwood Reade (1872)

"To his inferiors the Prophet was ever indulgent."[5]

– Simon. H. Leeder (1917)

Knowledge of People

"... nature, rather than experience, had endowed him with one gift more to be envied than any other: knowledge of mankind.

---

amply demonstrated in the ḥadīth literature. His pagan antagonists, however, oppressed and fought him for years.

[1] Gibbon, *Decline and Fall*, vol. v, 101-02.

[2] A "page" is a young servant or attendant in Old English.

[3] Deutsch, *Literary Remains*, 72.

[4] Reade, *Martyrdom of Man*, 266.

[5] Simon. H. Leeder, "The Tenderness of the Prophet." Leeder (d. 1930) was an English author, best known for the title *Modern Sons of the Pharaohs* where he discusses Muslim-Christian relations in Egypt.

His instinctive judgment of men and people was rarely, we might say never, wrong."¹
— D. S. Margoliouth (1905)

Commanding in War

"A man of great patience, prudence and trustworthiness, of retentive memory, strong character, and with the disposition of a judge—a very commander of men."²
— Arthur Glyn Leonard (1909)

"What the Prophet's public life attests should be noted; proven will, self-control, moderation and prudence, perspicacity and readiness to forgive, patience and forethoughtfulness, in short all the capacity to maneuver of a chief in war and a chief of state."³
— Louis Massignon (1922)

Lovable

"The depth of feeling in his dark black eye, and the winning expression of a face otherwise attractive, gained the confidence and love even of a stranger."⁴
— William Muir (1861)

"If I had to choose a single adjective for the description of his private character, I think I should prefer 'lovable'. Muhammad ... from the cradle to the grave was eminently lovable, and no

---

[1] Margoliouth, *Mohammed and the Rise of Islam*, 63.

[2] Leonard, *Islam: Her Moral and Spiritual Value*, 72.

[3] Louis Massignon, *Essay on the Origins of the Technical Language of Islamic Mysticism*, 98. Massignon (d. 1962) was a French scholar of Islamic and Arabic Studies and a Catholic priest.

[4] Muir, *Life of Mahomet*, vol. iv, 302.

man in this world has ever been more truly loved; not alone by those who spoke with him and knew him well, whose love still thrills in every word that they have left concerning him; but also by the millions who have never known him in the flesh, but have received his message and perused the story of his life."[1]

– Marmaduke Pickthall (1918)

"Born an orphan and blessed with no worldly goods, he was loved by all."[2]

– K. S. Ramakrishna Rao (1989)

"He was loved by children who clung round his knees, climbed up into his arms, and played with him."[3]

– Annie Besant (1932)

MANIFESTATION OF GOD'S REVELATION IN PRACTICE

"The teachings of the Holy Koran received practical demonstration in the life of Mahomet who, whether in times of suffering and persecution, or in times of worldly triumph and prosperity, displayed the noblest moral qualities which a human being could possibly possess."[4]

– Lord Headley (1914)

---

[1] Pickthall, "The Prophet's Character."

[2] Rao, *Muhammad: the Prophet of Islam*, 20.

[3] Besant, *The Life and Teachings of Muhammad*, 28.

[4] Lord Headley, *A Western Awakening to Islam*, 69-70. The purpose of God's revelation, compiled in the form of the Qur'an, was to shape human character in accordance with divine guidance. In this sense, the divine revelation was reflected in the character and personality of Prophet Muhammad. It is often said that a man is best known by those who are closest to him. Years after the Prophet left this world, 'Ā'isha, his youngest wife, was asked to describe the character of her late husband. In her response, she used only three words, but they proved to be sufficient, both for her

Marital Life

A Perfect Marriage

"Mahomet, being married, seemed to give himself up totally to the satisfaction of his spouse; never was [a] husband more tender or more obliging than he shewed himself to Cadijah; as on her side, never was a rich lady so submissive to a man, who could boast no wealth when she made him her husband; being constantly attentive to lull his cares, and sooth him into a sweet forgetfulness of all his former toils, by the pleasure and tranquility of a plentiful house."[1]

– Henry Stubbe (1671)

"Mahomet's house was a model of conjugal happiness and domestic virtue; Khadija made an ideal wife for Mahomet, who was the best of husbands."[2]

– Emile Dermenghem (1930)

"one of the most beautiful pictures of a perfect wedded life that history gives us."[3]

– T. W. Arnold (c. 1910s)

Equal Treatment of Wives

"Every day, after finishing the afternoon prayers, he made the entire round of the private apartments of his wives, to inquire how they were; and when it had become evening, he went to spend the night with her whose turn it was. As regards sustenance and portions and all things within his power, he observed a

---

students at the time and for others throughout history: *Kana khuluquhu al-Qur'an*—"His character was the Qur'an."

[1] Stubbe, *An Account of the Rise and Progress of Mahometanism*, 227.

[2] Dermenghem, *The Life of Mahomet*, 52.

[3] T. W. Arnold, in Leeder, "The Tenderness of the Prophet."

careful equality; and he used to say, 'O God, this is my portion in that which I possess: do thou not blame me in that which I do not possess...'"[1]

– S. W. Koelle (1888)

"Enemies of Islam have insisted in depicting Muhammad as a sensual individual ... They refuse to take into consideration the fact that during those years of his life when by nature the sexual urge is strongest,[2] although he lived in a society like that of the Arabs, where the institution of marriage was almost non-existent, where polygamy was the rule, and where divorce was very easy indeed, he was married to one woman alone, Khadija, who was much older than himself, and that for twenty-five years he was her faithful, loving husband. Only when she died and when he was already fifty years old did he marry again and more than once. Each of these marriages had a social or a political reason, for he wanted through the women he married to honor pious women, or to establish marriage relations with other clans and tribes for the purpose of opening the way for the propagation of Islam.

"He was man and not God, and the desire of a son may also have brought him to other marriages, for unfortunately the ones born to Khadija had died. Without too many resources, he took upon his shoulders the heavy burden of maintaining a large family, but always, in spite of the number of his wives, he observed a perfect equality towards all of them, nor did he ever use in

---

[1] Koelle, *Mohammed and Mohammedanism*, 392. To explain, in this supplication, the Prophet was humbling himself before God and acknowledging his human weakness. While expressing that he was doing his best to maintain strict equality between his wives in matters within his control, such as providing material provisions, time, etc., at the same time, he asked God to forgive him for things beyond his control, such as feeling more love for one wife over another.

[2] From the age of 25 until he was 50, the Prophet did not take a second wife. After his first wife Khadīja passed away at the age of 65, he married subsequent wives. Historians note that these marriages were primarily to establish ties of kinship with other tribes, thereby ensuring peace, or to care for widows in need of support.

respect of any one of them the right of separation. He acted under the sanction of revered ancient patriarchs like Moses and others, to whose plural marriages nobody seems to take exception. Could this be because we do not have the particulars of their daily lives, while in the case of Muhammad we know all about his life within the family?"[1]

— Laura Vaglieri (1925)

Expressing Affection

"Be it known that his apostolic Excellency was the best amongst the people, as regards the beauty of intercourse and kindness of companionship with his wives. That prince was exceedingly demonstrative of affection towards his wives; and when they came to solicit a command from him, and there was no obstacle in the way, he granted their request liberally. It is firmly established that sometimes, when Aisha the faithful drank water from her cup, that Excellency would take the cup out of her hand, and drink exactly from that place from which she had been drinking, and when she was eating meat from a bone, he would take the bone out of her hand and would put his blessed mouth exactly on the spot where Aisha had put hers, in order to eat the meat."[2]

— S. W. Koelle (1888)

Loving

"the story of their marriage[3] is altogether a graceful intelligible one ... [he] seems to have lived in a most affectionate, peaceable,

---

[1] Vaglieri, *An Interpretation Of Islam*, 67-68.

[2] Koelle, *Mohammed and Mohammedanism*, 390-91.

[3] Referring to the Prophet's marriage to Khadīja, his first wife and fifteen years his senior. They had a blissful marriage for 25 years, and he did not take another wife until after her death, when she was about 65 years old.

wholesome way with this wedded benefactress; loving her truly, and her alone."[1]

— Thomas Carlyle (1840)

Soft and Light-Hearted

"It is recorded that when Aisha became angry, that prince would lay his blessed hand upon her shoulder, and say, 'May God forgive her sins, subdue the wrath of her heart, and free her from excitement!' Sometimes ... when he was in the midst of the entire company of his pure wives, he would stretch out his blessed hand after one of them and make some fun and jest."[2]

— S. W. Koelle (1888)

MERCY

"Muhammad's loving kindness extended over all beings. He was noted for his love of children, and used to greet them in the street and play with them ... when one of his companions saw him kiss Hasan [his grandson], and remarked with disdain, 'I have ten boys but have never kissed any of them,' the Prophet thereupon replied: 'He who does not show mercy will not receive mercy.'"[3]

— Annemarie Schimmel (1984)

"No one can claim the quality of mercy who has never had anyone at his mercy, and there is no character in history which can be so safely held up for inspection and illustration of this particular quality as the Holy Prophet Mahomet."[4]

— Lord Headley (1914)

---

[1] Carlyle, *On Heroes,* 60.

[2] Koelle, *Mohammed and Mohammedanism,* 391-92.

[3] Schimmel, *And Muhammad Is His Messenger,* 48-49.

[4] Lord Headley, *A Western Awakening to Islam,* 70.

Military Leader

"When, after repeated efforts at conciliation had utterly failed, circumstances arose that dragged him into the battlefield purely in self-defense, the Prophet of Islam changed the whole strategy of the battlefield. The total number of casualties in all the wars that took place during his lifetime, when the whole Arabian Peninsula came under his banner, does not exceed a few hundreds in all."[1]

– K. S. Ramakrishna Rao (1989)

"Mohammed ... showed high talents as a general in every battle or skirmish in which he took part. He was brave too and, in spite of his age, able to undergo hardships with the youngest of his soldiers."[2]

– R. V. C. Bodley (1945)

"The battles he fought, the judgments he made, and the feats he accomplished leave no doubt about his endowment with a strong personality, deep convictions, dedication, and other qualities that make leaders of men."[3]

– Phillip K. Hitti (1969)

"He had studied at no military academy; yet he could organize his forces against tremendous odds and gained victories through the moral forces which he marshalled."[4]

– K. S. Ramakrishna Rao (1989)

Mission-Driven

"The central point is that until he breathed his last he was

---

[1] Rao, *Muhammad: the Prophet of Islam*, 9.

[2] Bodley, *The Messenger: The Life of Mohammed*, 153.

[3] Phillip K. Hitti, *Islam: A Way of Life*, 24.

[4] Rao, *Muhammad: the Prophet of Islam*, 20.

struggling for his God, for the salvation of his people—even all of humanity—and that he never lost faith in his divine mission."[1]

– Theodor Noldeke (1860)

"He was the messenger of the One God, and never to his life's end did He forget who he was, or the message which was the marrow of his being. He brought his tidings to his people with a grand dignity, sprang from the consciousness of his high office, together with a most sweet humility, whose roots lay in the knowledge of his own weakness ... no man was ever more thoroughly filled with the sense of his mission or carried out that mission more heroically."[2]

– Stanley Lane-Poole (1883)

MODEST

"'He was more bashful,' says Ayesha, 'than a veiled virgin; and if anything displeased him, it was rather from his face, than by his words, that we discovered it.'"[3]

– William Muir (1861)

"He was more modest than a virgin behind the curtain."[4]

– Winwood Reade (1872)

MODERN (AHEAD OF HIS TIME)

"Mohammed, without a shadow of a doubt, was centuries before his age. In his God concept, in his rejection of the ancient myth of immaculate conception, in his refusing to acknowledge

---

[1] Noldeke, *The History of the Qur'an*, 4.

[2] Lane-Poole, *Studies In A Mosque*, 84-85.

[3] Muir, *Life of Mahomet*, vol. iv, 305.

[4] Reade, *Martyrdom of Man*, 266.

Christ's divinity, he was essentially a modern—a modern of the twentieth century. It was this catholicity therefore that made Islam blossom into a spiritual energy that embraces so many national units."[1]
– Arthur Glyn Leonard (1909)

Money and Wealth (Perspectives On)

"Far from considering worldly possessions an indication of divine favour, Mahomet was troubled by them, for he did not wish to receive all his reward in this world; and we ought not be deceived by the prosperity of the wicked. 'What I fear most for you,' he often said to his adherents, 'are the things that are given you in this world.' ... he went on to say that riches were only desirable if they had been come by honestly and if they were employed in a godly manner in helping the poor. If not, riches were a curse, and in any case, a great temptation. 'The richest in this world will be the poorest in the next, unless they distribute thus: (and the Prophet made a gesture, first in front of him, then to the right and left, as if he were distributing gifts profusely)."[2]
– Emile Dermenghem (1930)

"One may not gather that the Prophet considered wealth *per se* to be an evil, or he would not have assented to the notion of man's temporary possession of God's goods. Rather, his insistence is against its abuse, its use as occasion for pride and arrogance (96:6,7), for unworthy discrimination (80:5,6), and for gluttony. One must not trust in it at all (111:2; 104:3; 92:11; 69:28; 3:8,12), nor compete for it (102:1), nor hoard it (104:2; 9:34), for it is for man only a transient asset, and is so likely to lead him into forgetfulness of God (63:9). Since God is the chief concern, all else

---

[1] Leonard, *Islam: Her Moral and Spiritual Value*, 109-10.

[2] Dermenghem, *The Life of Mahomet*, 263-64.

falls properly into secondary place."[1]

— John Clark Archer (1924)

MONOTHEISM (ABSOLUTE AND UNCOMPROMISING)

"With just reason then did Mahomet, following the example of all the prophets, condemn the worship of the stars; not as a perfect prevarication relating to the corruption of the will; but as an abuse of the common notion, and universal idea of the divinity: since the order of natural things is nothing else than the execution of the will of the omnipotent. A will, neither mutable, nor occational, but determined by an eternal decree, to which the motion of the first movers is as subject as the last of the things that are moved."[2]

— Henri de Boulainvilliers (1730)

"The unity and indivisibility of the Godhead formed the basis of his creed."[3]

— Charles Mills (1817)

"Arabia was idolatrous when Muhammad, seven centuries after Jesus Christ, introduced to it the religion of the God of Abraham, Ishmael, Moses, and Jesus Christ ... Muhammad declared that there was only one God, who had neither father nor son and that the Trinity imported an idea from paganism ... He rescued more souls from false gods, overturned more idols, and pulled down more pagan temples in fifteen years than the adherents of Moses and Jesus Christ had in fifteen centuries."[4]

— Napoleon Bonaparte (*c.* 1821)

---

[1] Archer, *The Mystical Elements of Mohammed*, 53.

[2] Boulainvilliers, *Life of Mohammed*, 241.

[3] Mills, *An History of Muhammedanism*, 276.

[4] Cole, *Napoleons's Egypt*, 129-30.

"he called upon them to renounce their idolatry, and to embrace the more pure, simple, and reasonable belief of the unity of God."[1]

– Charles Mills (1817)

"The great doctrine, then, of the Koran is the 'unity' of God, to restore which, Mohammed asserted, was the chief end of his mission."[2]

– John Davenport (1869)

"Islamism [preached by Prophet Muhammad], which is the purest production of Semitic genius, and which may be looked upon as the ideal of monotheism, suppressed all curiosity, all inquiry into first causes."[3]

– Ernest Renan (1886)

"The religion thus established by the Koran is a stern and severe monotheism: it has nothing abstract and indistinct in its primary notion of the Godhead. Allah, so far from being a mere philosophic first cause regulating the universe by established laws, while itself stands aloof in unapproachable majesty; is an ever-present, ever working energy."[4]

– John Davenport (1869)

"Other men have been monotheists in the midst of idolaters, but no other man has founded a [more] strong and enduring monotheistic religion."[5]

– Marcus Dods (1887)

---

[1] Mills, *An History of Muhammedanism*, 14.

[2] Davenport, *An Apology for Mohammed and the Koran*, 74.

[3] Ernest Renan, *Studies in Religious History*, 45.

[4] Davenport, *An Apology for Mohammed and the Koran*, 78.

[5] Dods, *Mohammed, Buddha, and Christ*, 18.

"The Muslim faith is summed up in a lapidary double formula: 'There is no God but Allah; Muhammad is the Prophet of Allah.' The whole of Islam ... is contained *in nuce* in this double affirmation. An absolute, uncompromising monotheism, for which *shirk*—the association of any emanation or offspring with God—is the depth of impiety ... Muslim monotheism set out to surpass even that of the Jews in rigour."[1]

— Francesco Gabrieli (1968)

"Muhammad from the beginning of his claim to the prophetic office showed himself to be irreconcilably opposed to polytheism in whatever form, and to be the bitter enemy of all idol-worship."[2]

— William St. Clair Tisdall (1910)

"The Arabic prophet with a voice which was inspired by a deep communion with his Master, preached the purest monotheism to the worshippers of fetish and the followers of a corrupt Christianity and Judaism."[3]

— Laura Vaglieri (1925)

MORALITY (SUPERIOR TYPE)

"Besides these specific regulations for moral conduct, the exhortations to virtue are numerous in the Koran and Sonna ... Vice is considered to consist in a sinful thought and look, and men are rewarded according to the merit of their intentions. Pride, anger, and covetous are held in abhorrence. Faith is to be kept even with infidels. Gentleness of manners, and a modest deportment, are every where enjoined. Forgiveness of injuries will meet with its

---

[1] Gabrieli, *Muhammad and the Conquests of Islam*, 85-86.

[2] William St. Clair Tisdall, *The Religion of the Crescent*, 17. Tisdall (d. 1928) was an Anglican priest, linguist and historian.

[3] Vaglieri, *An Interpretation Of Islam*, 30.

reward; and mankind are exhorted to pray for, and not to curse, offenders."¹

– Charles Mills (1817)

"There is no greater except him who, in proclaiming earlier the same dogma, had promulgated at the same time a purer morality; who did not draw the sword in aid of the word, that sole weapon of the mind; who gave up his own blood instead of spilling that of his brethren; and who was a martyr instead of being a conqueror. But this latter personage, men, accordingly, have judged to be too great to be submitted to the common measure of humanity; and if his human nature and his doctrine have made him a prophet even among skeptics, his virtue and his sacrifice have made him a god."²

– Alphonse de Lamartine (1854)

"Through mockery and persecution the Prophet keeps unflinchingly in his path; no threats, no injuries, hinder him from still preaching to his people the unity and the righteousness of God, and exhorting to a far purer and better morality than had ever been set before them."³

– Edward Freeman (1856)

"The ideas of morality taught by the great Teacher were quite noble. 'It is not righteousness that ye turn your faces in prayer towards the East and the West; but righteousness is of him who believeth in God, and the last day and the Angels and the Scriptures and the Prophets; who giveth money for God's sake unto

---

[1] Mills, *An History of Muhammedanism*, 329-30.

[2] Lamartine, *History of Turkey*, vol. i, 155-56. Lamartine's concluding words, 'made him a god,' may be offensive to Muslims who regard Prophet Muhammad as no more than a human prophet. The author, however, obviously used this expression as a figure of speech to emphasize that such a collection of noble attributes in Prophet Muhammad is unmatched by any other human being.

[3] Freeman, *History and Conquests of the Saracens*, 35.

his kindred, and unto orphans, and the needy, and the stranger, and those who ask, and for redemption of captives; who is constant at prayer, and giveth alms; and of those who perform their covenant when they have covenanted, and who behave themselves patiently in adversity, and hardships, and in times of violence; these are they who are true, and these are they who fear God.';[1] 'Wrong not your brother', 'defend the weak from the injury', 'All things shall perish; God alone will survive.' This simple, clear, definite declaration relating all actions to the source is the fabric of a simple and noble morality."[2]

– Annie Besant (1932)

A Mortal (Denied Divinity)

"In a hadith of Umm Salma the prophet freely admits his fallibility: 'I am only mortal, and when you come disputing before me perhaps some of you are more eloquent in argument than others, and I give judgement according to what I hear. But whoso receives judgement in this way to the detriment of his brother's rights let him not take it, for if he does I have reserved a place in hell for him.' ... Rāfi' b. Khadīj: 'The prophet of God came to Medina when they were fecundating the date-palms, and asked what was being done. It was replied that this was custom. 'Perhaps it would be better if you did not do it,' said he. So they left the trees as they were and the crop was deficient. When the people told him of this, he said, 'I am only mortal. If I give you an order in the domain of your religion then receive it; but if I give you an order from my own opinion (*rai*) then am I but mortal.'"[3]

– Alfred Guillaume (1924)

---

[1] Q. 2:177.

[2] Besant, *The Life and Teachings of Muhammad*, 32-33.

[3] Guillaume, *The Traditions of Islam*, 154-55.

"He had but one answer for his worshippers[1], 'I am no more than a man, I am only human.' 'Do none enter Paradise save by the mercy of God?' asked A'isha. 'None, none, none,' he answered. 'Not even thou by thy own merits?' 'Neither shall I enter Paradise unless God cover[s] me with His mercy.' He was a man like unto his brethren in all things save one, and that one difference served only to increase his humbleness, and render him the more sensitive to his shortcomings. He was sublimely confident of this single attribute, that he was the messenger of the Lord of the Worlds, and that the words he spake came verily from Him."[2]

– Stanley Lane-Poole (1883)

"As for Mohammed himself, the Koran repeatedly disclaims on his behalf anything that savours of the superhuman. He is but a mortal man, commissioned with the sole duty of conveying God's warning and message of salvation. He has no knowledge beyond what is revealed to him, and has been granted no miraculous powers. He is commanded to seek pardon for his faults and to be patient under adversity. Yet he is a noble pattern to those who hope in God, his decisions must be accepted in matters of faith and conduct, belief in his revelation and obedience to him are necessary to salvation."[3]

– Hamilton A. R. Gibb (1948)

Moral Perfection (A Model For)

"the moral excellence of Mohammed shines out as a brilliant."[4]

– Arthur Glyn Leonard (1909)

---

[1] More correctly, "for any would be worshipper." Muslims are strict monotheists and worship God alone.

[2] Lane-Poole, *Studies In A Mosque*, 81.

[3] Gibb, *Mohammedanism: An Historical Survey*, 60.

[4] Leonard, *Islam: Her Moral and Spiritual Value*, 73.

His Character

"In war and peace, at home and in the world, in the religious sphere as in every phase of working and acting, the Prophet is the ideal model of moral perfection. Whatever he did remains exemplary for his followers."[1]

– Annemarie Schimmel (1984)

"The greatest success of Muhammed's life was affected by sheer moral force without the stroke of a sword."[2]

– K. S. Ramakrishna Rao (1989)

Mothers (Respect and Care For)

"one should not forget the high veneration shown by the Prophet to mothers. It is told that when the Prophet was informed once that the monk Juraij did not care for his mother, who wanted to see him, Muhammad said: 'If Juraij were a learned, knowing monk he would have known that it is part of the service of God to answer one's mother's call.' Tradition also ascribed to him the beautiful saying 'Paradise lies beneath the feet of the mothers.'"[3]

– Annemarie Schimmel (1984)

Obeyed Like no Other Man Ever Was

"A poor, hard-toiling, ill-provided man; careless of what vulgar men toil for ... something better in him than *hunger* of any sort [for worldly things],—or these wild Arab men, fighting and jostling three and twenty years at his hand, in close contact with him always, would not have reverenced him so! They were wild men, bursting ever and anon into quarrel, into all kinds of fierce sincerity; without right worth and manhood, no man could have

---

[1] Schimmel, *And Muhammad Is His Messenger*, 54.

[2] Rao, *Muhammad: the Prophet of Islam*, 8.

[3] Schimmel, *And Muhammad Is His Messenger*, 51.

commanded them ... he stood there face to face with them; bare, not enshrined in any mystery; visibly clouting his own cloak, cobbling his own shoes; fighting, counseling, ordering in the midst of them: they must have seen what kind of a man he *was,* let him be called what you like! No emperor with his tiaras was obeyed as this man in a cloak of his own clouting, during three and twenty years of rough actual trial. I find something of a veritable Hero necessary for that, of itself."[1]

– Thomas Carlyle (1840)

"His followers were bound to him by the ties of love, not fear."[2]
– Marmaduke Pickthall (1917)

Orator

"Before he spoke, the orator engaged on his side the affections of a public or private audience. They applauded his commanding presence, his majestic aspect, his piercing eye, his gracious smile, his flowing beard, his countenance that painted every sensation of the soul, and his gestures that enforced each expression of the tongue ... The son of Abdallah was educated in the bosom of the noblest race, in the use of the purest dialect of Arabia; and the fluency of his speech was corrected and enhanced by the practice of discreet and seasonable silence."[3]

– Edward Gibbon (1788)

Orphanage (Institutionalized)

"Orphanages have sprung for the first time, it is said, under the teaching of the Prophet of Islam. The world owes its orphanages

---

[1] Carlyle, *On Heroes,* 79-80.

[2] Pickthall, "The Prophet's Gratitude."

[3] Gibbon, *Decline and Fall,* vol. v, 102.

to this Prophet who was himself born an orphan."¹
— K. S. Ramakrishna Rao (1989)

ORPHANS (TREATMENT OF)

"He, once a poor orphan, always had a place in his heart for the underprivileged:

> Therefore the orphan oppress not
> And the beggar drive not away."²
> — Phillip K. Hitti (1969)

OSTENTATION (FREE OF)

"He ... does not pretend to be what he is not. There is no ostentatious pride in him."³
— Thomas Carlyle (1840)

"He was most unostentatious and selfless to the core."⁴
— K. S. Ramakrishna Rao (1989)

PATIENCE

Calm Even at Uncouth Behavior

"He put up with the improprieties of the Bedouins. Once when a Bedouin was making water in the very mosque, Mahomet protected him from the others who wanted to make him pay for this outrage ... On another occasion a Bedouin pulled at Mahomet's

---

[1] Rao, *Muhammad: the Prophet of Islam*, 16.

[2] Hitti, *Islam: A Way of Life*, 24; quoting Q. 93:9-10.

[3] Carlyle, *On Heroes*, 80.

[4] Rao, *Muhammad: the Prophet of Islam*, 25.

cloak with such force that his skin was badly scratched. 'O Mahomet, give me some of Allah's riches that you hold in your power,' he cried. Mahomet turned to him laughingly and gave him a present."[1]

– Emile Dermenghem (1930)

With Women

"[He had] almost unfailing patience which he displayed even under provocation, and the gentleness with which he attended to the griefs of all sorts of women and comforted them, even at times to the extent of revising his legislation."[2]

– Hamilton A. R. Gibb (1948)

PATRIOTISM-NATIONALISM REJECTED

"his example shows us that to serve Allah truly is to serve humanity. Personal ambition, national ambition, tribal jealousy—all the passions which compose what we call patriotism—he abjured as criminal. Instead he preached the brotherhood of all believers."[3]

– Marmaduke Pickthall (1917)

PARENTS (RESPECT AND CARE FOR)

"'Health, peace, and competence, are all that are desirable.' (Koran, ii, iv, v) ... [Muhammad's teachings] do not violate the obligation of humanity; and Muhammed declares, that a man is

---

[1] Dermenghem, *The Life of Mahomet*, 169-70.

[2] Gibb, *Mohammedanism: An Historical Survey*, 33.

[3] Pickthall, "Address on the Prophet's Birthday." On the subject of nationalism, see footnote on page 177.

bound to maintain his parents when [they are] in want, although they should be idolaters."[1]

– Charles Mills (1817)

"Mohammed emphasized reverence and gratitude toward one's parents: Show 'kindness to your parents ... and say not to them, Fie!, neither reproach them. And defer humbly to them out of tenderness and say: Lord, have compassion on them both, even as they reared me when I was little' (17:24-25)."[2]

– Tor Andrae (1932)

PEACEMAKER

"He also said, 'Ye cannot enter Paradise, except ye believe; and ye cannot believe, except ye make friendship with each other. Mark therefore the means I indicate to you for securing mutual friendship, namely, the open declaration of peace both to the known and to the unknown.' He also said, 'Give peace to the little and to the great; to the few and to the many; to the standing and to the sitting!' It is also recorded that that prince once entered into a company of boys, and another time into a company of women, and on both occasions he saluted by giving the peace."[3]

– S. W. Koelle (1888)

"As a paradigmatic personality, Muhammad has important lessons, not only for Muslims, but also for Western people. His life was a jihad: as we shall see, this word does not mean "holy war," it means "struggle." Muhammad literally sweated with the effort to bring peace to war-torn Arabia, and we need people who are prepared to do this today. His life was a tireless campaign against

---

[1] Mills, *An History of Muhammedanism*, 330-31.

[2] Andrae, *Mohammed: The Man and His Faith*, 107.

[3] Koelle, *Mohammed and Mohammedanism*, 399.

greed, injustice, and arrogance."[1]

– Karen Armstrong (2006)

PERSEVERANCE

"we must admire the perseverance with which he retained his faith in his divine mission, not discouraged by twelve years of humiliation, nor by the repudiation of the "People of Scripture," upon whom he had relied as his principal witnesses, nor yet by numbers of temporary rebuffs during his struggle for the dominion of Allah and His Messenger, which he carried on through the whole of Arabia."[2]

– C. Snouck Hurgronje 1916)

"Nor indeed was it a light task to break with the past and set at naught the old traditions deriving their weight and importance from remote and ageless antiquity ... but only one like Mohammed, burning with divine love and fired with holy zeal, could have assumed mission and undertaken duties involving such immense personal sacrifices. The rude polytheism of Arabia, the grossly sensual and epicurean life of the Arabs, his higher nature could not tolerate ... It was a stake of life and death, but he threw himself into the conflict with all the force that was in him only to emerge from it purified, exalted, fortified, and illumined."[3]

– Alfred von Kremer (1873)

"Mohammed may stand [in] comparison with the most courageous of the heroic prophets of Israel. For the truth's sake he risked his life, he suffered daily persecution for years, and

---

[1] Karen Armstrong, *Muhammad: A Prophet for Our Time*, 7. Armstrong (b. 1944) is a prolific British author who specializes in comparative religion.

[2] C. Snouck Hurgronje, *Mohammedanism*, 47. Fluent in Arabic, Hurgronje (d. 1936) was a Dutch scholar of oriental culture and languages and taught at Leiden University.

[3] Alfred von Kremer, *Contributions to the History of Islamic Civilization*, 146-47.

eventually banishment, the loss of property, of the goodwill of his fellow-citizens, and of the confidence of his friends—he suffered, in short, as much as any man can suffer short of death, which he only escaped by flight, and yet he unflinchingly proclaimed his message. No bribe, threat or inducement could silence him."[1]

– Marcus Dods (1887)

POLITE

"His politeness to men of all conditions who approached him, was gentle and respectful."[2]

– Alphonse de Lamartine (1854)

"His politeness to the great, his affability to the humble, and his dignified demeanour to the presumptuous, procured him respect, admiration, and applause."[3]

– Charles Mills (1817)

"His manner was that of the perfect Arab gentleman, who knows no distinction of ranks, and is as courteous and formally polite to rags as to purple."[4]

– Marcus Dods (1887)

POLITICAL INSTITUTION (WORK OF A GENIUS)

"The Judaic law, which still subsists, and that of the child of Ishmael,[5] which, for ten centuries, has ruled half the world, still

---

[1] Dods, *Mohammed, Buddha, and Christ*, 17-18.

[2] Lamartine, *History of Turkey*, vol. i, 152.

[3] Mills, *An History of Muhammedanism*, 38.

[4] Dods, *Mohammed, Buddha, and Christ*, 90.

[5] i.e., Prophet Muhammad.

proclaim the great men who laid them down; and, while the pride of philosophy or the blind spirit of faction sees in them no more than lucky impostures, the true political theorist admires, in the institutions they set up, the great and powerful genius which presides over things made to endure."[1]

– Jean-Jacques Rousseau (1762)

"Mahomet held very sane views, and linked his political system well together; and, as long as the form of his government continued under the caliphs who succeeded him, that government was indeed one, and so far good."[2]

– Jean-Jacques Rousseau (1762)

POMP OF ROYALTY (SHUNNED)

"The good sense of Mahomet despised the pomp of royalty; the apostle of God submitted to the menial offices of the family."[3]

– Edward Gibbon (1788)

"Nothing in him or around him announced the sovereign or the conqueror; all was in simple keeping with the apostle."[4]

– Alphonse de Lamartine (1854)

"A vulgar impostor would have claimed miraculous powers or have decked himself in the pomp of earthly royalty. But Mahomet still only proclaimed himself as God's Prophet; personal honours he disclaimed; his demeanour was as courteous and equable as ever; the friends of his adversity were never forgotten. Crown and sceptre, court and palace, he had none; the lord of

---

[1] Jean-Jacques Rousseau, *The Social Contract & Discourse*, Chapter VII: The Legislator.

[2] Rousseau, *The Social Contract & Discourse*, Chapter VII: The Legislator.

[3] Gibbon, *Decline and Fall*, vol. v, 148.

[4] Lamartine, *History of Turkey*, vol. i, 151.

Arabia lived in the humblest dwelling, on the plainest fare, accessible to the meanest of believers. The master of thousands of willing slaves still patched his own shoes and milked his own cattle."[1]

    – Edward Freeman (1856)

"He used to … avoid as much as possible anything that gave him the air of being a king. He had neither court nor ministers, only advisers and several secretaries, and a seal on a silver ring bearing these words: 'Mahomet, the Messenger of God.'"[2]

    – Emile Dermenghem (1930)

PIETY (GENUINE AND SINCERE)

"To the last he was a pious Muslim, simple in his habits, regular in prayer…"[3]

    – Marmaduke Pickthall (1917)

"The genuineness and sincerity of Mohammed's piety, and the honesty of his belief in his religious call, are indisputable."[4]

    – Tor Andrae (1932)

THE POOR (TENDERNESS FOR)

"The appurtenances of his house, the porticoes adjacent to the mosque, the courts of the edifice, were one vast hospital, where the poor, the widows, the orphans, the infirm, could be seen waiting for nourishment or medicine. They were called the 'guests of the bench,' because they passed their life seated or lying on the

---

[1] Freeman, *History and Conquests of the Saracens*, 37.

[2] Dermenghem, *The Life of Mahomet*, 166.

[3] Pickthall, "The Prophet's Gratitude."

[4] Andrae, *Mohammed: The Man and His Faith*, 260.

benches of the prophet's house. Every night the prophet visited them, comforted them, clad them, fed them with his barley bread and dates. He brought daily a certain number of them into the house, to take their repast with him. He distributed the others, as guests of God, among the wealthiest of his disciples."[1]

– Alphonse de Lamartine (1854)

"This good custom [of taking care of the poor by Muslims] ... is founded on the tradition that tells of the Prophet's tenderness for the poor. When he went to his meals he nearly always called some such folk to join him."[2]

– Simon. H. Leeder (1917)

"Like all noble characters, Mohammed certainly felt a real and sincere concern for the poor and neglected."[3]

– Tor Andrae (1932)

A Practical Illustration for Human Life

"[His objective was] to give practicable rules of guidance to men living and working in the world and to illustrate them by his noble example. If he had not led armies he could not have served as a model for a general leading armies into battle; if he had not fought personally he could not have been an exemplar to a soldier laying down his life in the cause of truth, justice, and freedom; if he had not made laws for the guidance of his followers he could never have been regarded as an outstanding example to a legislator; if he had not decided cases he could not have served as a light to judges and magistrates; if he had not married he would have left men unguided practically in half of their everyday duties and could not have shown how to be a kind and affectionate

---

[1] Lamartine, *History of Turkey*, vol. i, 152.

[2] Leeder, "The Tenderness of the Prophet."

[3] Andrae, *Mohammed: The Man and His Faith*, 103.

husband and a loving father; if he had not taken revenge on tyrants for the wrongs inflicted on innocent persons, if he had not overcome his persecuting enemies and forgiven them, if he had not overlooked the faults of those attached to him, he could not have been an excellent exemplar and a perfect model, as the Qur'an pronounced him to be. Indeed, it is the distinguishing characteristic of his life that he not only gave practical rules of guidance in all walks of life, but gave by his life a practical illustration of all those rules."[1]

— Marmaduke Pickthall (1917)

"As husband, father, neighbour, friend, he was a pattern for all ages, no less than as a ruler and *imam*."[2]

— Marmaduke Pickthall (1918)

PRAGMATIC

"But Mohammed was not altogether 'quietistic.' He displayed no exaggerated 'dependence' upon God. He was a practical prophet. He was not in the hands of God as the corpse is in the washer's hands. He was no mere 'child of the day' with no thought of the morrow. Nor was he indifferent to the things of the body, to sufferings and to buffetings. He had ends in view which demanded strength both of body and of spirit. He put his confidence in God, but did not neglect 'to tie the camel's leg.' He lamented the dishonesty and greed of his time, the indifference of his people to spiritual values, but he did not recommend as a cure for all this the denial of the world entirely."[3]

— John Clark Archer (1924)

"When Islam [as preached by Prophet Muhammad] gives man a

---

[1] Pickthall, "The Holly Prophet As An Example."

[2] Pickthall, "The Prophet's Character."

[3] Archer, *The Mystical Elements of Mohammed*, 85.

moral perspective to which he can turn in desperation, it does not go beyond the limits of reality, nor does it present an ideal of virtue which would be unreachable save by the few elect. Instead it establishes healthy principles of life which prove in their application to be of a genuine and admirable practicability. By presenting a model of integrity and honesty, it does not depart from the law of life, but remains close to human nature and takes into consideration the just aspiration of an honest happiness. Far from creating a difference between the religious life of the individual and his behavior in the world, it looks towards the creation of a society where man is at the same time a member of it and also a devoted servant of God."[1]

– Laura Vaglieri (1925)

"Practical advice to his people is not lacking either. When a Bedouin asked him whether, since he trusted in God and His protection, he could let his camel roam loose, the Prophet answered briefly: *I'qilhā wa tawakkal*, 'First tether it, and then trust in God.' The importance of activity in this world, as contrasted to an unhealthy fatalism that leads in the long run to a lack of responsibility, is expressed best in the oft-repeated hadith: 'This world is the seedbed for the next world;' every action upon which man embarks here will bring its fruits—good or bad—in the next world, at the day of Resurrection. Furthermore, every faithful Muslim should be reminded to appropriate the Prophet's short prayer 'Oh Lord, increase my knowledge!'"[2]

– Annemarie Schimmel (1984)

Preacher

"Gifted men with a genius for preaching are rare. Descartes included the perfect preacher among the rarest kind in the world ...

---

[1] Vaglieri, *An Interpretation Of Islam*, 59.

[2] Schimmel, *And Muhammad Is His Messenger*, 47.

In the person of the Prophet of Islam the world has seen this rarest phenomenon on the earth, walking in flesh and blood."[1]

– K. S. Ramakrishna Rao (1989)

"[Islam's] abiding influence on the common relations of mankind in the affairs of everyday life, its deep power over the masses, its regulation of their conceptions of rights and duty, its suitability and adaptability to the ignorant savage and the wise philosopher alike: [these] are characteristic features of the teachings of the Prophet of Islam."[2]

– K. S. Ramakrishna Rao (1989)

PRACTICED WHAT HE PREACHED

"The interdiction of wine was confirmed by his example."[3]
– Edward Gibbon (1788)

"His prohibition of wine was enforced by his example."[4]
– Charles Mills (1817)

"Muhammad never preached what he himself did not practise."[5]
– Simon. H. Leeder (1917)

"Islam, in a word, is a creed of practice not theory. By practice it was formed. On practice it has lived. It was because Mohammed practised what he preached, that the small seed of his original idea blossomed at last into the mighty 'Igdrasil' of the East—the

---

[1] Rao, *Muhammad: the Prophet of Islam*, 21.

[2] Ibid., 29.

[3] Gibbon, *Decline and Fall*, vol. v, 149.

[4] Mills, *An History of Muhammedanism*, 41.

[5] Leeder, "The Tenderness of the Prophet."

great banyan tree of existence."¹

– Arthur Glyn Leonard (1909)

PRISONERS OF WAR (TREATMENT OF)

"It was the Arab custom to slay the defeated foe. When his followers asked the Prophet what was to be done with the prisoners taken in battle, he replied: 'Nay, show mercy to the fallen, and shed no blood. Treat these men as brothers.' The result of this teaching was that the conquerors who had with them dates and bread (the latter being considered a dainty in Arabia) contented themselves only with the dates and divided the bread among the conquered foe. What a noble example of mercy to a fallen foe? This is the first time in history that conquerors had been feeding the conquered."²

– Annie Besant (1932)

PURITY OF SOUL

"it was the purest humanity [of the Prophet] which dictated the law, that in the sale of captives, the infant should not be separated from the mother."³

– Charles Mills (1817)

PROACTIVE

"Unquestionably too he looked ahead—he made provision for the future. His whole apostolic life was one long and arduous

---

[1] Leonard, *Islam: Her Moral and Spiritual Value*, 106.

[2] Besant, *The Life and Teachings of Muhammad*, 30.

[3] Mills, *An History of Muhammedanism*, 40.

preparation for coming events."[1]

– Arthur Glyn Leonard (1909)

RACISM (ABOLISHED)

"It is, indeed, one of the most striking proofs of the strength of the creed of Islam that it does thus force into the background—at any rate, to a considerable degree—the distinguishing racial characteristics of the peoples to which it has come, and supersede them by a mind, a character, a life which is primarily and unmistakably the outcome of the creed itself. The Mohammedan type of character is as definite and clear cut a thing as possible, and can be traced directly to the doctrinal and ethical teaching of the creed itself, in a measure that it would, I think, be difficult to parallel in the case of the adherents of any other religion."[2]

– G. A. Lefroy (1907)

"Mohammed denounced and abolished caste, class, color, and race distinctions. The greatest evidence of the democratic policies of Islam is in the pilgrimage to Mecca. Here Europeans and Asiatics and Africans, coolies, princes, merchants, and warriors, meet in the same humble garb which Mohammed and his followers wore for the last pilgrimage in 632. They all eat the same food, share the same tents, and are treated with no distinction ... They follow the example of the founder of their faith who ruled Arabia but had no compunction about dining with a slave or sharing his dates with a beggar. Could a man who was not inspired have brought such an international brotherhood into being?"[3]

– R. V. C. Bodley (1945)

---

[1] Leonard, *Islam: Her Moral and Spiritual Value*, 94.

[2] Lefroy, *Mankind and the Church*, 281-82.

[3] Bodley, *The Messenger: The Life of Mohammed*, 343-44.

"... Islam has achieved a larger measure of success in dealing with the racial problem than Christianity."[1]

– Phillip K. Hitti (1969)

RATIONAL

"On the saddest day of Mohammed's life, when the light of it seemed to have gone down in the grave of his little boy Ibrahim, an eclipse of the sun occurred as he went home, and his friends spoke of it as a kind of token of the sympathy of Heaven. A vulgar impostor would have accepted the flattery, but Mohammed simply said, 'The sun and the moon are amongst the signs appointed by the Lord. They are not eclipsed on the death of any one.'"[2]

– Marcus Dods (1887)

"In order to lead men to a belief in one God, he did not delude them with tales of happenings which deviate from the normal course of nature—the so-called miracles; nor did he compel them to keep quiet by using celestial threats which only undermine man's ability to think. Rather, he simply invited them, without asking them to leave the realm of reality, to consider the universe and its laws."[3]

– Laura Vaglieri (1925)

REALIST

"Mohammed was a realist. Had he lived in the twentieth century, he and his theories would have fitted in comfortably with those

---

[1] Hitti, *Islam: A Way of Life*, 29.

[2] Dods, *Mohammed, Buddha, and Christ*, 22.

[3] Vaglieri, *An Interpretation Of Islam*, 30-31.

of the Modernists. He would most likely have been their leader."[1]
– R. V. C. Bodley (1945)

RECONCILE (READY TO)

"Always ready for reconciliation and compromise, he was unshakably firm in the intuition which was the centre of his life, the uncontaminated *tawhid*, the proclamation of the divine unity."[2]
– Francesco Gabrieli (1968)

REFINED AND CULTURED

"Taciturn and reserved, he was yet in company distinguished by a graceful urbanity."[3]
– William Muir (1858)

"He never yawned at prayer. When he sneezed he did so with a subdued voice, covering his face."[4]
– William Muir (1861)

"What is recorded of his tastes and habits exhibits ordinarily a high degree of refinement and delicacy. He abhorred anything that produced an evil odour: garlic and onions were described by him as evil vegetables,[5] and his loathing of anything that tainted

---

[1] Bodley, *The Messenger: The Life of Mohammed*, 84.

[2] Gabrieli, *Muhammad and the Conquests of Islam*, 23. The Prophet was always flexible and sought peace by avoiding conflict, but he never compromised in matters of faith and obedience to God.

[3] Muir, *Life of Mahomet*, vol. ii, 30.

[4] Muir, *Life of Mahomet*, vol. iv, 327.

[5] Margoliouth's choice of words is sometimes inaccurate. The Prophet did not refer to any vegetable that God made permissible as "evil." His disapproval of garlic, onion, or leek was limited to consuming them raw and then approaching a gathering of people, such as in a mosque, where their odor might disturb people. This is what he said

the breath was used as a lever by members of his harem. When sovereign he found fault with those whose hair was untidy, or whose clothes were dirty, being himself particular as to his appearance. He disliked yellow teeth, and almost made the use of the toothpick a religious ordinance."[1]

— D. S. Margoliouth (1905)

"It was one of the Prophet's habits that when he made 'Atsa,' that is, when he sneezed, he made a moderate noise, covering his blessed face with his robe-sleeve and putting his blessed hand before his nostrils. He used to say, 'God loves sneezing, but detests yawning: let every one who sneezes say, *Praise be to God!* and let him who hears him rejoin, *God have mercy on him!*'"[2]

— S. W. Koelle (1888)

"In the familiar offices of life he scrupulously adhered to the grave and ceremonious politeness of his country ... and the habits of courtesy were imputed to personal friendship, or universal benevolence."[3]

— Edward Gibbon (1788)

"A remarkable feature was the urbanity and consideration with which Mahomet treated even the most insignificant of his followers."[4]

— William Muir (1861)

---

according to one report: "Ibn 'Umar reported that the Messenger of Allah (ﷺ) said, 'Whoever eats of this plant (referring to garlic) should not approach our mosque, till its odor dies.'" (Authenticated by Muslim)

[1] Margoliouth, *Mohammed and the Rise of Islam*, 64.

[2] Koelle, *Mohammed and Mohammedanism*, 400.

[3] Gibbon, *Decline and Fall*, vol. v, 102.

[4] Muir, *Life of Mahomet*, vol. iv, 305.

His Character

Reformer

In Moral Life

"In the moral life of his countrymen he effected a remarkable reform. He abolished drunkenness and gambling, vices to which the Arabs had been specially addicted. He abolished the practice of infanticide, and also succeeded in rendering its memory detestable ... whatever laws he made respecting women and slaves were made with the view of improving their condition."[1]

– Winwood Reade (1872)

Established Brotherhood

"The immediate result of the Prophet's teaching was the dissolution of the tribal system and the foundation of the brotherhood of Islam. We are far from saying that the tribal system completely disappeared from the Arabs after Islam, but it lost, without a doubt, its darker and uglier features."[2]

– Alfred von Kremer (1873)

---

[1] Reade, *Martyrdom of Man*, 268.

[2] Von Kremer, *Contributions to the History of Islamic Civilization*, 154. Von Kremer is mistaken here, for the Prophet did not abolish tribes, nor was that his intention. What he successfully achieved was the end of inter-tribal warfare and bloodshed, under the overarching principle of Islam that there is no superiority of one tribe over another, nor one race over another, nor one skin color over another; that might does not make right; and that any conflicts between tribes or people must be resolved according to the laws set forth by God, the Provider and Sustainer of all mankind.

There is nothing inherently wrong with the tribal system, which developed organically since the dawn of humanity, providing essential protection and other benefits to people. It continues to exist in many parts of the world. What is problematic, however, is the modern nation-state system—developed by post-Enlightenment Europe—where people are grouped along artificial and inorganic boundaries, each promoting its own "national interests" under the banner of "nationalism," often at the expense of other nation-states. This system has fueled arms races, conflicts, and bloodshed,

Infighting Replaced with Friendship

"Mahomet ... breathed among the faithful a spirit of charity and friendship, recommended the practice of the social virtues, and checked, by his laws and precepts, the thirst of revenge and the oppression of widows and orphans. The hostile tribes were united in faith and obedience, and the valor which had been idly spent in domestic quarrels was vigorously directed against a foreign enemy."[1]

– Edward Gibbon (1788)

Large-Scale Reform in the Society

"He put forth a new religion; so have others before and since; but his religion was not destined to influence a single sect or a single nation; it was to stamp the mind and the destiny of the whole oriental world ... No man was ever more emphatically a reformer in the history of his own age and country."[2]

– Edward Freeman (1856)

"With the leaders of the Reformation, Mohammed, the greatest of all Reformers, meets with little sympathy..."[3]

– R. Bosworth Smith (1874)

"it was undoubtedly to Islam, that simple yet majestic creed of which no unprejudiced student can ignore the grandeur, that they owed the splendid part which they were destined to play in the history of civilization. In judging of the Arabian Prophet,

---

consuming valuable resources that could otherwise benefit the well-being of humanity. Indeed, it has even brought the world to the brink of global destruction and the potential annihilation of humanity.

[1] Gibbon, *Decline and Fall*, vol. v, 169.

[2] Freeman, *History and Conquests of the Saracens*, 6.

[3] Smith, *Mohammed and Mohammedanism*, 59-60.

Western critics are too often inclined to ignore the condition from which he raised his country, and to forget that many institutions, such as slavery and polygamy, which they condemn were not introduced but only tolerated by Islam. The early Muslims were very sensible of the immense amelioration in their life effected by Muhammad's teaching."[1]

— Edward G. Browne (1902)

"For the first twelve years of his mission he endured such cruel persecution and distress as would have killed or driven mad a man of slighter faith. Then came the Hijrah, the flight from Makkah to Medinah, when he was fifty two. In the ten years remaining of his life he succeeded in reforming all Arabia; he destroyed idolatry; raised women from the utmost degradation to an honoured and assured position, abolished useless bloodshed, made strict rules for war, and for the first time in the history of the world made universal brotherhood a principle and fact of common law."[2]

— Marmaduke Pickthall (1920)

"That he ... did have so large and so effective a program of reform for this world is a matter of continuing wonder and admiration, not to be explained by any casual theory of the abnormal."[3]

— John Clark Archer (1924)

Elevated Women

"He consecrated the rights of property in women, who had been thitherto disinherited of all right and of all possessions of their own in the conjugal community. He commended the widows to

---

[1] Browne, *A Literary History of Persia*, 186.

[2] Pickthall, "A Sermon."

[3] Archer, *The Mystical Elements of Mohammed*, 85.

their sons. 'A son,' says the Koran, 'obtains paradise at the feet of his mother.'"[1]

– Alphonse de Lamartine (1854)

"whatever laws he made respecting women and slaves were made with the view of improving their condition."[2]

– Winwood Reade (1872)

"he undoubtedly secured for them [i.e., women] by laws the rights of inheriting and holding property, which under the older system were precarious."[3]

– D. S. Margoliouth (1905)

"Woman was elevated to a status she had never enjoyed previously, either in the East or the West. Her rights were safeguarded by the law, and her husband had no claim on the fruits of her labour or on her property, while as wife she held certain legal claims on her husband he could not repudiate and none might take from her."[4]

– John Parkinson (1917)

"The historical truth is this, that the Prophet of Islam was perhaps the greatest feminist the world has ever known, considering the country and the age in which he lived."[5]

– Marmaduke Pickthall (1917)

---

[1] Lamartine, *History of Turkey*, vol. i, 153. This statement is not from the Qur'an but is based on a narration from Prophet Muhammad. Once, a man came to him expressing his desire to join the battlefield. "Do you have a mother?" he asked him. "Yes," the man replied. "Then stay with her, for Paradise is beneath her feet," said the Prophet. (Paraphrased from a report authenticated by al-Nasā'ī)

[2] Reade, *Martyrdom of Man*, 268.

[3] Margoliouth, *Mohammed and the Rise of Islam*, 461.

[4] Parkinson, "Muhammad As Social Reformer."

[5] Pickthall, "Islam and Progress."

"In the religious history of the world there is no person who has done so much to elevate the position of the fair sex as Muhammad."[1]

– Simon. H. Leeder (1917)

"He also raised woman from the condition of being a property to that of a proprietor, and he constituted her as the first 'legal' sharer whose interests the Muhammadan law has to consult ... The married woman is in a better legal position than the married Englishwoman, and she can give evidence in attestation of a birth, marriage, or death, which is still denied to a woman in Republican France."[2]

– G. W. Leitner (c. 1914)

"he certainly benefitted them [women] incalculably by setting up laws that enabled them to inherit and hold property;"[3]

– R. F. Dibble (1926)

"Indisputably, Mahomet's preachings brought about a great progress in Arabian life as regards both the family and hygiene. Woman's status, as we shall see, was greatly improved. Prostitution, temporary marriage and free love were forbidden as well as the forcing of captives into prostitution to enrich their masters."[4]

– Emile Dermenghem (1930)

"I often think that woman is more free in Islam than in Christianity. Woman is more protected by Islam than by the faith which preaches monogamy. In Al Quran the law about woman is juster and more liberal. It is only twenty years that Christian England

---

[1] Leeder, "The Tenderness of the Prophet."

[2] Leitner, "Religious Systems of the World."

[3] Dibble, *Mohammed*, 243.

[4] Dermenghem, *The Life of Mahomet*, 259.

has recognized the right of women to property, while Islam has allowed this right from all times."¹

– Annie Besant (1932)

"It is a fact, concluded A. Reville,² that 'when we take into consideration the times and the country there is no reform more worthy or more fearless than that in which Mahomet showed his initiative in favour of women ... The Oriental woman owes much to the Prophet.'"³

– Emile Dermenghem (1930)

"That his reforms enhanced the status of women in general by contrast with the anarchy of pre-Islamic Arabia is universally admitted."⁴

– Hamilton A. R. Gibb (1948)

"[The Prophet of] Islam came as the defender of the weaker sex and entitled women to share in the inheritance of their parents. It gave women, centuries ago, the right of owning property. Yet it was only 12 centuries later, in 1881, that England, supposed to be the cradle of democracy, adopted this institution of Islam and an Act was passed, called, 'The Married Women's Act'."⁵

– K. S. Ramakrishna Rao (1989)

In Hygiene

"Indisputably, Mahomet's preachings brought about a great

---

[1] Besant, *The Life and Teachings of Muhammad*, 25.

[2] Albert Réville (d. 1906) was a French Protestant theologian and a historian of religions. He is known for his 4-volume *Historie des Religions*.

[3] Dermenghem, *The Life of Mahomet*, 297fn1.

[4] Gibb, *Mohammedanism: An Historical Survey*, 33.

[5] Rao, *Muhammad: the Prophet of Islam*, 15.

progress in Arabian life as regards both the family and hygiene."[1]

– Emile Dermenghem (1930)

In Every Sphere of Life

"The reforms effected by the Prophet can only be rightly estimated by a reference to the history—social and religious—of the Arabs before the introduction of Islam. Whether we regard him as a divinely-inspired Prophet or a bold and far-sighted reformer, no individual figure in the history of the East is so impressive as that of Mohammed."[2]

– Alfred von Kremer (1873)

"In every sphere of life Islam effected a change for the better, nor were the early Muslims insensible of the immense amelioration wrought by Islam ... Islam taught the Arabs purity of life and straightforwardness of conduct. It broadened their thoughts and widened their sympathies. It breathed into them catholic charity and rendered them God-fearing. It instilled in them virtue and valour, which made them the conquerors of the world and the models of knighthood. It emphasized the necessity of good living and right thinking ... From gross fetichism to severe and unbending monotheism—such was the religious reform effected by [the Prophet of] Islam."[3]

– Alfred von Kremer (1873)

REFUSED NONE

"He found it almost impossible to say 'No' to any petitioner, and he never declined the invitation or small offering even of the

---

[1] Dermenghem, *The Life of Mahomet*, 259.

[2] Von Kremer, *Contributions to the History of Islamic Civilization*, 146.

[3] Ibid., 163.

meanest of the people."[1]

— Marcus Dods (1887)

"One day a woman gave him a cloak, which he needed badly, but when some one asked him for the cloak to make a shroud, Mahomet gave it up, for 'he could refuse nothing.'"[2]

— Emile Dermenghem (1930)

"He disliked to say *No*; if unable to reply to a petitioner in the affirmative, he preferred to remain silent."[3]

— William Muir (1861)

"His kindness, liberality, and generosity, were such that he never sent any beggar empty away from his door."[4]

— S. W. Koelle (1888)

"Never a suppliant came but he got more than he deserved or desired."[5]

— Lord Headley (1914)

Resolve

"Mohammed's greatness lies in the clearness of his vision and in the boldness of his resolve. The enormity of the task he was undertaking cannot be adequately measured by us at this distance of time. It was almost Herculean. It meant the entire subversion of the tribal system with its narrow ties and limited sympathies, the dethronement of the idols sanctified by age and tradition, the

---

[1] Dods, *Mohammed, Buddha, and Christ*, 90.

[2] Dermenghem, *The Life of Mahomet*, 163.

[3] Muir, *Life of Mahomet*, vol. iv, 305.

[4] Koelle, *Mohammed and Mohammedanism*, 380.

[5] Lord Headley, *A Western Awakening to Islam*, 80.

sweeping away of old and cherished ideals, and finally, what was most distasteful to the heathen Arabs, the imposition of fast and prayer and wholesome restraint upon the free, gay and unbridled license in social intercourse. Difficult and perilous as the task was, the inward power of genuine conviction irresistibly impelled the prophet to grapple with the situation, to face and conquer the obstacles that lay in his path..."[1]

– Alfred von Kremer (1873)

"Behind the quiet and unobtrusive exterior of Mahomet, lay hid a high resolve, a singleness and unity of purpose, a strength and fixedness of will, a sublime determination..."[2]

– William Muir (1858)

RESPECT FOR PEOPLE

Cultural Sensitivity

"From whatever tribe men came to follow him, he would speak to them in their own language."[3]

– S. W. Koelle (1888)

Valuing Others' Opinions

"He would take counsel with his friends about things; and Aisha the faithful declared, 'I have not seen any one amongst the people

---

[1] Von Kremer, *Contributions to the History of Islamic Civilization*, 148.

[2] Muir, *Life of Mahomet*, vol. ii, 31. These qualities are not unique to Prophet Muhammad but are characteristic of all prophets of God. They were entrusted with a mission by Him and remained focused on that mission until their death.

[3] Koelle, *Mohammed and Mohammedanism*, 393. By "language," Koelle must have meant "dialect." The Prophet spoke only Arabic, as did all the tribes in the Arabian Peninsula, each using varying dialects.

who so readily asked advice as that Excellency.'"¹

— S. W. Koelle (1888)

Avoiding Disturbing People

"When he went to a house at night, he saluted in a manner that those who were awake could hear him, but that those asleep were not awakened."²

— S. W. Koelle (1888)

Respecting Privacy

"Of all the habits of that prince one was that when he went to any one's house, he did not place himself opposite the door, but stood either on the right or on the left hand side of it, asking permission to enter ... He [would say], 'If ye go to any one's house, first give the peace; and do not admit any one into your house, who, in coming, does not first give you the peace.' ³ He also said, 'Greeting is before asking: if any one begins by asking anything of you, without first giving you the peace, then do not answer him.' ... once some one came to that prince's house asking, 'Shall I enter?' But he sent some one out to him, saying, 'Teach that person the way of asking permission, and let him first say, 'Peace be upon you!' and afterwards, 'May I come in?.'"⁴

— S. W. Koelle (1888)

---

[1] Ibid., 393.

[2] Ibid., 399.

[3] His reason for standing to the left or right of the door while awaiting permission was to ensure he was not in direct view of the interior of the house when the door was opened. Such refined mannerism and respect for people's privacy is remarkable, even by modern standards.

[4] Koelle, *Mohammed and Mohammedanism*, 398.

His Character

RESPECT FOR ALL ABRAHAMIC FAITHS

Disclaimed as Founder of a New Faith

"So far from professing to bring a new revelation Mohammed insisted that the Scripture given to him was but a restatement of the faith delivered to the Prophets before him, confirming their Scriptures and itself confirmed by them. Yet the originality of Islam is none the less real, in that it represents a further step in the logical (if not philosophical) evolution of monotheistic religion. Its monotheism, like that of the Hebrew Prophets, is absolute and unconditioned, but with this it combines the universalism of Christianity. On the one hand, it rejects the nationalist taint from which Judaism as a religion did not succeed in freeing itself; for Islam never identified itself with the Arabs, although at times Arabs have identified themselves with it. On the other hand, it is distinguished from Christianity, not so much (in spite of all outward appearances) by its repudiation of the trinitarian concept of the Unity of God, as by its rejection of the soteriology of Christian doctrine and the relics of the old nature cults which survived in the rites and practices of the Christian Church."[1]

– Hamilton A. R. Gibb (1948)

Previous Prophets of God

"Mohammed never gave himself out as the founder of a new religion, but, on the contrary, he maintains (chapters 2, 3, 16, 26, &c.) his religion to be that of Abraham, which was revealed to him (Mohammed) by the Angel Gabriel (chapter 33). The sole object of the Koran is that of correcting the Scriptures [that became corrupted by the hands of men]."[2]

– John Davenport (1869)

---

[1] Gibb, *Mohammedanism: An Historical Survey*, 69.

[2] Davenport, *An Apology for Mohammed and the Koran*, 74.

"Mohammed never, at any time, suggested that the religion which he preached was his idea. He never attributed to himself anything godly. None of his followers worship him. Accordingly to his lights, he was a prophet like Noah or Moses, sent by God to restore into the right path His people who, from time to time, strayed."[1]

– R. V. C. Bodley (1945)

"the liberality of Mahomet allowed to his predecessors[2] the same credit which he claimed for himself; and the chain of inspiration was prolonged from the fall of Adam to the promulgation of the Koran."[3]

– Edward Gibbon (1788)

Revenge (Never Took)

"Attempts were made at his life a number of times, but he never took revenge. He was always ready to forgive personal injuries."[4]

– Annie Besant (1932)

Rights (Discharging Of)

Giving All Things Its Due

"The Prophet said: 'The best among you is not the one who forgets the life after death in order to enjoy the present, nor the one who does the contrary; the best among you is the one who takes

---

[1] Bodley, *The Messenger: The Life of Mohammed*, 83.

[2] i.e., Gibbon, judging from a secular perspective, considers this recognition of all previous prophets a "liberality" of Prophet Muhammad. However, any genuine prophet of God would necessarily confirm them since they are all sent by the same God to the same humanity.

[3] Gibbon, *Decline and Fall*, vol. v, 106-07.

[4] Besant, *The Life and Teachings of Muhammad*, 32.

from both.' To a too fervent youngster he said: 'Your body has its rights and your wife has her rights and your guest has his rights.' To the one who one day asked his advice about alms, he said: 'Give one-third because one-third is already enough. It is better to leave your descendants provided for than to compel them to go begging.'"[1]

– Laura Vaglieri (1925)

Giving Everyone His Due

"Hosein Ibn Ali[2] narrates: When I asked my father how the Prophet lived in public, he answered, 'He kept his tongue from what is unprofitable, conciliated and pleased his companions, and did not offend them. He treated the honourable men of the people with distinction, and gave to the people their due. He never neglected good manners, duly saluted his companions, and inquired after their state. He approved of what was good, and condemned what was bad. Those nearest to him were the best of the people; and the most honoured those who were most benevolent to the Mussulmans.'"[3]

– S. W. Koelle (1888)

ROLES (PERFORMED MANY)

---

[1] Vaglieri, *An Interpretation Of Islam*, 61. Here, Vaglieri is paraphrasing from the hadith. Under Islamic law, the estate of the deceased is distributed among specific inheritors in prescribed ratios, and one may not bequeath more than one-third of the estate to charity. This restriction is based on an incident during the Prophet's time. One of his companions, Sa'd ibn Abī Waqqāṣ, was severely ill and feared imminent death. When the Prophet visited him, Sa'd expressed his desire to bequeath all or the bulk of his estate to charity. The Prophet limited him to no more than one-third, advising that it would not be wise to leave his heirs in poverty.

[2] Ḥussayn's father was Alī, who was the Prophet's son-in-law.

[3] Koelle, *Mohammed and Mohammedanism*, 378.

The Most Praised Man

"As long as Muhammad lived he performed the functions of prophet, lawgiver, religious leader, chief judge, commander of the army and civil head of the states—all in one."[1]
– Phillip K. Hitti (1937)

"Mohammed was not only spiritual. He, like every human being, had a material side to his character. Not only was he a preacher and a prophet; not only was he a lawgiver—a law and a light unto his people to this very day; but as one who himself rigidly practised self-denial and economy and condemned extravagance, who possessed the organizing ability to administer the estate of others, and who could command preferably in peace, but if necessary in war, he was a statesman and an economist."[2]
– Arthur Glyn Leonard (1909)

"But amid all the duties of general, legislator, judge, and diplomatist, the Prophet did not neglect those of preacher and teacher: his advice was demanded on all possible questions, and the occasions were few on which he failed to give it."[3]
– D. S. Margoliouth (1905)

"Judged only by achievement, Muhammad the man, the teacher, the orator, the author, the statesman, and the warrior stands out as one of the ablest men in all history. He laid the basis of a religion—Islam; initiated a state—the caliphate; prompted a culture—the Arabic-Islamic culture; and founded a nation—the Arab nation. He is still a living force in the lives of millions of men."[4]
– Phillip K. Hitti (1969)

---

[1] Hitti, *History of the Arabs*, 139.

[2] Leonard, *Islam: Her Moral and Spiritual Value*, 93-94.

[3] Margoliouth, *Mohammed and the Rise of Islam*, 463-64.

[4] Hitti, *Islam: A Way of Life*, 24.

His Character

ROLE MODEL

"Napoleon Bonaparte, as we have seen, was an admirer of Muhammad. Indeed ... for Bonaparte the prophet was something of a role model: stirring orator, brilliant general, sage statesman."[1]

– John V. Tolan (2019)

"Serious or trivial, his daily behaviour has instituted a canon which millions observe at this day with conscious mimicry. No one is regarded by any section of the human race as [this] Perfect Man has been imitated so minutely. The conduct of the Founder of Christianity has not so governed the ordinary life of His followers. Moreover, no Founder of a religion has been left on so solitary an eminence as the Muslim Apostle."[2]

– David Geroge Hogarth (1921)

"The imitation of the noble actions and thoughts that Muhammad, the 'beautiful model,' had taught his community by his personal example was meant to form each and every Muslim, as it were, into a likeness of the Messenger. This is so that each, like him, should give witness of God's unity through his or her whole being and existence ... It is this ideal of the *imitatio Muhammadi* that has provided Muslims from Morocco to Indonesia with such a uniformity of action: wherever one may be, one knows how to behave when entering a house, which formulas of greeting to employ, what to avoid in good company, how to eat, and how to travel."[3]

– Annemarie Schimmel (1984)

---

[1] Tolan, *Faces of Muhammad*, 13.

[2] David Geroge Hogarth, *Arabia*, 52. Hogarth (d. 1927) was an English archaeologist and diplomat. In 1919, he served as the British commissioner at the Middle East Commission of the Paris Peace Conference.

[3] Schimmel, *And Muhammad Is His Messenger*, 55.

Ruler

"when we regard him as a ruler and lawgiver, we can only wonder and admire. He established for the first time in history a United Arabia."[1]

– Winwood Reade (1872)

Sacrifice

"It was a stake of life and death, but he threw himself into the conflict with all the force that was in him..."[2]

– Alfred von Kremer (1873)

"For the truth's sake he risked his life, he suffered daily persecution for years, and eventually banishment, the loss of property, of the goodwill of his fellow-citizens, and of the confidence of his friends—he suffered, in short, as much as any man can suffer short of death..."[3]

– Marcus Dods (1887)

Saintly

"Muhammad appears as a saintly man ... He preached that slaves should be set free, that fathers should not kill unwanted baby girls, that those oppressed by society inherit the earth, that peace is better than war, that justice prevails ... on one occasion, when a deputation of Christians visited him, he said, when time for prayers arrived, 'Conduct your service here in the mosque. It is a place consecrated to God.'"[4]

– James A. Michener (1955)

---

[1] Reade, *Martyrdom of Man*, 268.

[2] Von Kremer, *Contributions to the History of Islamic Civilization*, 147.

[3] Dods, *Mohammed, Buddha, and Christ*, 17-18.

[4] Michener, "Islam: The Misunderstood Religion."

His Character

SANE

Sanity is not easily defined, and the transition from sanity to insanity may not always be discernible. Only a perfectly wholesome individual in all respects might be considered fully "sane." If this is a correct definition, it could be argued that *everyone* has some level of "insanity"—something lacking or undesirable in their character, manner, temperament, wisdom, judgment, or emotional and spiritual health. However, if there ever was a human being who exemplified complete wholesomeness and could be considered fully sane, it would undoubtedly be Prophet Muhammad.

"If ever a man was sane and healthy, he was."[1]
– Arthur Glyn Leonard (1909)

"Muhammad ... was as sane and practical in the last days of his life as he had been when he first received his mission."[2]
– Marmaduke Pickthall (1917)

"If ever there was a man who was clearly sane, it was Mohammed."[3]
– R. V. C. Bodley (1945)

SELFLESS

"He was most unostentatious and selfless to the core. What were the titles he assumed? Only two, Servant of God, and His Messenger; Servant first and then a Messenger."[4]
– K. S. Ramakrishna Rao (1989)

---

[1] Leonard, *Islam: Her Moral and Spiritual Value*, 43.
[2] Pickthall, "The Prophet's Gratitude."
[3] Bodley, *The Messenger: The Life of Mohammed*, 72.
[4] Rao, *Muhammad: the Prophet of Islam*, 25.

"From the hour when he received his call until he died the Prophet lost all thought of his own interests. No other man in the whole history of the world, however mighty his enthusiasm for a cause, has served that cause so single-heartedly as did Muhammad. In the hour of triumph, as of that of adversity, he was the faithful servant of the Most High, doing his Master's work without a taint of selfish motive."[1]

– Marmaduke Pickthall (1920)

SERVANTS (TREATMENT OF)

"Excellence of his Morals—A servant maid being once long in returning from an errand, Mahomet was annoyed and said, 'If it were not for the law of retaliation, I should have punished you with this toothpick' (i.e. with an inappreciably light punishment.)"[2]

– William Muir (1861)

"He was kind and forgiving to all. 'I served him from the time I was eight years old,' said his servant Anas, 'and he never scolded me for anything, though I spoiled much.'"[3]

– R. Bosworth Smith (1874)

"The good manners of that prince were such, that he never grieved any one of his friends and servants. Uns Ibn Malik says, 'I served that prince for ten years, both at home and on journeys, and he never said to me, 'Why didst thou do this ? or why didst thou not do that?'"[4]

– S. W. Koelle (1888)

---

[1] Pickthall, "A Sermon."

[2] Muir, *The Life of Mahomet*, vol. iv, 326-27.

[3] Smith, *Mohammed and Mohammedanism*, 85.

[4] Koelle, *Mohammed and Mohammedanism*, 377-78.

His Character

SHARING

"The little food that he had was always shared with those who dropped in to partake of it. Indeed, outside the Prophet's house was a bench or gallery, on which were always to be found a number of the poor who lived entirely on the Prophet's generosity, and were hence called the 'people of the bench'."[1]

— R. Bosworth Smith (1874)

"Dates and water were his usual fare, and milk and honey his luxuries. When he travelled, he divided his morsel with his servant."[2]

— Charles Mills (1817)

"He shared his food, even in times of scarcity, with others; and was sedulously solicitous for the personal comfort of every one about him."[3]

— William Muir (1861)

SINCERE

"A silent great soul; he was one of those who cannot but be in earnest; whom Nature herself has appointed to be sincere. While others walk in formulas and hearsays, contented enough to dwell there, this man could not screen himself in formulas; he was alone with his own soul and the reality of things ... Such sincerity as we named it, has in very truth something of divine. The word of such a man is a Voice direct from Nature's own Heart. Men do and must listen to that as to nothing else;—all else is wind in comparison."[4]

— Thomas Carlyle (1840)

---

[1] Smith, *Mohammed and Mohammedanism*, 85-86.

[2] Mills, *An History of Muhammedanism*, 39.

[3] Muir, *Life of Mahomet*, vol. iv, 305.

[4] Carlyle, *On Heroes*, 60-61.

"It is strongly corroborative of Mahomet's sincerity that the earliest converts to Islam were his bosom friends and the people of his household; who, intimately acquainted with his private life, could not fail otherwise to have detected those discrepancies which, more or less, invariably exist between the professions of the hypocritical deceiver abroad, and his actions at home."[1]
– William Muir (1858)

"Muḥammad's life and work unconditionally presuppose the sincerity of his commission."[2]
– Theodor Noldeke (1860)

"It is a striking proof of his sincerity that his earliest and most devoted disciples were those of his own household, and his familiars, who had known him in all circumstances and scanned him in all moods—his wife, his slave, his cousin, his father-in-law—the latter themselves men of character and position."[3]
– Marcus Dods (1887)

"Mohammed's sincerity and fixity of purpose is a fact we cannot get away from. It is this which has chained his followers as with the sure cord of God to the Faith."[4]
– Arthur Glyn Leonard (1909)

"There can be no question of the profound sincerity of the man."[5]
– James A. Montgomery (1917)

"… Muhammad before he began his mission was highly esteemed by his own countrymen for integrity of conscience and

---

[1] Muir, *Life of Mahomet*, vol. ii, 97.

[2] Noldeke, *The History of the Qur'an*, 24.

[3] Dods, *Mohammed, Buddha, and Christ*, 21.

[4] Leonard, *Islam: Her Moral and Spiritual Value*, 106.

[5] Montgomery, *Religions of the Past and Present*, 221.

purity of life ... how could it be that Muhammad could have threatened liars and hypocrites with the eternal fire in the burning words of the Quran if he himself had been a liar. How could he have dared to preach, in spite of the insults of his countrymen, if he, a man of simple nature, had not been continuously urged on by inner forces? How could he have started a struggle which looked hopeless? How could he have carried it on for over ten years at Mecca with very little success and countless sorrows, if he had not the very deep conviction of the truth of his mission? How could so many noble and intelligent Muslims have believed in him and thrown in their lot with him, joined the new faith and consequently associated themselves with a society made up for the most part of slaves, freedmen and indigent people if they had not felt in his word the sincerity of the Truth? We do not need to say more, for even among Occidentals the truth is well accepted that the sincerity of Muhammad was deep and true."[1]

– Laura Vaglieri (1925)

"To-day we cannot question his sincerity. His whole life ... proves that he believed profoundly in his mission and that he accepted it heroically as a burden of which he was to bear the heavier portion."[2]

– Emile Dermenghem (1930)

"Above all, there is Muhammad's absolute sincerity in feeling himself the recipient of a special contact with the divine, and the transmitter of a message which was, in the beginning at least, infinitely higher than any ambition or interest of his own."[3]

– Francesco Gabrieli (1968)

---

[1] Vaglieri, *An Interpretation Of Islam*, 27-28.

[2] Dermenghem, *The Life of Mahomet*, 249.

[3] Gabrieli, *Muhammad and the Conquests of Islam*, 22.

Serving Humanity

"An unusually delicate consideration for the feelings and comfort of those about him betrayed itself in his whole manner ... With all reverence we may say, he was among men as he that serveth."[1]

– Marcus Dods (1887)

"No man ever served humanity as this man did, whose sole aim was to serve Allah. And his example shows us that to serve Allah truly is to serve humanity. Personal ambition, national ambition, tribal jealousy—all the passions which compose what we call patriotism—he abjured as criminal. Instead he preached the brotherhood of all believers."[2]

– Marmaduke Pickthall (1917)

Serving Others First

"When he had company who had to be served with water or sherbet, he gave them first, himself drinking after them, and it is established that he said, 'He who gives drink to the people, drinks after them.'"[3]

– S. W. Koelle (1888)

Simplicity

"In his habits he was extremely simple, though he bestowed great care on his person. His eating and drinking, his dress and his furniture, retained, even when he had reached the fulness of power, their almost primitive nature. He made a point of giving away all 'superfluities.' The only luxuries he indulged in were, besides

---

[1] Dods, *Mohammed, Buddha, and Christ*, 90.

[2] Pickthall, "Address on the Prophet's Birthday."

[3] Koelle, *Mohammed and Mohammedanism*, 389.

arms, which he highly prized, certain yellow boots, a present from the Negus of Abyssinia."[1]

– Emanuel Deutsch (1869)

"the lord of Arabia lived in the humblest dwelling, on the plainest fare, accessible to the meanest of believers. The master of thousands of willing slaves still patched his own shoes and milked his own cattle."[2]

– Edward Freeman (1856)

"A patriarchal simplicity pervaded his life."[3]

– William Muir (1861)

"His house, his dress, his food—they were characterized by a rare simplicity."[4]

– Gustav Weil (1866)

"The simplicity of his private life was in keeping with his public life."[5]

– R. Bosworth Smith (1874)

"It is recorded that the abstinence of that prince was such that if the entire world had been offered unto him, he would not have looked at it; and when he departed from this world, his armour had been pawned to a Jew; and for three successive days his stomach did not taste bread. It is likewise recorded that, for two days in succession, he could not satisfy himself with barley-bread. It might happen in the Prophet's family that no fire was lit for a whole month, but that they lived upon dates and water. So

---

[1] Deutsch, *Literary Remains*, 72.

[2] Freeman, *History and Conquests of the Saracens*, 37.

[3] Muir, *Life of Mahomet*, vol. iv, 304.

[4] Weil, *A History of Islamic Peoples*, 28.

[5] Smith, *Mohammed and Mohammedanism*, 236.

also it could happen that his Excellency laid himself down at night hungry, when on the following day he was going to fast."¹

— S. W. Koelle (1888)

Slaves (Treatment Of)

"He but rarely made use of the hand of his slave for the most disagreeable services of the house. He went to fetch water from the well, swept and washed the boards of his floor. Seated on the ground, upon his mat of straw, he mended himself his sandals, and stitched his worn garments."²

— Alphonse de Lamartine (1854)

"He was ... most patient and kindly to his slaves."³

— Marcus Dods (1887)

"[The Prophet said] 'Your slaves are your brothers. Give them the same food and the same clothing that you wear. Do not force them to work beyond their strength.'"⁴

— Emile Dermenghem (1930)

"The Prophet's admonition concerning the treatment of slaves— 'Let them wear what you wear, and let them eat what you eat'— was quite popular in later centuries, as several anecdotes prove."⁵

— Annemarie Schimmel (1984)

---

[1] Koelle, *Mohammed and Mohammedanism*, 379.

[2] Lamartine, *History of Turkey*, vol. i, 152.

[3] Dods, *Mohammed, Buddha, and Christ*, 90.

[4] Dermenghem, *The Life of Mahomet*, 259.

[5] Schimmel, *And Muhammad Is His Messenger*, 48.

SLAVERY

"The law of Islam [as established from the teachings of Prophet Muhammad] regulated the position of slaves with much equity, and there is a great body of testimony from people who have spent a part of their lives among Mohammedan nations which does justice to the benevolent treatment which bondmen generally receive from their masters there. Besides that, we are bound to state that in many Western countries or countries under Western domination whole groups of the population live under circumstances with which those of Mohammedan slavery may be compared to advantage."[1]

– Snouck Hurgronje (1916)

"The Prophet had a great zeal for the *manumission of slaves*, and pointed out its meritoriousness. He gave liberty to a number of male and female slaves."[2]

– S. W. Koelle (1888)

"His slaves he always freed."[3]

– William Muir (1861)

"whatever laws he made respecting women and slaves were made with the view of improving their condition."[4]

– Winwood Reade (1872)

"The following sayings [of Prophet Muhammad] will illustrate the traditional policy and attitude of Muslims towards their slaves: 'The slave must be given food and clothing. He must not be given a task which he is unable to perform.' 'It is your

---

[1] Hurgronje, *Mohammedanism*, 129.

[2] Koelle, *Mohammed and Mohammedanism*, 414.

[3] Muir, *Life of Mahomet*, vol. iv, 336.

[4] Reade, *Martyrdom of Man*, 268.

brethren that God has put beneath your hands. He who has one thus subjected to him by God must feed him from what he eats himself, and clothe him in his own clothes. He must not give him a task beyond his strength. If he does, then he must help him himself.' Again, 'He who beats a slave for a fault he has not committed or slaps his face must make atonement by setting him free.' 'Whoso separates a woman from her child (the commentator explains, by selling, giving, &c.) God will separate him from his loved ones on the resurrection day.' It is related that the apostle of God gave Ali a slave, saying: 'Do not beat him, for I have ordered that those who pray shall not be beaten, and I have seen this slave at prayer.' ... 'We will slay him who slays his slave, and we will maim him who maims him.'"[1]

– Alfred Guillaume (1924)

"He tolerated slavery but he also regulated it. To free a slave he cited as a good action; for certain infractions of the ritual the freeing of a slave was the penance. [The Prophet said] 'Whoever frees a slave shall be exempted from hell; for every member of the liberated slave, a member of the liberator shall be freed, even to the secret parts of his body . . . Your slaves are your brothers. Give them the same food and the same clothing that you wear. Do not force them to work beyond their strength.'"[2]

– Emile Dermenghem (1930)

"The Koran like the Old Testament takes slavery for granted. So deeply rooted was the institution in the socioeconomic life of the ancient society that no other course could have been possible. Not only did Muhammad dam a main source of slavery by prohibiting inter Moslem raiding and warring, but he introduced more humane treatment for slaves. 'Be kind unto parent ... and unto those whom your right hands own' (4:40, 16:73, 24:33). No

---

[1] Guillaume, *The Traditions of Islam*, 105-6.

[2] Dermenghem, *The Life of Mahomet*, 259.

Moslem could enslave a fellow Moslem. If a slave (*'abd*) embraced Islam he was not automatically freed, but manumission of slaves in general was inculcated as something pleasing to Allah; it could be regarded as an expiation for sins committed. It is generally believed that on the whole slaves fared better under Islam than in Christendom."[1]

— Phillip K. Hitti (1969)

Social Intercourse

Gave Everyone Full Attention

"When he turned towards you, it was never partially but with the whole body."[2]

— William Muir (1858)

"The same habit [of thoroughness] pervaded his manner in social intercourse. If he turned in conversation towards a friend, he turned not partially, but with his full face and his whole body. 'In shaking hands, he was not the first to withdraw his own; nor was he the first to break off in converse with a stranger, nor to turn away his ear.'"[3]

— William Muir (1861)

Shared in Their Feelings

"He understood both joy and sorrow, and—conclusive proof of his wide and genuine humanity—had an equally ready sympathy for both."[4]

— Marcus Dods (1887)

---

[1] Hitti, *Islam: A Way of Life*, 29.

[2] Muir, *Life of Mahomet*, vol. ii, 30.

[3] Muir, *Life of Mahomet*, vol. iv, 303.

[4] Dods, *Mohammed, Buddha, and Christ*, 90.

"What his companions admired, he also admired; and when they laughed, he either was silent or smiled. He would laugh so that his teeth could be seen."[1]

– S. W. Koelle (1888)

Made Everyone Feel Valued

"He possessed the rare faculty of making each individual in a company think that he was the most favoured guest. When he met any one rejoicing, he would seize him eagerly and cordially by the hand. With the bereaved and afflicted he sympathized tenderly."[2]

– William Muir (1861)

"He showed regard and honour to those coming to the assemblies; and sometimes would let them sit upon his own cushion. He would mention his companions by their patronymics and call them by the names they liked best."[3]

– S. W. Koelle (1888)

SOCIAL JUSTICE AND WELFARE

"'There is but one God.' ... Asserting that everlasting truth, he did not engage in vain metaphysics, but applied himself to improving the social condition of his people by regulations respecting personal cleanliness, sobriety, fasting, prayer. Above all other works he esteemed almsgiving and charity."[4]

– John William Draper (1861)

---

[1] Koelle, *Mohammed and Mohammedanism*, 393.

[2] Muir, *Life of Mahomet*, vol. iv, 305.

[3] Koelle, *Mohammed and Mohammedanism*, 380.

[4] John William Draper, *A History of the Intellectual Development of Europe*, vol. i, 330. Draper (d. 1882) was an English-born American scientist, philosopher, physician, chemist, and historian.

His Character

"By the force of his extraordinary personality, Muhammad revolutionized life in Arabia and throughout the East ... He lifted women from the bondage in which desert custom held them and preached general social justice."[1]

– James A. Michener (1955)

"The morality which the Koran proclaims is apparently of a definitely social nature. The duty of being kind and helpful is especially stressed. The wealthy have the responsibility of aiding the poor with their surplus. Since Mohammed frequently insists that an occasional gift is not sufficient, that alms-giving must be regarded as a perpetual responsibility, a sort of permanent institution, and that the believer is to give the needy man 'a share' of his possessions, it is quite understandable that Hubert Grimme, in a book which attracted a great deal of attention in its day, championed the idea that Mohammed should be treated as a social rather than as a religious reformer. According to Grimme, the social injustices prevailing at the time in Mecca, where the wealthy merchants oppressed the poor and allowed them to perish in their misery, aroused the flaming wrath of the Prophet, and he arose to establish a new and better social order."[2]

– Tor Andrae (1932)

STATE AND GOVERNMENT

"[An] aspect of the Prophet's biography that may appear repellent to Western tastes and is correspondingly difficult to assess correctly is his blending of religion and politics, of *din wa daula* ... What seems to the non-Muslim a contradiction, that is, Muhammad's role as prophet and statesman, is according to the Muslim's conviction the very proof of Muhammad's unique role as God's messenger, evidencing his greatness and the truth of his message. How could it happen that God, who sent him, should

---

[1] Michener, "Islam: The Misunderstood Religion."

[2] Andrae, *Mohammed: The Man and His Faith*, 101-02.

not grant him ultimate success and inspire him to guide his community well?"[1]

    – Annemarie Schimmel (1984)

"His humanity and foresight were also manifested in more important matters. Blood-feuds—the time-honored and almost ineradicable system of tribal revenge for homicide—he endeavored, with partial success, to wipe out by emphasizing the brotherhood of Islam, and by advocating the acceptance of money as a partial compensation; ethical and legislative essays that gradually led to a saner and more peaceful system of government."[2]

    – R. F. Dibble (1926)

"If a Western observer, brought up in the liberal tradition of post-Enlightenment thought, claims that religion and politics (in the widest sense of the word) should be separated and that religion is a personal, interiorized, and exclusively private affair, a matter of the heart alone, the traditional Muslim will explain to him that, rather, religion and state belong together like the two sides of a coin. If Muhammad—as it was said at some point in Islamic history—is the axis around which the *Heilsgeschichte* of the human race is revolving, then the political and social aspects of life too belong to that process. Muhammad's political acumen, his battle for social improvement in Mecca and even more in Medina, his "constitution" of Medina, which is praised today as a model of modem democratic institutions, and his activities in the economic sector—all these appeal to the modern Muslim as examples by which he too should shape his life and that of his community. There is no room in Islam for the dualism of a good spiritual realm and an evil material sphere..."[3]

    – Annemarie Schimmel (1984)

---

[1] Schimmel, *And Muhammad Is His Messenger*, 52.

[2] Dibble, *Mohammed*, 242-43.

[3] Schimmel, *And Muhammad Is His Messenger*, 52-53.

His Character

STRUCK NONE

"He never struck any one in his life. The worst expression he ever made use of in conversation was, 'What has come to him? May his forehead be darkened with mud!' When asked to curse some one, he replied, 'I have not been sent to curse, but to be a mercy to mankind.'"[1]

– Emanuel Deutsch (1869)

"He never struck a human being in his life."[2]

– Marmaduke Pickthall (1917)

"Ayesha [reports] 'he never smote any one but in the service of the Lord, not even a woman or a servant.'"[3]

– William Muir (1861)

"The sources praise Muhammad's concern for the weak, and his kindliness is always highlighted: 'He did not beat a servant, nor a maid servant, and none of his wives,' says the tradition."[4]

– Annemarie Schimmel (1984)

SUPERNATURAL POWERS (DENIED HAVING)

"the most miraculous thing about Mohammed is that he never claimed the power of working miracles."[5]

– R. Bosworth Smith (1874)

"With admirable sagacity and sincerity he declined to give himself out as a worker of miracles. To those who asked for signs,

---

[1] Deutsch, *Literary Remains*, 72.

[2] Pickthall, "Address on the Prophet's Birthday."

[3] Muir, *Life of Mahomet*, vol. iv, 305.

[4] Schimmel, *And Muhammad Is His Messenger*, 46.

[5] Smith, *Mohammed and Mohammedanism*, 237-38.

he replied, 'Signs are in the power of God alone, and I am no more than a public preacher.'"[1]

– Marcus Dods (1887)

"He never attributed to himself anything godly."[2]

– R. V. C. Bodley (1945)

"Mohammed rejected every request to pose as a wonder-worker, and emphatically denied all superstitions in regard to his own person. He is only a man like other men; he has no recourse to heavenly resources; he is not even the master of his own fate, to say nothing of the fate of others ... At all events, in important matters he did not attempt to advance his authority or safeguard his position by means of alleged miracles."[3]

– Tor Andrae (1932)

"Mohammed remained steadfast in his refusal to do anything supernatural. He declared and redeclared that he was nothing more than a man who had been chosen like any of the other prophets in history to help the people to salvation ... he continued to assert all through his life, and to deny that he had any divine attributes. He was a human being like any other and never anything more than the mouthpiece of the Almighty."[4]

– R. V. C. Bodley (1945)

SUPERSTITION (WIPED OUT)

"In the fifteenth and sixteenth centuries the great reformer

---

[1] Dods, *Mohammed, Buddha, and Christ*, 28.

[2] Bodley, *The Messenger: The Life of Mohammed*, 83.

[3] Andrae, *Mohammed: The Man and His Faith*, 251. For a discussion on the nature and limitations of miracles, see our book, *The Book of Miracles: Extraordinary Facts from the Qur'an Indicating Divine Origin*.

[4] Bodley, *The Messenger: The Life of Mohammed*, 72-73.

Maring Luther followed up in north Europe what Muhammad had started over nine hundred years before in Arabia, viz. the clearing away of that which was founded on superstition and bigotry and uptting in its place *a faith of simple trust and belief in God.*"[1]

— Lord Headley (1914)

"Foolish acts of cruelty which were connected with old superstitions were swept away by him with other institutions of paganism."[2]

— D. S. Margoliouth (1905)

"If greatness consists in reforming those wrapt in a degrading superstition and pernicious practices of every kind, the Prophet of Islam has wiped out superstitions and irrational fear from the hearts of millions."[3]

— K. S. Ramakrishna Rao (1989)

TALENTS OF A SUPERIOR ORDER

"He possessed talents of a superior order—his perception was quick and active, his memory capacious and retentive, his imagination lively and daring, his judgment clear and perspicuous, his courage dauntless…"[4]

— John Davenport (1869)

TOLERANCE (RELIGIOUS)

"As Mahomet persecuted none for Religion, who beleived one

---

[1] Lord Headley, "Simplicity of Faith."

[2] Margoliouth, *Mohammed and the Rise of Islam*, 458-59.

[3] Rao, *Muhammad: the Prophet of Islam*, 21.

[4] Davenport, *An Apology for Mohammed and the Koran*, 11.

God & the day of Judgement, so lest of all the Christians, who, as we have seen before, enjoyed more of his Favours then any of the other Religions."[1]
— Henry Stubbe (1671)

"the Prophet himself gave guarantees to the Christians of Nejran that their Christian institutions would be preserved and gave orders to the head of an expedition to Yemen that no Jews be molested in his Judaism ... [subsequent Muslim] generals followed Muhammad's example in making agreements with the conquered peoples. By virtue of these agreements, the conquered were granted the freedom of following the old religion and traditions, provided that those who did not accept Islam would pay the government a fair tax, jizya. This tax was lighter than the taxes which the Muslims were liable to pay to their own government. In return these subjects (called Dhimmi) were granted protection not different from that enjoyed by the Muslim community itself. Consequently, as the practices followed by the Prophet and by the first orthodox Caliphs became law itself for later Muslims, it is no exaggeration to insist that Islam was not satisfied with preaching religious tolerance, but that it made tolerance a part of its religious law."[2]
— Laura Vaglieri (1925)

"Muhammad, always following these divine principles, was very tolerant, particularly towards the followers of monotheistic religions. He knew how to show patience with the pagans, always waiting in the belief that time would complete his work of conversion. He was satisfied with what we would call a purely formal conversion of the Bedouins, because he knew that these sons of the desert were impatient by nature of checks of any kind. He well knew that God would finally enter into the human heart.

---

[1] Stubbe, *An Account of the Rise and Progress of Mahometanism*, 188.
[2] Vaglieri, *An Interpretation Of Islam*, 26.

'Why do you want to push men to believe when faith can only come from God?', he said one day to one of his followers."[1]

– Laura Vaglieri (1925)

"Islam triumphed because it brought a message [of tolerance] that was needed by the Oriental world ... the People of the Book, both Jew and Christian, by paying tribute, had a right to protection, could practise their faith freely, and were considered a part of the community. 'He who wrongs a Jew or a Christian,' said Mahomet, 'will have me as his accuser.' The Koran and the *hadiths* are replete with counsels of tolerance ... When 'Omar entered Jerusalem, he ordered the Christians not to be molested, neither them nor their churches, and he showered favours upon the patriarch. When the patriarch invited him to pray in the cathedral he refused only because he feared that this might be used later as a pretext for seizing the church.

"What a contrast, we cannot help saying, with the entry of the crusaders, advancing in a river of blood up to the knees of the knights and the bridles of the horses, deciding to cut the throats of all Mussulmen who had escaped the first slaughter!"[2]

– Emile Dermenghem (1930)

"[Islam has] its record of broad tolerance of diversity within its own community, refusal to persecute those of other communities, and the dignity with which it has endured moments of eclipse."[3]

– Hamilton A. R. Gibb (1948)

"Once a Jew came to the prophet and protested that Muhammad's chief assistant had outraged Jews by claiming that Muhammad was more exalted than Moses. The prophet said to his

---

[1] Ibid., 25.

[2] Dermenghem, *The Life of Mahomet*, 331.

[3] Gibb, *Mohammedanism: An Historical Survey*, 3-4.

assistant, 'You should not have said this. The feeling of other people must be respected.'"[1]

— James A. Michener (1955)

Travelling

"He began and concluded a journey by uttering pious ejaculations. As he was coming back, his friends would go out to meet him, taking their children and wives with them. When returning from a journey, he never entered the city at night and also forbade his friends from doing so. He would have a camel or a bullock slain, to regale those who came to welcome him back. On his return, he first entered the mosque and said two genuflexions of prayers. To travellers he would say, 'Start at night; for to those who do so the road is shortened.' He also advised, 'It is proper that no less than three companions should set out together, so that they may appoint one of their number for a commander.' If any one came to bid him farewell before starting on a journey, he would say, 'I commend to God thy religion and the result of thy labours;' or sometimes also, 'May God increase thy piety, pardon thy sins, and prosper thee wherever thou turnest!?'"[2]

— S. W. Koelle (1888)

Tried and Tested

"We may regard the Holy Prophet of Arabia as a real character—a real personality, who at every step was tried and weighed, but was never found wanting."[3]

— Lord Headley (1914)

---

[1] Michener, "Islam: The Misunderstood Religion."

[2] Koelle, *Mohammed and Mohammedanism*, 390.

[3] Lord Headley, *A Western Awakening to Islam*, 76.

His Character

TRUE TO ALL

"Mohammed was no mere spiritual peddler, no vulgar time-serving vagrant, but one of the most profoundly sincere and earnest spirits of any age or epoch ... True, moreover, because he was true to himself, to his people, and above all to his God."[1]

– Arthur Glyn Leonard (1909)

"A man who is true to his fellowmen, who never lies, whose word is trusted, that man has in himself a truth which would not be deceived by Him who is Truth Himself."[2]

– Annie Besant (1932)

TRUTHFUL

"from an early age, he had been remarked as a thoughtful man. His companions named him '*Al Amin*, The Faithful.'[3] A man of truth and fidelity; true in what he did, in what he spake and thought."[4]

– Thomas Carlyle (1840)

"His whole life is one long argument for his loyalty to truth."[5]

– Stanley Lane-Poole (1883)

"the man himself was sincere and faithful ... he in person drew them not alone by sheer force of will and character, but by a force

---

[1] Leonard, *Islam: Her Moral and Spiritual Value*, 21.

[2] Besant, *The Life and Teachings of Muhammad*, 9.

[3] Even before his prophetic mission began, Muhammad (ﷺ) was known for his high moral character and integrity. He was renowned for never telling a lie and for always honoring any trust placed in him, which earned him the title *al-ṣādiq al-amīn*—The Truthful, The Trustworthy—from his community.

[4] Carlyle, *On Heroes*, 59.

[5] Lane-Poole, *Studies In A Mosque*, 81.

which was even stronger, the force of sincerity and truth."[1]
— Arthur Glyn Leonard (1909)

TRUSTWORTHY

Keeping Trust

"The very name of Faithful, by which he was always distinguished, proves beyond a doubt what manner of man he was."[2]
— Arthur Glyn Leonard (1909)

"[In his teachings] Faith is to be kept even with infidels."[3]
— Charles Mills (1817)

"His neighbours called him *Al Amin*, the trustworthy, the testimony to the character of which any man might be proud."[4]
— Annie Besant (1932)

Fulfilling Promise

"he was ... a fulfiller of promises, a diligent servant of God, and one seeking after Divine approval."[5]
— S. W. Koelle (1888)

Maintaining Secrets of People

"he was of a kindly disposition and noble acts, keeping secrets

---

[1] Leonard, *Islam: Her Moral and Spiritual Value*, 50.
[2] Ibid., 79.
[3] Mills, *An History of Muhammedanism*, 329-30.
[4] Besant, *The Life and Teachings of Muhammad*, 7.
[5] Koelle, *Mohammed and Mohammedanism*, 383.

hid, and yet the confidant of heaven..."¹

— S. W. Koelle (1888)

UNCIVILIZED PEOPLE (TREATMENT OF)

"Many of the hadith already cited will have shown the good sense, amiability, and liberality of the prophet. 'Aisha [reports]: A man asked permission to see the prophet of God, who said, 'Let him come in though he is of an evil tribe.' When the man sat with him the prophet showed him a bright countenance and conversed agreeably with him. After he had gone 'Aisha asked: 'How is it that you treated him so kindly when you had thus spoken of him?' He replied: 'When have you known me immoderate in speech? The worst men in God's sight on the day of resurrection will be those whom men forsake through dread of their wickedness.'"²

— Alfred Guillaume (1924)

"A remarkable feature was the urbanity and consideration with which Mahomet treated even the most insignificant of his followers."³

— William Muir (1861)

UNFLINCHING

"Through mockery and persecution the Prophet keeps unflinchingly in his path; no threats, no injuries, hinder him from still preaching to his people the unity and the righteousness of God, and exhorting to a far purer and better morality than had ever

---

[1] Ibid., 383.

[2] Guillaume, *The Traditions of Islam*, 150-51. 'Ā'isha was a wife of the Prophet.

[3] Muir, *Life of Mahomet*, vol. iv, 305.

been set before them."[1]

– Edward Freeman (1856)

"The courage of Mohammed, which is one of the outstanding traits throughout his career, points in the same direction. The opposition which his rebellious utterances aroused and which in time became threatening did not swerve him from his path."[2]

– James A. Montgomery (1917)

Unifier of Humanity

"it being laid down by him that there never was nor ever can be more than one true, orthodox religion, that although the particular laws or ceremonies are only temporary and subject to alteration, according to the divine direction, yet the substance of it being eternal truth, is not liable to change, but continues immutably the same, and that whenever this religion became neglected or corrupted in essentials, God vouchsafed to re-inform and re-admonish mankind thereof by several prophets, of whom Moses and Jesus were the most distinguished, till the appearance of Mohammed."[3]

– John Davenport (1869)

"However great a weight one may give to political and economic factors, it was religion, Islam, which in a certain sense united the hitherto hopelessly divided Arabs, Islam which enabled them to found an enormous international community; it was Islam which bound the speedily converted nations together even after the shattering of its political power, and which still binds them today

---

[1] Freeman, *History and Conquests of the Saracens*, 35.

[2] Montgomery, *Religions of the Past and Present*, 221.

[3] Davenport, *An Apology for Mohammed and the Koran*, 74.

when only a miserable remnant of that power remains."[1]

– Snouck Hurgronje (1916)

"Islam came at a time when people were divided into religious sects, when they were fighting and cursing each other, each sect believing itself to be the sole repository of the word of God—at a time when fighting and fanaticism were considered a necessary part of religious life. Islam came and proclaimed that religion had at all times, and by the mouths of all the prophets, been simply one—that in essence it had taught always the same things; to hold God alone in His sovereignty, to submit to His will, and to obey His commandments, practising good and keeping away from evil. Furthermore, Islam insisted that the variety of forms and rituals which different religions presented, proceeded from the mercy of God, Who gave to each people in each particular time a religion suited to its needs and susceptible of development along with the progress of the human mind; but it insisted that at last, when mankind had been prepared by events and had reached a state of maturity and were in a position to comprehend a divine Teaching, which appealed not only to the emotions but also to the intellect, Muhammad had appeared to reconcile all these teachings for the benefit of humanity, to settle the differences between the 'people of the book', which means Christians and Jews, and to guide men towards the attainment of happiness both in this life and in the one beyond."[2]

– Laura Vaglieri (1925)

Unpretentious

"So unpretentious was he that he would receive from his companions no special mark of reverence, nor would he accept any

---

[1] Hurgronje, *Mohammedanism*, 16.

[2] Vaglieri, *An Interpretation Of Islam*, 39.

service from his slave which he could do himself."[1]
— Gustav Weil (1866)

"He was gracious, unassuming, most patient and kindly to his slaves, adored by his followers, captivating to strangers."[2]
— Marcus Dods (1887)

"Even in the height of his glory Muhammad led, as in his days of obscurity, an unpretentious life..."[3]
— Phillip K. Hitti (1937)

Victor (A Most Odd)

"The entry of an eastern victor is ordinarily the signal for plunder and massacre, alike of the armed and the unarmed, of the innocent and the guilty. Mahomet had his wrongs to avenge; but they are satisfied by a handful of exceptions to a general amnesty, and the majority even of these are ultimately forgiven. It is the temple of God desecrated by idols which he had come to ransom ... He reared no palace for his own honour by the side of the temple which he had recovered to the honour of God. The city of his fathers, the metropolis of his race, the shrine of his religion, was again deserted for his humble dwelling among those who had stood by him in the day of trial."[4]
— Edward Freeman (1856)

Visiting the Sick

"he used to say, 'Do not force the sick to take food or drink

---

[1] Weil, *A History of Islamic Peoples*, 28.

[2] Dods, *Mohammed, Buddha, and Christ*, 90.

[3] Hitti, *History of the Arabs*, 120.

[4] Freeman, *History and Conquests of the Saracens*, 37-38.

against their will: for God is giving them food and drink.' ... He also said, 'Cheer up the sick with pleasant words, and free their minds from grief and sadness.'"¹

– S. W. Koelle (1888)

"He visited the sick and was full of sympathy for all..."²

– Gustav Weil (1866)

"Be it known that his apostolic Excellency also paid visits to the sick, and commanded his friends to do the same. When he went to see a sick person, he used to say, 'Please God, no misfortune, but purification,' or 'Atonement and purification'. He seated himself on the sick person's cushion, and inquired, 'How art thou? What is thy condition? Hast thou a fancy for anything?' If the person fancied a thing that was not hurtful, he ordered it to be given. He would lay his right hand on the sick person's body, and say,

'Remove the ban, thou Lord of man!
O Healer, heal, relieve!
There is no cure, besides Thy cure:
Help, Helper, we believe.'"³

– S. W. Koelle (1888)

WARFARE (RULES OF)

"Mohammed ... ever spared the innocent blood of women, maidens and infants. In short, he strictly commanded his followers never to molest, but to treat as brethren, all who would accept

---

[1] Koelle, *Mohammed and Mohammedanism*, 403-04.

[2] Weil, *A History of Islamic Peoples*, 28.

[3] Koelle, *Mohammed and Mohammedanism*, 412. The original supplication of the Prophet out of which Koelle made this poem are: "O Allah, Lord of mankind! Remove his distress, for Thou are the Healer. There is no healing but from You, a healing that leaves behind no trace of the ailment." (Authenticated by al-Bukhārī)

and obey the Koran. Moses, on the contrary, slaughtered whole nations, without offering or accepting any conditions of mercy; an example never followed by Mohammed, although in many instances by Christian Powers, and more especially by the Spaniards in their conquest of Peru and Mexico. Nowhere throughout the Koran can be found attributed to the Deity commands wholly opposed to all human ideas of justice and mercy..."[1]

– John Davenport (1869)

"Sometimes victorious, sometimes defeated, every incident created an appropriate occasion for the noble Prophet to manifest different phases of his grand character. One has simply to digest and codify them and the world will find in them laws and rules of war more humane and appropriate than could ever be imagined by the promoters of the Hague Conference. Never a sword was drawn but as a last resort to defend human life."[2]

– Lord Headley (1914)

"His generosity in the days of his final triumph exhibited a greatness of soul rare indeed in the pages of history. He commanded his soldiers to spare the feeble, the old, women and children; he forbade their destroying houses, making off with harvests or cutting down fruit trees ... He prescribed the use of the sword only in cases of necessity. We see him publicly condemning some of his captains and giving recompense for the damage done by them. 'The gaining of a single soul,' he declared, 'is worth more than the richest conquest.'"[3]

– Emile Dermenghem (1930)

---

[1] Davenport, *An Apology for Mohammed and the Koran*, 136. Davenport then proceeds to cite from the Bible, Exodus 31:27, Joshua 10:40, I Samuel 15:3, and Deuteronomy 20:17 as vindicating "in the murder of twelve millions of Indians" by the Spaniards using "the example of the Israelites towards the people of Canaan."

[2] Lord Headley, *A Western Awakening to Islam*, 80.

[3] Dermenghem, *The Life of Mahomet*, 174-75.

"Mohammed commanded his troops to spare monks, women, children and blind people, and forbade the destroying of houses and cutting down of trees or other wanton waste."[1]

– James A. Montgomery (1917)

"In an age of barbarism, the battlefield itself was humanised and strict instructions were issued not to embezzle, not to cheat, not to break trust, not to mutilate, not to kill a minor child or a woman or an old man, not to hew down date palm nor burn it, not to cut down a fruit tree, not to molest monks and persons engaged in worship."[2]

– K. S. Ramakrishna Rao (1989)

"The seizing of booty was the natural outcome of all combats and, with commerce and herding, formed, we might well say, the national industry of the Arabs. Mahomet tolerated it in his people 'because of their weakness'; but the dividing of the spoils was strictly regulated; the greater part went to charity and the upkeep of the army. He forbade the separating of captive children from their mothers."[3]

– Emile Dermenghem (1930)

WISE AND PRUDENT

"He was as pre-eminently wise as he was devout. He utilized his wisdom to the fullest extent of his capacity..."[4]

– Arthur Glyn Leonard (1909)

---

[1] Montgomery, *Religions of the Past and Present*, 332 (footnote).

[2] Rao, *Muhammad: the Prophet of Islam*, 10.

[3] Dermenghem, *The Life of Mahomet*, 175.

[4] Leonard, *Islam: Her Moral and Spiritual Value*, 43.

"'The dust of the actual' covered the way he trod, and prudence was a constant companion on the journey."[1]

– John Clark Archer (1924)

Work Ethics

Accomplisher of Tasks

"Thorough and complete in all his actions, he never took in hand any work without bringing it to a close. The same habit pervaded his manner in social intercourse."[2]

– William Muir (1861)

Did His Own Work

"His custom was to do every thing for himself. If he gave an alms he would place it with his own hand in that of the petitioner. He aided his wives in their household duties; he mended his own clothes; he tied up the goats; he even cobbled his sandals."[3]

– William Muir (1861)

Women (Treatment Of)

"The whole personal teaching of the Prophet is opposed to cruelty, especially towards woman ... Indeed, the Prophet made a husband's treatment of his wife the test of his general conduct by his saying, 'The best of you is he who is best to his wife.'"[4]

– Marmaduke Pickthall (1917)

---

[1] Archer, *The Mystical Elements of Mohammed*, 85.

[2] Muir, *Life of Mahomet*, vol. iv, 303.

[3] Ibid., 304.

[4] Pickthall, "Islam and Progress."

WRONGED NONE

"He did good continually. He is the only conqueror and ruler in all history of whom it can be truly said that he never wronged a fellow creature in the least respect."[1]

– Marmaduke Pickthall (1920)

"As soon as he was conscious of his danger,[2] he edified his brethren by the humility of his virtue or penitence. 'If there be any man,' said the apostle from the pulpit, 'whom I have unjustly scourged, I submit my own back to the lash of retaliation. Have I aspersed the reputation of a Musulman? Let him proclaim my thoughts in the face of the congregation. Has any one been despoiled of his goods? The little that I possess shall compensate the principal and the interest of the debt.' 'Yes,' replied a voice from the crowd, 'I am entitled to three drams[3] of silver.' Mahomet heard the complaint, satisfied the demand, and thanked his creditor for accusing him in this world rather than at the day of judgment."[4]

– Edward Gibbon (1788)

YIELDING TO OTHERS AND ADMITTING MISTAKES

"the ability to cling stubbornly and willfully to a decision that has once been made, or to a previous opinion, even when it contradicts all reason, is not a sign of a superior spiritual personality. There are many absolute fanatics among religiously inspired persons who cling with an iron consistency to the most unfortunate and senseless ideas. But Mohammed was no fanatic. To a great extent the secret of his unique ability to attract men is explained

---

[1] Pickthall, "A Sermon."

[2] i.e., approaching death.

[3] *Dirham*, or silver coin.

[4] Gibbon, *Decline and Fall*, vol. v, 143-44.

by a wise yielding which was never deterred by principles. He had the courage to surrender a position which could not be held honourably."[1]

    – Tor Andrae (1932)

"The Prophet never in any way tried to conceal any possible mistake he might have made ... [Once] A poor and blind man had gone to him and asked for teaching. The Prophet was talking to a man of high rank at the time, and he took no notice of this poor man. Three times the man asked and three times he was disregarded. The next morning the Prophet sent for this man and told him that he had a message [from God] in the night, which is now in the Al Quran, that he had repulsed a poor man who cried out for knowledge and that he had not done well. Then the Lord Muhammad took him, placed him in a seat of honour and treated him always with the greatest courtesy because he said that 'on account of this man my Lord rebuked me.' Now that kind of thing, the humility of thought, the readiness to repair a blunder, the frank admission of a mistake, is not so common among the great Teachers of the world and yet you find it in him over and over again."[2]

    – Annie Besant (1932)

---

[1] Andrae, *Mohammed: The Man and His Faith*, 89-90.

[2] Besant, *The Life and Teachings of Muhammad*, 13-14.

The Religion He Preached

Sound and Rational Doctrines

"In a word, with respect to the essential doctrines of religion, all that he has laid down is true;"[1]

– Henri de Boulainvilliers (1730)

"there would not have been a more plausible system of doctrine than his, more agreeable to the light of reason, more comfortable to the righteous, or more terrible to willful and careless sinners; and that in the exercise of the worship he has establish'd, we manifestly discover the cause of that unconquerable affection the Mahometans bear to their religion: an attachment of heart, which our missionaries have greatly experienc'd; who are oblig'd to confess the little progress they make among them."[2]

– Henri de Boulainvilliers (1730)

Based on Reason

"One of the glories of Islam is that it is founded upon reason, and that it never demands from its followers an abnegation of that important mental faculty. Unlike certain other faiths, which insist upon their votaries implicitly accepting certain dogmas without independent inquiry, but simply on the authority of 'The Church,' Islam courts inquiry and counsels its disciples to study, search, and investigate prior to acceptance ... [The Prophet said:] 'Allah hath not created anything better than reason, or anything more perfect or more beautiful than reason, the benefits which Allah giveth are on its account, and understanding is begotten of it.'"[3]

– Henri M. Leon (1915)

---

[1] Boulainvilliers, *Life of Mohammed*, 243.

[2] Ibid., 244.

[3] Henri. M. Leon, "Islam: A Rational Faith." Prof. Léon (d. 1932), also known as William Henry Abdullah Quilliam, was a successful solicitor in Liverpool, England,

His Character

"I firmly believe that if all the best intellects of Europe could be brought into play in a search for a religion which should be based on worldly reason or common sense, no less than on the inspired writings of Divinely inspired prophets, the unanimous selection would be in favour of Islam, the simplicity and grandeur of which is quite without question. Is it not a blessing to be very grateful for to have the chance of embracing a religion which appeals to the reason as well as to the heart and inward longings of mankind, and is at the same time free from sacerdotalism and other complications?"[1]

— Lord Headley (1914)

FREE OF MYSTERY

"It is a religion, moreover, stripped of all controversy, and which, proposing no mystery to offer violence to reason, restricts the imagination of men to the being satisfied with a plain, invariable worship, notwithstanding the fiery passions and blind zeal that so often transported them beyond themselves. Lastly, it is a religion from which all worship of saints and martyrs, relics and images, all mystery and metaphysical subtlety; all monastic seclusion and enthusiastic penance is banished."[2]

— John Davenport (1869)

FREE OF DOGMA

"dogma—in the religious sense—is a definite form of doctrine

---

as well as a newspaper editor, diplomat, and later Dean of the London School of Physiology. Fluent in several languages and highly talented in multiple disciplines, he authored numerous books and articles and received several distinguished awards. He converted to Islam in 1887 and in the same year established, in Liverpool, England's first mosque.

[1] Lord Headley, *A Western Awakening to Islam*, 30.

[2] Davenport, *An Apology for Mohammed and the Koran*, 78.

affirmed positively by and promulgated by the authority of some particular religious sect ... Islam seems to stand alone in its freedom from dogma, belief in and submission to God and beneficence to all one's fellow creatures being sufficient for salvation ... [without] the necessity for any mediation because ... God is ever present with each one of us and is accessible to all."[1]
– Lord Headley (1914)

APPEALS TO IGNORANT AND LEARNED ALIKE

"The highways of philosophy and mysticism are open to few. And yet who would imagine that the truths of Islam, so noble and dignified, could exist outside the confines of lofty and profound philosophy ... how so simple yet all-embracing a faith has conquered ignorant and learned alike."[2]
– Neville J. Whymant (1914)

WELL-SUITED FOR INTELLECTUAL/SPIRITUAL DEVELOPMENT

"We must offer our deepest admiration to a religion which does not stop with a theory suited to the aspirations of human nature, nor with establishing a code of the highest rules which man can live by, but which goes on to inculcate a philosophy of life; which puts the basic principles of morality on a systematic and positive basis; which translates the duty of man towards himself and others into precise rules, which are capable of evolution and are compatible with the highest intellectual development; and, to crown it all, which provides a sanction for these laws. The

---

[1] Headley, "What Is Dogma."

[2] A. Neville J. Whymant, "The Philosophy of War in Comparative Religion." Whymant (d. 1970) was an English journalist, editor, linguist, diplomat, and professor of Oriental literature and philosophy at the Universities of Tokyo and Peking. He converted to Islam during the First World War and authored several books on China and the Chinese language.

influence of such a religion upon the lives of men generally, but more particularly upon those of the ignorant and the uneducated, is both continuous and healthy, since for them moral precepts have little value unless they are enunciated with the precision of a law and carry with them well defined penalties. Islam is such a religion."[1]

– Laura Vaglieri (1925)

SPIRITUALLY HIGHEST

"On the whole, we will repeat that this Religion of Mahomet's ... has a genuine element of what is spiritually highest looking through it ... For these twelve centuries, it has been the religion and life-guidance of the fifth part of the whole kindred of Mankind. Above all things, it has been a religion heartily believed. These Arabs believe their religion, and try to live by it! No Christians, since the early ages, or only perhaps the English Puritans in modern times, have ever stood by their Faith as the Moslem do by theirs,—believing it wholly, fronting Time with it, and Eternity with it."[2]

– Thomas Carlyle (1840)

SIMPLICITY

"There was no sacrament [in the religion the Prophet preached], consequently no priest to administer it; Islam has always been the lay religion *par excellence*. Teaching and exhortation are the only spiritual help that the pious Mohammedan wants, and this simple care of souls is exercised without any ordination or consecration."[3]

– C. Snouck Hurgronje (1916)

---

[1] Vaglieri, *An Interpretation Of Islam*, 63.

[2] Carlyle, *On Heroes*, 85.

[3] Hurgronje, *Mohammedanism*, 58.

"Islam is the religion of grand simplicity; it satisfies the noblest longings of the soul, and in no way contravenes the teachings of Moses or Christ."[1]
— Lord Headley (1914)

Purity Restored

"The abolition of idolatry and superstition, and the restoration of religion to what he called its pristine purity, were the avowed and plausible objects of the Arabian Prophet."[2]
— Charles Mills (1817)

Balanced

"A famous tradition[3] says, 'There is no monasticism in Islam.' As a matter of fact, Islam does not care for asceticism with its useless mortification of the flesh, its unnecessary privations as well as its continuous fasts and nights spent in prayer. In regard to marriage, the Islamic tradition asks for no more than an honest and constructive life in which the individual follows the middle of the road, remembering God on the one side and respecting, on the other, the rights and needs of the body, family, and society."[4]
— Laura Vaglieri (1925)

Peaceful

"the beauty and simplicity of the Muslim faith, which, in the writer's humble opinion, is free from the objections so apparent in many other religions ... the government of a nation or empire

---

[1] Lord Headley, *A Western Awakening to Islam*, 32.

[2] Mills, *An History of Muhammedanism*, 276.

[3] i.e., a statement attributed to the Prophet.

[4] Vaglieri, *An Interpretation Of Islam*, 60.

would go on more smoothly if such a peaceful religion were universally adopted."[1]

– Lord Headley (1914)

NO INTERMEDIARIES

"There is, as far as one can see, no class in the Mahomedan religion ... There are no popes, no bishops, and no ministers requiring large endowments and emoluments, for God Himself is the Head of this Church of the Spirit."[2]

– Lord Headley (1914)

"Every Muhammadan is a church in himself; every one is allowed to give an opinion on a religious matter, on the basis of the belief common to his co-religionists. They are not slaves to priests; they pray to God without an intermediary, and their place of worship is wherever they happen to be at the appointed hours of prayer ... There is no such thing as a Pope among them."[3]

– G. W. Leitner (c. 1914)

RELIGIOUS TOLERANCE

"... on the whole, unbelievers have enjoyed under Muhammadan rule a measure of toleration, the like of which is not to be found in Europe until quite modern times. Forcible conversion was forbidden, in accordance with the precepts of the Qur'an: 'Let there be no compulsion in religion' (Q. 2:256); 'Wilt thou compel men to become believers? No soul can believe but by the permission of God' (Q.10:99-100). The very existence of so many Christian sects and communities in countries that have been for

---

[1] Lord Headley, *A Western Awakening to Islam*, 23-24.

[2] Ibid., 20.

[3] Leitner, "Religious Systems of the World."

centuries under Muhammadan rule is an abiding testimony to the toleration they have enjoyed, and shows that the persecutions they have from time to time been called upon to endure at the hands of bigots and fanatics, have been excited by some special and local circumstances rather than inspired by a settled principle of intolerance."

– T. W. Arnold (1896)

"It is indeed sad for the Christian nations that religious tolerance, which is the great law of charity for one people towards another, was taught them by the Mussulmans."[1]

– Jean Hippolyte Michon (1853)

"In the chapter on 'Pilgrimage' in the Koran, the object of a religious war is declared to be the protection of 'mosques, synagogues, and churches,' for in them alike 'the name of God is frequently commemorated.' Is not this as tolerant a position as we have only reached after centuries?"[2]

– G. W. Leitner (c. 1914)

"The toleration of Islam has been recognized by all who have not brought prejudice to bear upon their study."[3]

– Dudely Wright (1919)

"Once agreements with the defeated peoples were made, the Muslims left them freedom of religion and did not use violence to compel conversions. The Muslim armies were not followed by a troop of insistent and unwanted preachers, nor did they place preachers in specially favored positions to expound or defend

---

[1] Jean Hippolyte Michon, *Voyage religieux en Orient* in Dermenghem, *The Life of Mahomet*, 331. Michon (d. 1881) was a French Catholic priest, archaeologist, and author. He is also considered as the father of graphology.

[2] Leitner, "Religious Systems of the World," referencing Q. 22:40.

[3] Dudely Wright, "Islam: The Faith of Progress." Wright (d. 1949) was an English writer and historian.

their creed ... Not only were Jews and Christians left to live in peace without any questioning of their religious beliefs, but they were named to offices in the government when their personal qualifications were of such a nature as to attract the notice of the rulers."[1]

– Laura Vaglieri (1925)

Manifested in Practice

"Bound up with these and other ritual observances, but not encumbered or obscured by them, the articles of the Muslim creed are incessantly finding outward manifestation in the life of the believer, and thus, becoming inextricably interwoven with the routine of his daily life, make the individual Musalman an exponent and teacher of his creed far more than is the case with the adherents of most other religions."[2]

– T. W. Arnold (1896)

No Persecution

"Islam has never interfered with the dogmas of any faith—never persecuted, never established an inquisition, never aimed at proselytism. It offered its religion, but never enforced it. 'Let there be no violence in religion.'"[3]

– John Davenport (1869)

Social Reform

"Slavery was not abolished; but the social position of the slave

---

[1] Vaglieri, *An Interpretation Of Islam*, 26.

[2] Thomas Walker Arnold, *The Preaching of Islam: A History of the Propagation of the Muslim Faith*, 418-19. Sir Arnold (d. 1930) was a British orientalist, historian, and Professor of Arabic at the University of London.

[3] Davenport, *An Apology for Mohammed and the Koran*, 78. The text quoted here is a verse from the Qur'an (2:256).

was entirely changed that he became practically one of the family ... Another valuable social reformation was the abolishing of all forms of gambling, one of the curses of present-day Christendom, another the total prohibition of strong drink, the most degrading and destructive habit of the West; evils that for generations have been enervating and debauching the manhood and womanhood of Europe. No religion save Islam has ever attempted their abolition."[1]

– Simon. H. Leeder (1917)

DEMOCRACY OF THE FIRST ORDER

"The Prophet of Islam brought the reign of democracy in its best form. Caliph Umar, Caliph Ali, the son-in-law of the Prophet, Caliph Mansur, Abbas, the son of the Caliph Mamun, and many other caliphs and kings had to appear before the judge as ordinary men in Islamic courts."[2]

– K. S. Ramakrishna Rao (1989)

"[An objective observer would recognize] the Islamic system a democracy of the first order, superior at any rate, to its modern Western counterpart."[3]

– Wael Hallaq (2013)

FREEDOM OF OPINION

"Islam allows you freedom of opinion and private right of

---

[1] Leeder, "The Tenderness of the Prophet."

[2] Rao, *Muhammad: the Prophet of Islam*, 12.

[3] Wael B. Hallaq, *The Impossible State: Islam, Politics, and Modernity's Predicament,* 52. Hallaq (b. 1955) is the Avalon Foundation Professor in the Humanities at Columbia University, specializing in ethics, law, political thought, Islamic legal theory, and modernity. He has authored numerous books and articles, many of which have been translated into over a dozen languages, and has received several awards for his work.

judgment ... To think is to differ, and the power of thinking was a Divine gift. Therefore Islam always respected difference of opinion. 'Difference of opinion in my followers is a blessing of God,' so say the generous Prophet of Islam."[1]

– Dudely Wright (1916)

LIBERATED MAN

"Thanks to Islam, paganism in its various forms was defeated. The concept of the universe, the practices of religion, and the customs of social life were each liberated from all the monstrosities which had degraded them, and human minds were made free of prejudice. Man finally realized his dignity. He humbled himself before the Creator, the Master of all mankind ... The spirit was liberated from prejudice, man's will was set free from the ties which had kept it bound to the will of other men, or other so-called hidden powers. Priests, false guardians of mysteries, brokers of salvation, all those who pretended to be mediators between God and man and consequently believed they had authority over other people's wills, fell from their pedestals. Man became the servant of God alone, and towards other men he had only the obligations of one free man towards other free men."[2]

– Laura Vaglieri (1925)

EQUALITY

"Islam, like any great Faith, and insight into the essence of man, is a perfect equalizer of men: the soul of one believer outweighs all earthly kingships; all men, according to Islam too, are equal."[3]

– Thomas Carlyle (1840)

---

[1] Wright, "Is Man Sinful By Nature?"

[2] Vaglieri, *An Interpretation Of Islam*, 33.

[3] Carlyle, *On Heroes*, 82.

"With regard to social gradations, the rich man is considered to be the natural protector of the poor, and the poor man takes his place at the table of the rich. Nowhere in Muhammadan society is there any invidious distinction between rich and poor; and even a Muhammadan slave is not only a member of the household, but has also far greater chances of rising to a position in the Government or in society than an English pauper."[1]

— G. W. Leitner (c. 1914)

"While previously men had suffered from the injustices of social differences, Islam proclaimed equality among human beings. Each Muslim was distinguished from other Muslims not by reason of birth or any other factor not connected with his personality, but only by his fear of God, his good deeds, his moral and intellectual qualities. The Quran states: 'O mankind, We have created you from a male and a female; and We have divided you into tribes and sub-tribes that you may recognize one of another. Verily, the most honourable among you, in the sight of Allah, is he who is the most righteous among you. (Surah 49, Verse 14)' A tradition[2] says: 'With Islam, God has caused the disappearance of pride, which was a characteristic of pagans, and of their habit of talking about their fathers: because man was born of Adam, and Adam of dust. According to God, the noblest of men is the one who is most fearful of Him.'"[3]

— Laura Vaglieri (1925)

"It was the first religion that preached and practised democracy ... the democracy of Islam is embodied five times a day when the peasant and king kneel side by side and proclaim, 'God alone is great' ... I have been struck over and again by this indivisible

---

[1] Leitner, "Religious Systems of the World."

[2] A statement of the Prophet.

[3] Vaglieri, *An Interpretation Of Islam*, 33-34.

unity of Islam that makes man instinctively a brother."[1]

– Sarojini Naidu

ELEVATES PEOPLE WITH JUSTICE AND FAIRNESS

"The acceptance of that religion, moreover, conferred equal rights with the conquering body and emancipated the vanquished states from the conditions which every conqueror, since the world existed up to the period of Mohammed, had invariably imposed. Islam put an end to infanticide then prevalent in the surrounding countries. It put an end to slavery, the adscription to the soil. It administered even-handed justice not only to those who professed its religion, but to those who were conquered by its arms. It reduced taxation, the sole tribute to the state consisting of one-tenth. It freed commerce from charges and impediments, it freed professors of other faiths from all fixed contributions to their church or their clergy, from all contributions whatsoever to the dominant creed. The repetition of a single phrase was the only form required or pledge exacted from proselytes."[2]

– John Davenport (1869)

COSMOLOGICAL MORALITY OF THE FIRST ORDER

"The Qur'an [provides] … a cosmology [that is] entirely grounded in *moral* natural laws, a cosmology with perhaps far more persuasive power than any of its Enlightenment metaphysical counterparts … [and] offers no less than a theory of cosmological morality of the first order, which is to say that Qur'anic cosmology is not only profoundly moral but is also itself constructed, both in form and content, out of a moral fiber. Everything that this universe contains was created for humans to enjoy,

---

[1] Sarojini Naidu in Rao, *Muhammad: the Prophet of Islam*, 11. Naidu (d. 1949) was an Indian poet and the 1st governor of the United Provinces after Indian independence.

[2] Davenport, *An Apology for Mohammed and the Koran*, 79.

not in a utilitarian manner but rather in ways that show deep moral accountability ... The entire enterprise of creation, re-creation, and death—that is, the series of laws governing the operation of the universe—is specifically designed by divine munificence and power for the *single purpose of challenging humans to do good.*"[1]

— Wael Hallaq (2013)

CIVILIZING EFFECTS

"Islam had done more for civilization than Christianity ... When Muhammadanism is embraced by a negro tribe, paganism, devil-worship, fetishism, cannibalism, human sacrifice, infanticide, witchcraft, at once disappear. The natives begin to dress, filth is replaced by cleanliness, and they acquire personal dignity and self-respect. Hospitality becomes a religious duty, drunkenness becomes rare, gambling is forbidden, immodest dances and the promiscuous intercourse of the sexes cease, female chastity is regarded as a virtue, industry replaces idleness, licence gives place to law, order and sobriety prevail, blood-feuds, cruelty to animals and to slaves, are forbidden. A feeling of humanity, benevolence, and brotherhood is inculcated. Polygamy and slavery are regulated, and their evils are restrained. Islam, above all, is the most powerful total abstinence association in the world ... Its restraining and civilizing effects are marvellous."[2]

— Isaac Taylor (1887)

ECONOMIC THEORY OF SOCIAL RESPONSIBILITY

"The paradigmatic Muslim *homo economicus* seeks wealth and

---

[1] Hallaq, *The Impossible State*, 83-84.

[2] Isaac Taylor, "What Islam Can Do." Rev. Taylor (d. 1901) was an ordained Anglican priest and Canon of York Minster. This excerpt is from a lecture he delivered in 1887 to a British audience, primarily composed of Anglican missionaries.

His Character

profit but remains materially and psychologically committed to social responsibility, as is abundantly evidenced in twelve centuries of Islamic socioeconomic history. Honor, prestige, nearness to God, and the love and respect of family and neighbor all paradigmatically intersect with this ethic of indebtedness to one's own community."[1]

– Wael Hallaq (2013)

"All contractual transactions under the Sharī'a are imbued with moral values. To be valid, contracts must presuppose ... wholehearted consent devoid of any trace of coercion or even reluctance. It presupposes fair dealing, good faith, and psychological ease by all contracting parties. Commerce and trade, being contractual, must be situated in this framework, one that requires forgiveness, magnanimity (*samāḥa*), rectitude, and avoidance of greed, avarice, and placing oppressive constraints on one's contractual partners ... This moral impulse is neither incidental nor does it hover at the margins of the legal culture. It is paradigmatic, surrounding and thoroughly permeating the fabric of the Sharī'ah's rules about property, contracts investments, commercial transactions, and anything having to do with profit."[2]

– Wael Hallaq (2013)

USHERED A NEW ERA OF MORAL & ECONOMIC PROSPERITY

"There unfolded before the eyes of an astonished world a new religion, a simple, easy one, which speaks to the heart and to the brain; a new form of government, far superior in its moral principles and qualities to those existing at that time, was established; gold that had been hidden in the safes of plutocrats began changing hands and going to the poor, starting a system of healthy circulation once again; educated, capable, intelligent men under the

---

[1] Hallaq, *The Impossible State*, 161.

[2] Ibid., *The Impossible State*, 149-50.

guidance of a government ruled by honest, democratic ideals found encouragement in the new order and were able to rise to the highest public offices ... a new era of prosperity and wealth was ushered in, a richness which Asia had not witnessed for centuries. The life of the conquered peoples, their civil rights and wealth received a degree of protection approximating to that enjoyed by the Muslims themselves."[1]

– Laura Vaglieri (1925)

A Sublime Path to God

"The advent of Mahomet, some six hundred years after Christ, exposed the unreality of all such ideas as atonements, priestly interventions, supplications to the saints, and those other cumbersome and involved methods of approaching the Almighty. However grand the Mosaic laws, however beautiful the gentle and forgiving precepts of the Holy Prophet of Nazareth, it must be admitted that the Mahomedan teaching contained the most sublime message, overriding by its very simplicity all obstacles in the way of the believer on his path to God."[2]

– Lord Headley (1914)

Promotes A Virtuous Life

"the exhortations to virtue are numerous in the Koran and Sonna[3] ... Gentleness of manners, and a modest deportment, are every where enjoined. Forgiveness of injuries will meet with its reward; and mankind are exhorted to pray for, and not to curse, offenders."[4]

– Charles Mills (1817)

---

[1] Vaglieri, *An Interpretation Of Islam*, 21.

[2] Lord Headley, *A Western Awakening to Islam*, 22.

[3] More correctly "Sunnah" which refers to the Prophet's statements and actions that constitute the second source of law in Islam after the Qur'an.

[4] Mills, *An History of Muhammedanism*, 329-30.

His Legacy

Transformation of People

"To the Arab Nation it was as a birth from darkness into light … a Hero-Prophet was sent down to them with a word they could believe: see, the unnoticed becomes world-notable, the small has grown world-great; within one century afterwards, Arabia is at Grenada on this hand, at Delhi on that;—glancing in valor and splendor and the light of genius, Arabia shines through long ages over a great section of the world … is it not as if a spark had fallen, one spark, on a world of what seemed black unnoticeable sand; but lo, the sand proves explosive powder, blazes heaven-high from Delhi to Grenada! I said, the Great Man was always as lightning out of Heaven; the rest of men waited for him like fuel, and then they too would flame."[1]
      – Thomas Carlyle (1840)

"how noble and sublime the work of this reformer really was, this reformer who, within the span of a few years, transformed a welter of idolatrous and barbarous people into a united monotheistic community, which was animated by the highest moral sentiments."[2]
      – Laura Vaglieri (1925)

"The Prophet of Islam thus brought about such a mighty transformation that the noblest and purest among Arabs by birth offered their daughters in marriage to this Negro slave … What a tremendous change was brought by Qur'an and Prophet Muhammed in the Arabs, the proudest people at that time on earth. This is the reason why Goethe, the greatest of German poets, speaking about the Holy Qur'an, declared that, 'This book will go on exercising through all ages a most potent influence.' This is also the reason why George Bernard Shaw says, 'If any

---

[1] Carlyle, *On Heroes,* 86.

[2] Vaglieri, *An Interpretation Of Islam,* 29.

religion has a chance of ruling over England, nay, Europe, within the next 100 years, it is Islam.'"[1]

— K. S. Ramakrishna Rao (1989)

"Islam, like a spring of pure and refined water, developed among barbarian people in a desolate and arid land far from the crossroads of civilization and human thought. So abundant was its volume that the spring fast became a creek, then a river, and finally overflowed and broke into thousands of channels, spilling out over the country. In those places where the miraculous water was sampled, people who had become divided were brought together again and disagreements were settled; and in place of the blood feud which was the supreme law and which served to keep together tribes of the same origin, a new sentiment began to make itself felt: a sentiment of brotherhood among men bound together by common ideals of morality and religion. As soon as this spring became an irresistible river, its pure and vigorous stream encircled mighty kingdoms representing old civilizations, and, before their peoples could realize the true import of the event, it overtook them, levelling countries, demolishing barriers, waking slumbering minds with its noise and making a united community out of the widest variety of nations. Such a phenomenon had never before been witnessed in history."[2]

— Laura Vaglieri (1925)

IMPACT AND INFLUENCE

Upon the Human Race

"Four years after the death of Justinian, 569 A.D., was born at Mecca, in Arabia, the man who, of all men, has exercised the

---

[1] Rao, *Muhammad: the Prophet of Islam*, 14.

[2] Vaglieri, *An Interpretation Of Islam*, 17.

greatest influence upon the human race—Mohammed..."[1]

– John William Draper (1861)

His Name a Mirror Image of the Religion Itself

"it is, without doubt, one of the most noticeable circumstances in the history of his religion, that his own person should have been so much bound up with it; that every caliph or sultan who has reigned over any tribe of his followers should have reigned in his name; that the recollection of a man should have so much more power than even the book which Mussulmans regard with such profound reverence; that the honor of a human chieftain should so markedly distinguish a religion which looks upon man as separated by an immeasurable distance from the object of his worship."[2]

– Frederick Maurice (1845)

"Mohammed *is* Islam, much more so than Moses is Judaism and Jesus is Christianity."[3]

– R. V. C. Bodley (1945)

"A rose by any other name may smell as sweet. But Islam without the halo of time-honoured sanctity that attaches to the name of Mohammed, would sound as but a hollow brass or a tinkling cymbal. Just, in fact, as the man himself was sincere and faithful, there is, and there will continue to be, a magic in his name more so even than that of Christ has for the Christian..."[4]

– Arthur Glyn Leonard (1909)

---

[1] Draper, *A History of the Intellectual Development of Europe*, vol. i, 329.

[2] Frederick Maurice, *Religions of the World*, 43. Maurice (d. 1872) was an English Anglican theologian and author.

[3] Bodley, *The Messenger: The Life of Mohammed*, 103.

[4] Leonard, *Islam: Her Moral and Spiritual Value*, 50.

"After all, Islam is essentially the lengthened shadow of one man. Mohammed founded it and his spirit dominates it still. He is the fountain head of all the main Islamic currents which have grooved and moistened the soil of many lands. His word and his life are a court of perpetual appeal on the part of his followers throughout the earth."[1]

– John Clark Archer (1924)

Greater than Jesus and St. Paul Combined

"Muhammad played a far more important role in the development of Islam than Jesus did in the development of Christianity. Although Jesus was responsible for the main ethical and moral precepts of Christianity (insofar as these differed from Judaism), it was St. Paul who was the main developer of Christian theology, its principal proselytizer, and the author of a large portion of the New Testament. Muhammad, however, was responsible for both the theology of Islam and its main ethical and moral principles ... It is probable that the relative influence of Muhammad on Islam has been larger than the combined influence of Jesus Christ and St. Paul on Christianity."[2]

– Michael H. Hart (1978)

ACCOMPLISHMENTS

Most Illustrious Achievements

"The religion of Mahomet is unquestionably of much larger extent than the Christian; its victories, its conquests, its triumphs, are incomparably more illustrious than anything the Christians can boast of in this kind of prosperity. The exploits of the

---

[1] Archer, *The Mystical Elements of Mohammed*, 5.

[2] Michael Hart, *The 100: A Ranking of the Most Influential Persons in History*, 9.

Mahometans are without doubt the most glorious things that history affords. What can we find more wonderful than the empire of the Saracens, which extended from the Straits of Gibraltar as far as the Indies ?"[1]
— Peter Bayle (1695)

"Graceful in his person, easy and insinuating in his manners, and endowed with a greatness of mind which could brave the storms of adversity and rise superior to the disadvantages of an illiterate education; he was in possession of accomplishments more valuable in themselves and capable of producing more illustrious effects, than all that the influence of wealth, or the authority of hereditary power could have bellowed."[2]
— Joseph White (1784)

Immense Achievement with Least Amount of Resources

"Never, in fine, did man accomplish in less of time so immense and so durable a revolution in the world; since, in less than two centuries after his preaching, Islamism, preached and armed, reigned over the three Arabias, conquered to the unity of the Godhead, Persia, Khorassan, Transoxiana, Western India, Syria, Egypt, Ethiopia, all the known continent of Northern Africa, several islands of the Mediterranean, Spain, and a part of Gaul."[3]
— Alphonse de Lamartine (1854)

"The more one reflects on the history of Muhammad and of early Islam, the more one is amazed at the vastness of his achievement. Had it not been for his gifts as seer, statesman, and administrator and, behind these, his trust in God and firm belief that God had

---

[1] Peter Bayle, *An Historical and Critical Dictionary*, vol. 1, 312. Bayle (d. 1706) was a French philosopher, author, and lexicographer.

[2] White, *Sermons Preached Before the University of Oxford*, 92.

[3] Lamartine, *History of Turkey*, vol. i, 154.

sent him, a notable chapter in the history of mankind would have remained unwritten."¹

– W. Montgomery Watt (1955)

"Mohammed's greatness lies in the clearness of his vision and in the boldness of his resolve. The enormity of the task he was undertaking cannot be adequately measured by us at this distance of time. It was almost Herculean."²

– Alfred von Kremer (1873)

United Vast Swaths of Humanity Under One Religion

"Within a brief span of mortal life Muhammad called forth out of unpromising material a nation never united before, in a country that was hitherto but a geographical expression; established a religion which in vast areas superseded Christianity and Judaism and still claims the adherence of a goodly portion of the human race; and laid the basis of an empire that was soon to embrace within its far-flung boundaries the fairest provinces of the then civilized world."³

– Phillip K. Hitti (1937)

Political Institutions

"No other religious leader has ever bound his creed so closely to definite political conceptions. Mahomet was not only the instrument of divine revelation, but he was also at the end of his life the head of a temporal state with minutest laws and regulations— chaotic it may be, but still binding so that Islamic influence extended over the whole of the lives of its adherents. This

---

[1] Watt, *Muhammad At Medina*, 335.

[2] Von Kremer, *Contributions to the History of Islamic Civilization*, 148.

[3] Hitti, *History of the Arabs*, 121-22.

constitutes its strength. Its leader swayed not only the convictions but the activities of his subjects."[1]

— Gladys M. Draycott (1916)

Established Man's Duties to God, Man & the Lower Creation

"Such were the life, the mission, and the death of Mahomet. Never did man propose to himself voluntarily or otherwise, an end more sublime, since this end was superhuman; to sap the superstitions interposed between the creature and the Creator, to bring back God to man and man to God, to restore the rational and holy idea of the Divinity amid that chaos of the material and disfigured deities of idolatry."[2]

— Alphonse de Lamartine (1854)

"Such, in brief outline, is the religion of Mohammad. It is a form of pure theism, simpler and more austere than the theism of most forms of modern Christianity, lofty in its conception of the relation of man to God, and noble in its doctrine of the duty of man to man, and of man to the lower creation."[3]

— Stanley Lane-Poole (1883)

FOUNDER (THREEFOLD)

"Mohammed is a threefold founder—'of a nation, of an empire, and of a religion.' Illiterate himself, scarcely able to read or write, he was yet the author of a book which is a poem, a code of laws, a Book of Common Prayer, and a Bible in one, and is reverenced to this day by a sixth of the whole human race as a miracle of

---

[1] Gladys M. Draycott, *Mahomet: Founder of Islam*, 6.

[2] Lamartine, *History of Turkey*, vol. i, 153.

[3] Lane-Poole, *Studies In A Mosque*, 99.

purity of style, of wisdom, and of truth."[1]

– R. Bosworth Smith (1874)

The Greatest Human Being Ever

A Man with a Unique Combination of Noble Qualities

"Mahomet was distinguished by the beauty of his person, an outward gift which is seldom despised, except by those to whom it has been refused. Before he spoke, the orator engaged on his side the affections of a public or private audience. They applauded his commanding presence, his majestic aspect, his piercing eye, his gracious smile, his flowing beard, his countenance that painted every sensation of the soul, and his gestures that enforced each expression of the tongue. In the familiar offices of life he scrupulously adhered to the grave and ceremonious politeness of his country: his respectful attention to the rich and powerful was dignified by his condescension and affability to the poorest citizens of Mecca ... and the habits of courtesy were imputed to personal friendship, or universal benevolence. His memory was capacious and retentive, his wit easy and social, his imagination sublime, his judgment clear, rapid, and decisive. He possessed the courage both of thought and action; and, although his designs might gradually expand with his success, the first idea which he entertained of his divine mission bears the stamp of an original and superior genius. The son of Abdallah was educated in the bosom of the noblest race, in the use of the purest dialect of Arabia; and the fluency of his speech was corrected and enhanced by the practice of discreet and seasonable silence."[2]

– Edward Gibbon (1788)

"Mohammed possessed that combination of qualities which

---

[1] Smith, *Mohammed and Mohammedanism*, 237.

[2] Gibbon, *Decline and*, vol. v, 101-02.

more than once has decided the fate of empires. A preaching soldier, he was eloquent in the pulpit, valiant in the field. His theology was simple: 'There is but one God.' ... Asserting that everlasting truth, he did not engage in vain metaphysics, but applied himself to improving the social condition of his people by regulations respecting personal cleanliness, sobriety, fasting, prayer. Above all other works he esteemed almsgiving and charity. ... To be the religious head of many empires, to guide the daily life of one-third of the human race, may perhaps justify the title of a messenger of God."[1]

– John William Draper (1861)

"A remarkable feature was the urbanity and consideration with which Mahomet treated even the most insignificant of his followers. Modesty and kindness, patience, self-denial, and generosity, pervaded his conduct, and rivetted the affections of all around him. He disliked to say No; if unable to reply to a petitioner in the affirmative, he preferred to remain silent. 'He was more bashful,' says Ayesha, 'than a veiled virgin; and if anything displeased him, it was rather from his face, than by his words, that we discovered it; he never smote any one but in the service of the Lord, not even a woman or a servant.' He was not known ever to refuse an invitation to the house even of the meanest, nor to decline a proffered present however small. When seated by a friend, 'he did not haughtily advance his knees towards him.' He possessed the rare faculty of making each individual in a company think that he was the most favoured guest. When he met any one rejoicing, he would seize him eagerly and cordially by the hand. With the bereaved and afflicted he sympathized tenderly. Gentle and unbending towards little children, he would not disdain to accost a group of them at play with the salutation of peace. He shared his food, even in times of scarcity, with others; and was sedulously solicitous for the personal comfort of every

---

[1] Draper, *A History of the Intellectual Development of Europe*, vol. i, 330.

one about him. A kindly and benevolent disposition pervades all these illustrations of his character."[1]

– William Muir (1861)

"Mohamed set a shining example to his people ... His house, his dress, his food—they were characterized by a rare simplicity. So unpretentious was he that he would receive from his companions no special mark of reverence, nor would he accept any service from his slave which he could do himself. Often and often indeed was he seen in the market purchasing provisions; often and often was he seen mending his clothes in his room, or milking a goat in his courtyard. He was accessible to all, and at all times. He visited the sick and was full of sympathy for all ... Unlimited was his benevolence and generosity, and so was his anxious care for the welfare of the community. Despite innumerable presents which from all quarters unceasingly poured in for him; despite rich booty which streamed in—he left very little behind, and even that be regarded as State property. After his death his property passed to the State and not to Fatima, his only daughter, the wife of Ali."[2]

– Gustav Weil (1866)

An Original Man

"He was genuinely sincere in spite of his deep consciousness of a lack of sincerity.[3] The great fact of existence overwhelmed him; he could not escape its grip. Others might ignore this fact, and live in empty vanity, but to him the reality of life seemed

---

[1] Muir, *The Life of Mahomet*, vol. iv, 305-06.

[2] Weil, *A History of Islamic Peoples*, 28.

[3] To explain, the Prophet was always subconsciously aware of his human fallibility despite having an impeccable character. His fear of making a slip and displeasing God stemmed from his humility and awe before the majesty of God. For further discussions on this, see Appendix II on page 291.

terribly wonderful, and a flaming vision before his eyes. Such a man is a great man. We may also call him an original man, a messenger who brings us news of the infinite and the unknown. We might call him a poet or a prophet, for we feel that the words which he speaks are not the words of an ordinary man. They have their immediate source in the inner reality of things, since he lives in constant fellowship with this reality."[1]

– Tor Andrae (1932)

A Genius of the Highest Degree

"If genius implies a keen psychological insight into the nature and inner consciousness of life's issues, added to inexhaustible energy, capacity for work and patience, then Mohammed was a genius ... he was without doubt a genius of the highest degree. The founder of a faith—one of the greatest the world has produced—spiritual commander of the faithful, his genius was essentially moral and religious. His whole life was one long labour of love and devotion to achieve his object, i.e. to proclaim God to the nations of the earth."[2]

– Arthur Glyn Leonard (1909)

The Greatest Hero

"We give Muhammad credit as a warrior, as a legislator, as a poet, as a man of uncommon genius, raising himself amidst great opposition to a pinnacle of renown ... he is, without doubt, one of the greatest heroes the world has ever seen;"[3]

– Thomas Patrick Hughes (1877)

---

[1] Andrae, *Mohammed: The Man and His Faith*, 247.

[2] Leonard, *Islam: Her Moral and Spiritual Value*, 115-16.

[3] Hughes, *Notes on Muhammadanism*, 5.

His Legacy

The Greatest Leader

"Leaders must fulfill three functions—provide for the well-being of the led, provide a social organization in which people feel relatively secure, and provide them with one set of beliefs. People like Pasteur and Salk are leaders in the first sense. People like Gandhi and Confucius, on one hand, and Alexander, Caesar and Hitler on the other, are leaders in the second and perhaps the third sense. Jesus and Buddha belong in the third category alone. Perhaps the greatest leader of all times was Mohammed, who combined all three functions."[1]

— Jules Masserman (1974)

The Best Example of One Man in History

"... we have reason to be astonished that he did so much. His career is the best example that can be given of the influence of the Individual in human history. That single man created the glory of his nation and spread his language over half the earth. The words which he preached to jeering crowds twelve hundred years ago are now being studied by scholars or by devotees in London and Paris and Berlin; in Mecca, where he laboured, in Medina, where he died; in Constantinople, in Cairo, in Fez, in Timbuctoo, in Jerusalem, in Damascus, in Bassora, in Baghdad, in Bokhara, in Cabul, in Calcutta, in Pekin, in the steppes of Central Asia, in the islands of the Indian Archipelago, in lands which are as yet unmarked upon our maps, in the oases of thirsty deserts, in obscure villages situated by unknown streams. It was Mahomet who did all this; for he uttered the book which carried the language; and he prepared the army which carried the book."[2]

— Winwood Reade (1872)

---

[1] Jules Masserman, "Who Were History's Great Leaders?"

[2] Reade, *Martyrdom of Man*, 268-69.

The Most Influential Figure

"Persons, dynasties, nations such as these, stand out conspicuously, and arrest our attention, in marked contrast to the dull succession of despot after despot, of dynasty after dynasty, whose names, to which we hardly attach an idea, are forgotten as soon as read. But far above all stands out that marvellous history on which we are now about to enter; the history of Mahomet and his Creed. Call him Prophet, Reformer, or Impostor, as we will, the camel-driver of Mecca, the conqueror of Medina, soars above every other man recorded in the history of the East. Nowhere in the history of the world can we directly trace such mighty effects to the personal agency of a single mortal."[1]

– Edward Freeman (1856)

"My choice of Muhammad to lead the list of the world's most influential persons may surprise some readers and may be questioned by others, but he was the only man in history who was supremely successful on both the religious and secular levels."[2]

– Michael H. Hart (1978)

"It is this unparalleled combination of secular and religious influence which I feel entitles Muhammad to be considered the most influential single figure in human history."[3]

– Michael H. Hart (1978)

The Most Influential Political Leader

"Muhammad (unlike Jesus) was a secular as well as a religious leader. In fact, as the driving force behind the Arab conquests, he

---

[1] Freeman, *History and Conquests of the Saracens*, 5.
[2] Hart, *The 100: A Ranking*, 3.
[3] Ibid., 10.

may well rank as the most influential political leader of all time."[1]

— Michael H. Hart (1978)

An Expression of the Creative Life of God

"Mohammed's religious integrity rests, then, upon the fact that he himself was one of those great personalities who are expressions of the creative life of God, and who have, therefore, an intuitive contact with this creative life, a spontaneous revelation of God."[2]

— Tor Andrae (1932)

The Greatest

"Mohammed should be contemplated and judged as a religious reformer and legislator living in Arabia in the seventh century after Christ, and he must then, most undoubtedly, be acknowledged as the very greatest man whom Asia can claim as her son, if not, one of the rarest and most transcendent geniuses the world itself ever produced."[3]

— John Davenport (1869)

"Looking at him and his work from every aspect, Mohammed was not merely a heroic prophet. He was much more. A king and a leader of men. A ruler and a judge over them. If we are to judge of him, to take him for what he is worth, by his work—the rich ripe fruit of his rare and strenuous effort—the Koran on the one hand, and, on the other, the mighty spiritual force he has left behind him in the Church of Islam, we must pronounce him to have

---

[1] Ibid., 9.

[2] Andrae, *Mohammed: The Man and His Faith*, 247.

[3] Davenport, *An Apology for Mohammed and the Koran*, iii-iv.

been a great and remarkable man. A man who, when his true value is understood and appreciated, will stand out in history as a political and religious reformer of a virile and heroic type. A man who will be regarded in even a greater light than he now is, when humanity shall have become less denominational and more rationally humanitarian. In reality Mohammed was an ultra great man. The difference (as it appears to me) between other great men and himself was wide."[1]

– Arthur Glyn Leonard (1909)

"Mohammed was ... one of the most profoundly sincere and earnest spirits of any age or epoch. A man not only great, but one of the greatest i.e. truest men that Humanity has ever produced. Great, i.e. not simply as a prophet, but as a patriot and a statesman: a material as well as a spiritual builder who constructed a great nation, a greater empire, and more even than all these, a still greater Faith. True, moreover, because he was true to himself, to his people, and above all to his God."[2]

– Arthur Glyn Leonard (1909)

"If the grandeur of the design, the pettiness of the means, the immensity of the results, be the three measures of human genius, who would dare to compare humanly the greatest men of modern times to Mahomet? The most famous of them have agitated but armies, laws, empires; they have founded (when they founded any thing) but physical potencies, often crumbled to the earth before themselves. Mahomet has recast armies, legislations, empires, peoples, dynasties, with millions of men throughout a third of the inhabited globe. More than this, he recast altars, gods, religions, ideas, creeds, souls. He has founded upon a *book*, of which every letter is become a law, a spiritual nationality which embraces peoples of every tongue and race, and he has stamped

---

[1] Leonard, *Islam: Her Moral and Spiritual Value*, 108-09.
[2] Ibid., 21.

as the indelible character of this Mussulman nationality, the hatred of false gods, and the passion of the one and true God. This patriotism, avengeful of the profanations of heaven, was the virtue of the children of Mahomet; the conquest of one third the world to his doctrine was his miracle; or rather, it was not the miracle of a man, but that of reason."[1]

— Alphonse de Lamartine (1854)

"A historian once said, a great man should be judged by three tests: Was he found to be of true mettle by his contemporaries? Was he great enough to rise above the standards of his age? Did he leave anything as permanent legacy to the world at large? This list may be further extended, but all these three tests of greatness are eminently satisfied to the highest degree in the case of Prophet Muhammed."[2]

— K. S. Ramakrishna Rao (1989)

"Some day, perhaps, when a love of truth shines clear enough to dispel the prejudice of the ages, Western writers will carry the study of the life of Muhammad past the point where they now allow his name to stand as a great figure in history, and will give him his just place in the golden book of humanity."[3]

— Simon. H. Leeder (1917)

"If for instance, greatness consists in the purification of a nation, steeped in barbarism and immersed in absolute moral darkness, that dynamic personality who has transformed, refined and uplifted an entire nation, sunk low as the Arabs were, and made them the torch-bearers of civilizations and learning, has every claim to that greatness. If greatness lies in unifying the discordant elements of society by the ties of brotherhood and charity, the Prophet of the desert has got every title to this distinction. If

---

[1] Lamartine, *History of Turkey*, vol. i, 154.

[2] Rao, *Muhammad: the Prophet of Islam*, 17.

[3] Leeder, "The Tenderness of the Prophet."

greatness consists in reforming those wrapt in a degrading superstition and pernicious practices of every kind, the Prophet of Islam has wiped out superstitions and irrational fear from the hearts of millions. If it lies in displaying high morals, Muhammad has been admitted by friends and foes as Al-Amin and As-Sadiq, the trustworthy and truthful. If a conqueror is a great man, here is a person who rose from a helpless orphan and a humble creature to be the ruler of Arabia, the equal of Khosros and Caesars, one who founded a great empire that has survived all these 14 centuries. If the devotion that a leader commands is the criterion of greatness, the Prophet's name even today exerts a magic charm over millions of souls, spread all over the world."[1]

– K. S. Ramakrishna Rao (1989)

"Compare Mohammed with the long roll of men whom the world by common consent has called 'Great'; while I admit that there is no one point in his character in which he is not surpassed by one or other, take him all in all, what he was, and what he did, and what those inspired by him have done, he seems to me to stand alone, above and beyond them all."[2]

– R. Bosworth Smith (1874)

"Philosopher, orator, apostle, lawgiver, warrior, conqueror of ideas, restorer of rational dogmas, of a worship without images, founder of twenty terrestrial empires, and of one spiritual empire—such was Mahomet. What man was greater, by all the scales on which we measure human greatness?"[3]

– Alphonse de Lamartine (1854)

"Where in all history is another such character?"[4]

– Marmaduke Pickthall (1918)

---

[1] Rao, *Muhammad: the Prophet of Islam*, 20-21.

[2] Smith, *Mohammed and Mohammedanism*, 233.

[3] Lamartine, *History of Turkey*, vol. i, 155.

[4] Pickthall, "The Prophet's Character."

A Prophet of God

We now arrive at the ultimate question: Was Muhammad (ﷺ) truly a prophet sent by God? Before answering this question, it is necessary to first understand the definition of prophethood.

From the perspective of the Abrahamic faiths, a prophet is a man appointed by God to deliver His message and preach it to the people. Moses and Jesus, for instance, were prophets sent to the Israelite tribes in Egypt and the Jews living in Palestine, respectively.

The core message conveyed by all prophets is fundamentally the same: to call people to worship God alone, obey Him in all matters, live by His laws in every aspect of life, perform righteous deeds, and exemplify good character, conduct, and morals. Nothing less can be expected from a prophet of God. A true prophet would not instruct people to worship and obey God in their private lives while disregarding or neglecting His guidance in other areas, such as commercial activities. Nor would a prophet's message allow for legislating laws or policies that contradict God's teachings, especially since such actions often have greater societal consequences than individual private deeds. Thus, the message of a prophet must be comprehensive, encompassing and guiding all aspects of human life.

Additionally, since the objective of a prophet is to cultivate people with good character and conduct, he himself must be endowed with noble qualities and serve as a role model for the people to whom he is sent. An essential test of prophethood, therefore, is the character of the prophet. If his character is not impeccable, he cannot be a true prophet. While a prophet, being human, may make inadvertent mistakes, a genuine prophet will never willfully disobey God in any matter, nor will he ever engage in any immoral behavior. His life must reflect the highest standards of integrity and righteousness, as his actions serve as a living example of the divine message he conveys.

While what is mentioned above are the core aspects of prophethood, there are two additional characteristics that may be looked into when judging whether one is a genuine prophet. First, if a prophet is given a scripture—and not all prophets are—its message must embody the principles outlined above, fostering the development of the best human character and society. Furthermore, the scripture must be internally consistent, free of contradictions, and reflective of divine wisdom. Second, a prophet may be granted miracles—though not all prophets are. These miracles, performed through God's power, transcend the natural laws of causality and serve as a testament to their divine appointment. The nature of these characteristics, so far as the Qur'an is concerned, has been discussed in another of our works, which interested readers may look into.[1]

When all these aspects of prophethood are examined in relation to Muhammad (ﷺ)—his exceptional character and conduct, his unparalleled reform efforts, his transformation of a lawless society into one of the most exemplary communities in human history, the comprehensive yet consistent message of the Qur'an, and its unique and miraculous attributes—there remains no room for doubt that he was indeed a genuine prophet sent by God. No other figure in human history embodies these qualities to such a comprehensive and extraordinary degree.

Non-Muslim Scholars on the Prophethood of Muhammad

Liberal scholars and academics who do not subscribe to the concept of divine agency, often regard Prophet Muhammad merely as a great man and reformer. Their ideological posture limits their ability to assess whether he could be a prophet of God. In contrast, numerous objective historians and scholars of oriental studies—particularly those who believed in a Creator Who is actively involved in human affairs, and had the ability to examine the original Arabic sources—came to the inescapable conclusion that Muhammad (ﷺ) could only have been a prophet of God.

As early as 1671, the English physician and historian Henry Stubbe wrote that it was "God [who] justly permitted Mahomet to sow a new doctrine in Arabia."[2] In 1840, the famous Scottish historian and philosopher Thomas Carlyle surprised the world with a lecture on

---

[1] *The Book of Miracles: Extraordinary Facts from the Qur'an Indicating Divine Origin.*

[2] Stubbe, *An Account of the Rise and Progress of Mahometanism*, 190.

Muhammad (ﷺ), calling him "The Hero" and a "true" prophet.[1] The German orientalist and scholar of Hebrew, Gustav Weil, wrote in 1843, "he may be regarded, even by those who are not Mohammedans, as a messenger of God."[2] In 1856, the English historian Edward Freeman stated that Prophet Muhammad "is truly a direct instrument in the hands of God and may be said to have a commission from Him."[3] In 1860, Theodor Noldeke boldly asserted, "That Muḥammad was a true prophet must be conceded if one considers his character carefully and without prejudice, and properly interprets the notion of prophethood."[4] Austrian orientalist Alfred von Kremer, in 1873, observed that the reform Muhammad (ﷺ) accomplished so swiftly "was a work which none but a divinely-inspired Prophet could have achieved."[5] English orientalist and Oxford University professor R. Bosworth Smith referred to him as "a very Prophet of God."[6] Sir E. Denison Ross, who directed the University of London's School of Oriental Studies, demonstrated uncommon boldness for his time in 1877, writing in the introduction to an edition of George Sale's translation of the Qur'an, "It is well for all who study the Koran to realize that the actual text is never the composition of the Prophet, but is the word of God addressed to the Prophet."[7]

The 20th century also saw a significant number of historians and scholars who considered Muhammad (ﷺ) to be a prophet of God. Notable Hungarian scholar of Islamic and Hebrew Studies, Ignac Goldziher, wrote around 1900, "I believed in the prophecies of Muhammad,"[8] while

---

[1] Carlyle, *On Heroes*, 47, 49.

[2] Gustav Weil, *Mohammed der Prophet, sein Leben und siene Lehre*, in Hurgronje, *Mohammedanism*, 24.

[3] Freeman, *History and Conquests of the Saracens*, 49.

[4] Noldeke, *The History of the Qur'an*, 2.

[5] Von Kremer, *Contributions to the History of Islamic Civilization*, 155.

[6] Smith, *Mohammed and Mohammedanism*, 238.

[7] George Sale and Edward Ross (Ed.), *The Koran and Sales's Preliminary Discourse*, vi. Sale (d. 1736) was a British orientalist and the first translator of the Qur'an into English from the original Arabic, which was published in 1734.

[8] Ignac Goldziher, *Tagebuch*, 71, in Tolan, *Faces of Muhammad*, 226.

Margoliouth, an English orientalist and Professor of Arabic at Oxford University, acknowledged, "there is a growing opinion among students of religious history that Muhammed may in a real sense be regarded as a prophet of 'certain truths.'"¹ Writing in the early 1910s, British orientalist scholar and academic G. W. Leitner stated that if the concept of God sending inspiration to mankind is indeed true, then the religion preached by Prophet Muhammad must be "inspired." He further remarked, "Indeed, I venture to state in all humility that if self-sacrifice, honesty of purpose, unswerving belief in one's mission, a marvellous insight into existing wrong or error, and the perception and use of the best means for its removal are among the outward and visible signs of inspiration, the mission of Muhammad was 'inspired.'"²

Italian orientalist and Professor of Arabic, Laura Vaglieri, emphasized that "the Quran could not be the work of an uneducated man, who had spent all his life in the midst of an unrefined society far away from men of learning and religion ... The Quran could have its source only in Him Whose knowledge comprehends everything in heaven and earth."³ French orientalist Emilie Dermenghem, in 1930, commented on the Prophet's divine stature: "his unique and real grandeur came from God, from his supernatural inspiration."⁴ In 1937, historian P. K. Hitti, a scholar of Islamic history and Semitic languages who taught at Princeton and Harvard, wrote that Muhammad (ﷺ) was "truly prophetic as any of the Hebrew prophets of the Old Testament,"⁵ while R. V. C. Bodley, in 1945, reflected on the Prophet's success in eliminating racism and establishing brotherhood, asking, "Could a man who was not inspired have brought such an international brotherhood into being?"⁶ Not long after,

---

¹ *Introduction* by Margoliouth in John M. Rodwell, *The Koran Translated*, viii. Rodwell (d. 1900) was an Anglican clergyman and a translator of the Qur'an from the original Arabic into English, which was first published in 1861.

² Leitner, "Religious Systems of the World."

³ Vaglieri, *An Interpretation Of Islam*, 41.

⁴ Dermenghem, *The Life of Mahomet*, 250.

⁵ Hitti, *History of the Arabs*, 113.

⁶ Bodley, *The Messenger: The Life of Mohammed*, 344.

Arberry, the renowned Arabic linguist from Cambridge University, stated in 1953, "I do not doubt at all that the Koran was a supernatural production."[1]

Recognition of Muhammad (ﷺ) as a prophet of God is not confined to historians and academics alone. A notable number of non-Muslim theologians, well-versed in the history of Islam and its Prophet, have also offered the same assessment. In a 1908 sermon, Pastor George Smith acknowledged Muhammad's (ﷺ) accomplishments as "one of the direct acts of God."[2] Well-known Catholic scholar Louis Massignon recognized the divine origin of the Qur'an in a work published in 1922, thanks to his access to Arabic which afforded him the ability to examine the original sources.[3] Soon after, American missionary and theologian John Clark Archer commented in 1924 that, granted the Prophet's sincerity—and he acknowledges that "no one questions his sincerity"—his experience could only be explained as "genuine revelation" through "direct and immediate experience."[4] English theosophist Annie Besant, in 1932, wrote that Muhammad (ﷺ) "must have been inspired by God, a true Prophet to the people to whom he came."[5] Jesuit theologian and Professor of Theology Jacques Dupuis regarded Muhammad (ﷺ) as a true prophet who received divine revelations, asserting that numerous contemporary theologians share this view.[6] Scottish historian and Anglican priest Montgomery Watt encouraged his fellow Christians to "regard Muhammad as correct in his belief, and therefore accept the Qur'an as truly a collection of revelations

---

[1] Arthur J. Arberry, *The Holy Koran: An Introduction with Selections*, 31. Arberry (d. 1969) was an eminent British scholar of Arabic and Persian literature. He was Head of the Department of Classics at Cairo University in Egypt, and subsequently taught at Cambridge University.

[2] Tolan, *Faces of Muhammad*, 237.

[3] Massignon, *Essay on the Origins*, 98n28.

[4] Archer, *The Mystical Elements of Mohammed*, 38.

[5] Besant, *The Life and Teachings of Muhammad*, 7.

[6] Jacques Dupuis, *Toward a Christian Theology of Religious Pluralism*, in Tolan, *Faces of Muhammad*, 248. Dupuis (d. 2004) was Professor of Theology at the Gregorian University in Rome.

from God."¹ Renowned Catholic theologian Hans Kung stated that Muhammad did not speak on his own, but that through him, God "has spoken to humanity."² Keith Ward, a retired professor of Divinity at the University of Oxford and a contemporary priest of the Church of England, affirmed, "I do think that Muhammad was a genuine prophet of God and that he was raised up by God and that the Qur'an is in some way an expression of God's revelation," noting that this position is "almost universally accepted" among his colleagues in the Anglican Church. Ward further acknowledged that many Roman Catholic priests "now officially believe Islam is a revelation of God."³

Dilemma for Some When Confronted with the Truth

Learned academics who through their studies and research arrive at the intellectual conviction that Muhammad (ﷺ) was a prophet sent by God or that the Qur'an is a revelation from God are inevitably faced with the choice of whether to accept Islam as their faith and model their lives based on its teachings. However, not all individuals make the choice to embrace Islam, even after reaching such a conclusion. Many factors can influence this decision, including potential backlash from family or society, hesitation to abandon a deeply ingrained cultural upbringing and identity, fear of losing one's position or social status, and other personal considerations. Cambridge scholar A. J. Arberry, who deeply admired the Qur'an, describing it as "indeed inimitable"⁴ and a "supernatural production," nonetheless confessed to his Muslim readers, "I am no Muslim, nor could ever be."⁵

Some choose to remain what is sometimes described as "submarine Muslims," secretly professing the faith without ever making it known

---

[1] W. Montgomery Watt, *A Christian Faith for Today*, 101.

[2] Tolan, *Faces of Muhammad*, 245.

[3] "Blogging Theology at 200K - looking back over the past 2 years" in YouTube.

[4] Arberry, *The Holy Koran*, 28.

[5] Ibid., 31.

publicly. Others never take that step, while some defer the decision indefinitely, postponing any serious consideration for a later time. Jerald Dirks, a Methodist minister who became convinced of Muhammad (ﷺ) as a genuine prophet of God and Islam as the true religion, initially hesitated to take that decisive step of embracing Islam. As he relinquished his ministerial role and his growing interest in Islam became more apparent, Dirks began receiving questions from those around him about whether he had converted to Islam. To avoid a direct answer, he developed a strategy of giving long, convoluted responses that left his questioners unsure of whether he still identified as a Christian or had become a Muslim. This ambiguous state persisted for several years.

Eventually, while traveling in a Muslim-majority country, Dirks encountered a moment of truth. On a narrow alleyway while exploring the old city, he crossed paths with a local Arab who, noticing his distinctly American appearance, directly asked him in Arabic, *"anta muslim?"* ("Are you a Muslim?"). Although Dirks understood the question, his limited Arabic vocabulary allowed only two possible answers: *na'am* (yes) or *la* (no). With no one around to interpret for him and no way to evade the question, he took a deep breath and braved for *"na'am"*—yes. From that moment onward, he publicly embraced his new faith and never looked back.[1]

---

[1] Jerald Dirks (d. 2019) earned a Master's degree in Divinity from Harvard University and subsequently became a minister in the United Methodist Church. As part of Harvard's Divinity program, he was required to study early Christianity, the history of the church, and the early texts and manuscripts. Ironically, the divinity program led him to see many contradictions in the Biblical texts and recognize striking similarities between the original teachings of Jesus and his early disciples and the teachings of Islam. Though he continued serving as a minister for a time, the conflict between what he had come to learn and what he was preaching from the pulpit to his church audience began to weigh heavily on his conscience. This inner turmoil ultimately led to his resignation from the church. Seeking a new career path, Dirks completed a Doctorate in Psychology from the University of Denver and became a clinical psychologist. A few years later, he converted to Islam. He authored several books on Islam and Christianity, published more than 60 scholarly articles in the field of clinical psychology, and contributed over 150 articles on Arabian horses—a subject of his passion.

Some resort to intricate wordplay in their writings. German scholar Tor Andrae, for instance, offers glowing praises for Muhammad (ﷺ) but dances around providing a definitive conclusion. He poses the question, "Was Mohammed's inspiration genuine?" and answers it himself: "That Mohammed acted in good faith can hardly be disputed by anyone who knows the psychology of inspiration. That the message which he proclaimed did not come from himself, from his own ideas and opinions, is not only a tenet of his faith but also an experience whose reality he never questioned."[1] Here Andrae describes the Prophet's thoughts but remains silent when it comes to his own verdict. Again, he writes, "It is the truth which he cannot question, because it bears the marks of the reality of experience. In my opinion this unshakable faith in the miracle of revelation cannot be psychologically understood unless we can assume that it came to the Prophet himself as something entirely unexpected and unsurmised. With complete honesty he can assure us that his Koran was in no wise composed or constructed [by humans]."[2] Here again, Andrae vividly describes how Muhammad (ﷺ) felt and his conviction in the divine origin of the Qur'an while skillfully avoiding revealing his own personal conclusion on whether *he* himself believed in its divine nature.

In the case of William Muir, it was clearly ideology that precluded his consideration of Islam. Muir's admiration for various aspects of Prophet Muhammad's character has been quoted in this book, and he wrote extensively on the authentic preservation of the Qur'an, even remarking, "There is probably in the world no other work which has remained twelve centuries with so pure a text."[3] Yet, despite his detailed study of Islam using original Arabic sources, he admitted that it was "incumbent" upon him to judge the question of Muhammad's (ﷺ) prophethood "from a Christian point of view."[4] His writings often revealed this bias, as he would refer to Jesus using terms like "our Lord" or "our blessed Saviour." While Muir acknowledged that the revelations

---

[1] Andrae, *Mohammed: The Man and His Faith*, 62-63.

[2] Ibid., 94-95.

[3] Muir, *The Life of Mahomet*, vol. i, xiv-xv.

[4] Muir, *The Life of Mahomet*, vol. ii, 90.

received by Muhammad (ﷺ) were "supernatural," he speculated whether they "may not have proceeded from God, but from the Evil One and his emissaries," an unscholarly and bizarre claim suggesting a satanic origin.[1] This led Emanuel Deutsch to quip that "a certain preconceived notion anent Satan seems to have taken somewhat too firm a hold upon his mind."[2] Muir later authored a book titled *The Testimony Borne by the Coran,* aimed at demonstrating how the Qur'an supports the Old and New Testaments—clearly an attempt to attract Muslims to Christianity. Regrettably for him, the book failed to gain traction among Muslim readers.

The result of such deep-seated prejudice was that Muir's analysis was severely compromised by his unquestioning adherence to dogmatic Christianity and his belief in Jesus as his Savior. He accepted the doctrines of the modern Church without scrutiny, even though these doctrines were established by St. Paul rather than Jesus himself. In contrast, the actual teachings of Jesus align closely with the teachings of the Qur'an— a fact increasingly uncovered by modern biblical scholarship. During Muir's lifetime, these insights had already begun to emerge. His contemporary and fellow orientalist Leitner, whom he must have known—for both worked in British India as civil servants—emphatically stated that what Jesus preached was "distinguished ... from the mystic creed of St. Paul" and that Islam is essentially the same as "original Christianity minus the teaching of St. Paul."[3] Muir was either unaware of these emerging facts or, more likely, his unwavering faith in Christian dogma prevented him from engaging with or acknowledging this growing body of research. Had he foreseen that subsequent academic and textual scholarship would definitively reveal the antagonistic nature of Pauline doctrines to the original teachings of Jesus, his *Life of Mahomet* might have been markedly different.

The case of Hungarian scholar Ignac Goldziher is particularly interesting. His studies led him to identify himself with Islam intellectually and emotionally. "My formal way of thinking," he wrote, "was through

---

[1] Ibid.

[2] Deutsch, *Literary Remains,* 119.

[3] Leitner, "Religious Systems of the World."

and through oriented toward Islam … I called my monotheism Islam, and I did not lie when I said that I believed in the prophecies of Muhammad."[1] While on a trip in Cairo and still formally a Jew, he attended the Friday prayer service with the help of a Muslim friend, donning traditional Muslim attire. Describing the profound experience of prostrating in prayer, he reflected, "Never in my life was I more devout, more truly devout, than on that exalted Friday."[2] Goldziher, however, never formally accepted Islam. He continued to identify as a Jew—albeit one deeply influenced by Islamic principles—and dedicated his career to advocating for reforms in Judaism inspired by the universal ideals of Islam.

In the course of life, human beings are often confronted with choices, some of which are difficult and require careful considerations. Certain choices, however, transcend cost-benefit analysis. For one who believes in God and accountability in the Afterlife, and is convinced of Muhammad (ﷺ) as a genuine prophet sent by Him, the only logical choice is to accept him as such and model life based on the divine message the Prophet brought, without reservation about potential losses in social status, prestige, power, or acceptance from family and friends. When the alternatives are between eternal success in Paradise or damnation in Hell—or between living the life gifted by God according to His chosen way for humanity or living it otherwise disregarding His way—the matter ceases to be a true dilemma.

Nevertheless, the decision remains one of free will, for "people must settle on their own paths as they alone will bear the future consequences of their deeds."[3]

---

[1] Goldziher, *Tagebuch*, 71, in Tolan, *Faces of Muhammad*, 226.

[2] Ibid.

[3] M. M. Al-Azami, *The History of the Qur'anic Text*, 342.

Appendix I: Selected Sayings of Prophet Muhammad

The statements and actions of Prophet Muhammad were collected, authenticated, and compiled into various volumes by early Muslim scholars. Among these, the six most authentic collections are those compiled by Ismail al-Bukhārī, Muslim ibn al-Ḥajjāj, Abū Dāwud al-Sijistānī, Muhammad ibn Isa al-Tirmidhī, Abū ʿAbd al-Raḥmān al-Nasāʾī, and Abū ʿAbd Allāh al-Qazwīnī (commonly known as Ibn Mājah).

Below is a small sample from the thousands of Prophet Muhammad's recorded sayings, offering the reader a glimpse of the profound wisdom he conveyed and kind of reform he initiated among his people which completely transformed their lives.

1

إِنَّ اللَّهَ جَمِيلٌ يُحِبُّ الجَمَالَ

"Allah[1] is beautiful and He loves beauty."[2]

2

يَا أَيُّهَا النَّاسُ إِنَّ اللَّهَ طَيِّبٌ وَلاَ يَقْبَلُ إِلاَّ طَيِّبًا

"O people! Allah is Pure, and He does not accept but what is pure."[3]

3

إِنَّ اللَّهَ رَفِيقٌ يُحِبُّ الرِّفْقَ فِى الأَمْرِ كُلِّهِ

"Allah is gentle and loves gentleness in all matters."[4]

---

[1] Prophet Muhammad referred to God as "Allāh," a unique and personal Name of the Creator that transcends gender and has no plural form. The same name, with minor variations, was historically used by earlier prophets in their respective Semitic languages. For example, in Aramaic—the language of Jesus—the word is "Alāh" or "Elāh," while in Hebrew, it is "Eloah." Muslims, therefore, are more authentic in calling the Creator "Allah."

[2] Authenticated by Muslim.

[3] Ibid.

[4] Authenticated by al-Bukhārī and Muslim.

4

إِنَّ اللَّهَ لاَ يَنْظُرُ إِلَى صُوَرِكُمْ وَأَمْوَالِكُمْ وَلَكِنْ يَنْظُرُ إِلَى قُلُوبِكُمْ وَأَعْمَالِكُمْ

"Verily Allah does not look at your appearances and your wealth, but He looks into your hearts and your deeds."[1]

5

مَثَلُ الَّذِى يَذْكُرُ رَبَّهُ وَالَّذِى لَا يَذْكُرُ مَثَلُ الْحَىِّ وَالْمَيِّتِ

"The similitude of the one who remembers his Lord and the one who does not is that of the living and the dead."[2]

6

اللَّهُمَّ إِنِّى أَعُوذُ بِكَ مِنْ عِلْمٍ لَا يَنْفَعُ وَمِنْ قَلْبٍ لَا يَخْشَعُ وَمِنْ نَفْسٍ لَا تَشْبَعُ وَمِنْ دَعْوَةٍ لَا يُسْتَجَابُ لَهَا

"O Allah, I seek refuge in You from knowledge that does not benefit, from a heart without god-consciousness, from an appetite that is insatiable, and from a supplication that is not answered."[3]

7

لاَ يَدْخُلُ النَّارَ أَحَدٌ فِى قَلْبِهِ مِثْقَالُ حَبَّةٍ خَرْدَلٍ مِنْ إِيمَانٍ ، وَلاَ يَدْخُلُ الْجَنَّةَ أَحَدٌ فِى قَلْبِهِ مِثْقَالُ حَبَّةٍ خَرْدَلٍ مِنْ كِبْرِيَاءَ

"None shall enter the Fire (of Hell) who has (as little as) the weight of a mustard seed of faith in his heart, and none shall enter Paradise who has (as little as) the weight of a mustard seed of pride in his heart."[4]

---

[1] Authenticated by Muslim.

[2] Authenticated by al-Bukhārī.

[3] Authenticated by Muslim.

[4] Ibid.

Appendix I

8

حُجِبَتِ النَّارُ بِالشَّهَوَاتِ وَحُجِبَتِ الْجَنَّةُ بِالْمَكَارِهِ

"The (Hell) Fire is surrounded by desires, while Paradise is surrounded by things that are undesirable."[1]

9

مَنْ أَحَبَّ لِقَاءَ اللَّهِ أَحَبَّ اللَّهُ لِقَاءَهُ وَمَنْ كَرِهَ لِقَاءَ اللَّهِ كَرِهَ اللَّهُ لِقَاءَهُ

"He who loves to meet Allah, Allah loves to meet him, and he who dislikes to meet Allah, Allah also dislikes to meet him."[2]

10

كُنْ فِي الدُّنْيَا كَأَنَّكَ غَرِيبٌ أَوْ عَابِرُ سَبِيلٍ

"Be in this world as if you are a stranger or a traveler."[3]

11

دَعْ مَا يَرِيبُكَ إِلَى مَا لاَ يَرِيبُكَ فَإِنَّ الصِّدْقَ طُمَأْنِينَةٌ وَإِنَّ الْكَذِبَ رِيبَةٌ

"Leave what makes you doubtful for what does not make you doubtful. The truth brings tranquility while falsehood sows doubt."[4]

12

اتَّقِ اللَّهَ حَيْثُمَا كُنْتَ وَأَتْبِعِ السَّيِّئَةَ الْحَسَنَةَ تَمْحُهَا وَخَالِقِ النَّاسَ بِخُلُقٍ حَسَنٍ

"Be conscious of Allah wherever you are, and follow an evil deed

---

[1] Authenticated by al-Bukhārī, this saying of the Prophet means that giving in to base desires and lawlessness is easier and more appealing than making the right choices in life, which often require effort, sacrifice, and curbing desires. The former path is easier but leads to Hell, while the latter is more challenging and rewarded with Paradise.

[2] Authenticated by Muslim.

[3] Authenticated by al-Bukhārī.

[4] Authenticated by al-Tirmidhī.

with a good one to erase it, and treat people with good behavior."[1]

13

أَكْمَلُ الْمُؤْمِنِينَ إِيمَانًا أَحْسَنُهُمْ خُلُقًا

"The most perfect believer in respect of faith is he who is best of them in manners."[2]

14

خَيْرُ النَّاسِ مَنْ طَالَ عُمُرُهُ وَحَسُنَ عَمَلُهُ

"The best of people is one whose life is long and his conduct is good."[3]

15

فِتْنَةُ الرَّجُلِ فِي أَهْلِهِ وَمَالِهِ وَوَلَدِهِ وَجَارِهِ تُكَفِّرُهَا الصَّلَاةُ وَالصَّوْمُ وَالصَّدَقَةُ وَالْأَمْرُ وَالنَّهْيُ

"Man is tested through his wife, wealth, children and neighbor. What expiates these is prayer, fasting, charity and by enjoining (what is good) and forbidding (what is evil)."[4]

16

مَا مِنْ مُصِيبَةٍ تُصِيبُ الْمُسْلِمَ إِلَّا كَفَّرَ اللَّهُ بِهَا عَنْهُ حَتَّى الشَّوْكَةِ يُشَاكُهَا

"No calamity befalls a Muslim but that Allah expiates some of his sins because of it, even if it is the prick of a thorn."[5]

17

أَكْثِرُوا ذِكْرَ هَاذِمِ اللَّذَّاتِ الْمَوْتِ

---

[1] Authenticated as ḥasan by al-Tirmidhī.

[2] Authenticated as ḥasan by Abū Dāwud.

[3] Authenticated as ḥasan by al-Tirmidhī.

[4] Authenticated by al-Bukhārī.

[5] Ibid.

"Remember death much, the destroyer of pleasures."[1]

18

عَلَيْكُمْ بِالصِّدْقِ فَإِنَّ الصِّدْقَ يَهْدِي إِلَى الْبِرِّ وَإِنَّ الْبِرَّ يَهْدِي إِلَى الْجَنَّةِ ، وَمَا يَزَالُ الرَّجُلُ يَصْدُقُ وَيَتَحَرَّى الصِّدْقَ حَتَّى يُكْتَبَ عِنْدَ اللَّهِ صِدِّيقًا ، وَإِيَّاكُمْ وَالْكَذِبَ فَإِنَّ الْكَذِبَ يَهْدِي إِلَى الْفُجُورِ وَإِنَّ الْفُجُورَ يَهْدِي إِلَى النَّارِ ، وَمَا يَزَالُ الرَّجُلُ يَكْذِبُ وَيَتَحَرَّى الْكَذِبَ حَتَّى يُكْتَبَ عِنْدَ اللَّهِ كَذَّابًا

"It is obligatory for you to tell the truth, for truth leads to virtue and virtue leads to Paradise. A man continues to speak the truth and endeavors to tell the truth until he is recorded as truthful with Allah. Beware of lying, for telling of a lie leads to obscenity and obscenity leads to Hell-Fire. A man keeps on lying and endeavors to tell a lie until he is recorded as a liar with Allah."[2]

19

مَنْ لَمْ يَدَعْ قَوْلَ الزُّورِ وَالْعَمَلَ بِهِ فَلَيْسَ لِلَّهِ حَاجَةٌ فِي أَنْ يَدَعَ طَعَامَهُ وَشَرَابَهُ

"Whoever does not give up false speech and bad behavior, Allah has not need of his leaving food and drink [during fasting in Ramadan]."[3]

20

لَيْسَ الشَّدِيدُ بِالصُّرَعَةِ إِنَّمَا الشَّدِيدُ الَّذِي يَمْلِكُ نَفْسَهُ عِنْدَ الْغَضَبِ

"The strong man is not one who wrestles well but the strong man is one who controls himself in a fit of rage."[4]

21

اللَّهُمَّ إِنِّي أَسْأَلُكَ الْهُدَى وَالتُّقَى وَالْعَفَافَ وَالْغِنَى

---

[1] Authenticated by al-Tirmidhī.

[2] Authenticated by Muslim.

[3] Authenticated by al-Bukhārī.

[4] Authenticated by Muslim.

"O Allah. I ask You for guidance, safety, chastity, and freedom from want."[1]

22

الرَّاحِمُونَ يَرْحَمُهُمُ الرَّحْمَنُ ، ارْحَمُوا أَهْلَ الأَرْضِ يَرْحَمْكُمْ مَنْ فِي السَّمَاءِ

"The Compassionate One has mercy on those who are merciful. Show mercy to those who are on earth, and He Who is in the heaven will show mercy to you."[2]

23

مَنْ لاَ يَرْحَمُ النَّاسَ لاَ يَرْحَمُهُ اللَّهُ

"One who is not merciful to people, Allah will not be merciful to him."[3]

24

خَيْرُكُمْ خَيْرُكُمْ لأَهْلِهِ وَأَنَا خَيْرُكُمْ لأَهْلِي

"The best of you is one who is best to his family, and I am the best of you to my family."[4]

25

إِذَا أَنْفَقَ الرَّجُلُ عَلَى أَهْلِهِ نَفَقَةً يَحْتَسِبُهَا فَهِيَ لَهُ صَدَقَةٌ

"If a man spends on his family, seeking reward from Allah, then it is (recorded as an act of) charity for him."[5]

26

مَنْ أَحَبَّ أَنْ يُبْسَطَ لَهُ فِي رِزْقِهِ وَيُنْسَأَ لَهُ فِي أَثَرِهِ فَلْيَصِلْ رَحِمَهُ

---

[1] Ibid.

[2] Authenticated by Abū Dāwud.

[3] Authenticated by al-Bukhārī and Muslim.

[4] Authenticated by al-Tirmidhī.

[5] Authenticated by al-Bukhārī and Muslim.

"Whoever loves that he be granted more wealth and his lease on life be prolonged, he should keep good relations with his kith and kin."[1]

27

لَيْسَ الْوَاصِلُ بِالْمُكَافِئِ وَلَكِنَّ الْوَاصِلَ الَّذِى إِذَا قُطِعَتْ رَحِمُهُ وَصَلَهَا

"The one who (truly) maintains ties of kinship is not the one who (only) reciprocates. The one who (truly) maintains ties of kinship is the one who, even when his relatives cut him off, still maintains ties of kinship."[2]

28

لاَ يُؤْمِنُ أَحَدُكُمْ حَتَّى يُحِبَّ لأَخِيهِ مَا يُحِبُّ لِنَفْسِهِ

"None of you is a (true) believer until he loves for his brother what he loves for himself."[3]

29

مَنْ كَانَ يُؤْمِنُ بِاللَّهِ وَالْيَوْمِ الآخِرِ فَلْيُحْسِنْ إِلَى جَارِهِ ، وَمَنْ كَانَ يُؤْمِنُ بِاللَّهِ وَالْيَوْمِ الآخِرِ فَلْيُكْرِمْ ضَيْفَهُ ، وَمَنْ كَانَ يُؤْمِنُ بِاللَّهِ وَالْيَوْمِ الآخِرِ فَلْيَقُلْ خَيْرًا أَوْ لِيَسْكُتْ

"Whoever believes in Allah and the Last Day, let him treat his neighbour well. And whoever believes in Allah and the Last Day, let him honor his guest. And whoever believes in Allah and the Last Day, let him say what is good or remain silent."[4]

30

مَنْ كَانَ فِي حَاجَةِ أَخِيهِ كَانَ اللَّهُ فِي حَاجَتِهِ

"He who meets the needs of his brother, Allah will meet his needs."[5]

---

[1] Authenticated by al-Bukhārī.

[2] Al-Bukhārī, *al-adab al-mufrad* (authenticated by al-Albānī).

[3] Authenticated by al-Tirmidhī.

[4] Authenticated by Ibn Mājah.

[5] Authenticated by Muslim.

31

$$\text{مَنْ أَنْظَرَ مُعْسِرًا أَوْ وَضَعَ عَنْهُ أَنْجَاهُ اللَّهُ مِنْ كُرَبِ يَوْمِ الْقِيَامَةِ}$$

"Whoever grants a respite to one who is in strained circumstances, or remits his debt, Allah will save him from the anxieties on the Day of Resurrection."[1]

32

$$\text{لاَ تَبَاغَضُوا وَلاَ تَحَاسَدُوا وَلاَ تَدَابَرُوا وَلاَ تَقَاطَعُوا، وَكُونُوا عِبَادَ اللَّهِ إِخْوَانًا، وَلاَ يَحِلُّ لِمُسْلِمٍ أَنْ يَهْجُرَ أَخَاهُ فَوْقَ ثَلاَثٍ}$$

"Do not harbor grudge against one another, nor jealousy, nor enmity; and do not show your backs to one another; and become as fellow brothers and slaves of Allah. It is not lawful for a Muslim to avoid speaking with his brother beyond three days."[2]

33

$$\text{إِيَّاكُمْ وَالظَّنَّ فَإِنَّ الظَّنَّ أَكْذَبُ الْحَدِيثِ، وَلاَ تَحَسَّسُوا وَلاَ تَجَسَّسُوا وَلاَ تَنَافَسُوا وَلاَ تَحَاسَدُوا وَلاَ تَبَاغَضُوا وَلاَ تَدَابَرُوا، وَكُونُوا عِبَادَ اللَّهِ إِخْوَانًا}$$

"Avoid suspicion, for suspicion is the gravest lie in talk. And do not be inquisitive about one another, nor spy upon one another, nor envy one another; nurse no malice, nor aversion, nor hostility against one another. Be servants of Allah in brotherhood."[3]

34

$$\text{لاَ يَسْتُرُ عَبْدٌ عَبْدًا فِي الدُّنْيَا إِلاَّ سَتَرَهُ اللَّهُ يَوْمَ الْقِيَامَةِ}$$

"There is no slave (of Allah) who conceals the faults of another slave in this world except that Allah will conceal his faults on the Day of Resurrection."[4]

---

[1] Ibid.

[2] Authenticated by al-Bukhārī and Muslim.

[3] Authenticated by Muslim.

[4] Ibid.

35

الْمُسْلِمُ مَنْ سَلِمَ الْمُسْلِمُونَ مِنْ لِسَانِهِ وَيَدِهِ ، وَالْمُهَاجِرُ مَنْ هَجَرَ مَا نَهَى اللَّهُ عَنْهُ

"A Muslim is the one who avoids harming (other) Muslims with his tongue or his hands. And a (true) emigrant is one who gives up all that Allah has forbidden."[1]

36

الْمُسْلِمُ أَخُو الْمُسْلِمِ ، لَا يَظْلِمُهُ وَلَا يَخْذُلُهُ وَلَا يَكْذِبُهُ وَلَا يَحْقِرُهُ ، التَّقْوَى هَاهُنَا وَيُشِيرُ إِلَى صَدْرِهِ ثَلَاثَ مَرَّاتٍ ، بِحَسْبِ امْرِئٍ مِنَ الشَّرِّ أَنْ يَحْقِرَ أَخَاهُ الْمُسْلِمَ ، كُلُّ الْمُسْلِمِ عَلَى الْمُسْلِمِ حَرَامٌ: دَمُهُ وَمَالُهُ وَعِرْضُهُ

"A Muslim is a brother of a Muslim: he does not oppress him, nor does he fail him, nor does he lie to him, nor does he hold him in contempt. Piety is right here [and he pointed to his chest three times]. It is enough evil for a man to hold his brother Muslim in contempt. Everything of a Muslim is inviolable for another Muslim: his blood, his property, and his honour."[2]

37

لاَ يَدْخُلُ الْجَنَّةَ مَنْ لاَ يَأْمَنُ جَارُهُ بَوَائِقَهُ

"He will not enter Paradise whose neighbor is not safe form his wrongful conduct."[3]

38

مَنْ لَمْ يَرْحَمْ صَغِيرَنَا وَيَعْرِفْ حَقَّ كَبِيرِنَا فَلَيْسَ مِنَّا

"Whoever does not show mercy upon our young, nor acknowledge the rights of our elders, is not from us."[4]

---

[1] Authenticated by al-Bukhārī.

[2] Authenticated by Muslim.

[3] Ibid.

[4] Al-Bukhārī, *al-adab al-mufrad* (authenticated by al-Albānī).

39

إِنَّ اللَّهَ حَرَّمَ عَلَيْكُمْ عُقُوقَ الْأُمَّهَاتِ وَمَنْعَ وَهَاتِ وَوَأْدَ الْبَنَاتِ، وَكَرِهَ لَكُمْ قِيلَ وَقَالَ وَكَثْرَةَ السُّؤَالِ وَإِضَاعَةَ الْمَالِ

"Allah has forbidden you to be undutiful to your mothers, to withhold (what you should give), to demand (what you do not deserve), to bury your daughters alive. And He dislikes your gossiping about others, your asking too many questions, and wasting wealth."[1]

40

مَنْ كَانَ لَهُ ثَلَاثُ بَنَاتٍ أَوْ ثَلَاثُ أَخَوَاتٍ أَوِ ابْنَتَانِ أَوْ أُخْتَانِ فَأَحْسَنَ صُحْبَتَهُنَّ وَاتَّقَى اللَّهَ فِيهِنَّ فَلَهُ الْجَنَّةُ

"Whoever has three daughters, or three sisters, or two daughters, or two sisters, and he keeps good company with them and fears Allah regarding them, then Paradise is for him."[2]

41

اللَّهُمَّ إِنِّي أُحَرِّجُ حَقَّ الضَّعِيفَيْنِ الْيَتِيمِ وَالْمَرْأَةِ

"O Allah, I declare inviolable the rights of the two weak ones: Orphans and women."[3]

42

فُكُّوا الْعَانِي وَأَجِيبُوا الدَّاعِيَ وَعُودُوا الْمَرِيضَ

"Set the captives free, accept the invitation, and visit the sick."[4]

43

إِذَا أَتَى أَحَدَكُمْ خَادِمُهُ بِطَعَامِهِ فَإِنْ لَمْ يُجْلِسْهُ مَعَهُ فَلْيُنَاوِلْهُ أُكْلَةً أَوْ أُكْلَتَيْنِ أَوْ

---

[1] Authenticated by al-Bukhārī.

[2] Authenticated as ḥasan by al-Tirmidhī.

[3] Authenticated as ḥasan by Ibn Mājah.

[4] Authenticated by al-Bukhārī.

لُقْمَةً أَوْ لُقْمَتَيْنِ فَإِنَّهُ وَلِيَ حَرَّهُ وَعِلَاجَهُ

"When your servant brings your food to you, if you do not ask him to join you, then at least ask him to take one or two morsels, or one or two handfuls, for he had been through its heat (while cooking it) and its preparation."[1]

44

مَنْ رَأَى مِنْكُمْ مُنْكَرًا فَلْيُغَيِّرْهُ بِيَدِهِ، فَإِنْ لَمْ يَسْتَطِعْ فَبِلِسَانِهِ فَإِنْ لَمْ يَسْتَطِعْ فَبِقَلْبِهِ وَذَلِكَ أَضْعَفُ الْإِيمَانِ

"Whosoever of you sees an evil, let him change it with his hand; and if he is not able to do so, then [let him change it] with his tongue; and if he is not able to do so, then with [at least] his heart, and that is the weakest of faith."[2]

45

إِذَا حَكَمَ الْحَاكِمُ فَاجْتَهَدَ ثُمَّ أَصَابَ فَلَهُ أَجْرَانِ وَإِذَا حَكَمَ فَاجْتَهَدَ ثُمَّ أَخْطَأَ فَلَهُ أَجْرٌ

"If a judge gives a verdict having striven (his best to ascertain the matter), then arrives at the correct ruling, he will have two rewards; and if a judge gives a verdict having striven (his best), then arrives at the wrong ruling, he will have one reward."[3]

46

إِنَّمَا أَنَا بَشَرٌ وَإِنَّكُمْ تَخْتَصِمُونَ إِلَيَّ، وَلَعَلَّ بَعْضَكُمْ أَنْ يَكُونَ أَلْحَنَ بِحُجَّتِهِ مِنْ بَعْضٍ، فَأَقْضِيَ لَهُ عَلَى نَحْوِ مَا أَسْمَعُ مِنْهُ فَمَنْ قَضَيْتُ لَهُ بِشَيْءٍ مِنْ حَقِّ أَخِيهِ فَلَا يَأْخُذَنَّهُ فَإِنَّمَا أَقْطَعُ لَهُ قِطْعَةً مِنَ النَّارِ

"Verily, I am only a human being, and you bring your disputes to me. It may be that some of you are more eloquent in presenting your

---

[1] Ibid.

[2] Authenticated by Muslim. Meaning, if a person's heart remains completely unmoved upon witnessing injustice, then it is entirely devoid of faith.

[3] Authenticated by al-Bukhārī and Muslim.

arguments than others, and I give judgment based on what I hear from you. So, if I give a judgment in favor of anyone that rightfully belongs to his (disputing) brother, he must not accept it, for (by doing so) I would be granting him only a portion of the (Hell) Fire."[1]

47

الْبَيِّنَةُ عَلَى الْمُدَّعِى وَالْيَمِينُ عَلَى الْمُدَّعَى عَلَيْهِ

"The proof is due from the claimant, and the oath is due from the one the claim is made against."[2]

48

لاَ يُؤْخَذُ الرَّجُلُ بِجَرِيرَةِ أَبِيهِ وَلاَ بِجَرِيرَةِ أَخِيهِ

"No man may be punished for the crime of his father or the crime of his brother."[3]

49

أَقِيمُوا حُدُودَ اللَّهِ فِي الْقَرِيبِ وَالْبَعِيدِ وَلاَ تَأْخُذْكُمْ فِي اللَّهِ لَوْمَةُ لاَئِمٍ

"Carry out the legal punishments, whether [the guilty be] close relatives or strangers. Do not let fear of criticism swerve you from the commands of Allah."[4]

---

[1] Ibid.

[2] Authenticated by al-Tirmidhī. Prophet Muhammad established the legal doctrine that the burden of proof is upon the accuser nearly 600 years before it was first adopted in the Western legal system (English common law) around the 13th century.

[3] Authenticated by al-Nasā'ī. The Qur'an categorically rejects the notion that one person can be held accountable for the crimes or sins of another. The verse "No bearer of burdens can bear the burden of another" (Q. 17:15) is repeated multiple times in the Qur'an, indicating the importance of this principle. This statement refutes the Christian concept of "original sin," which holds that every newborn child inherits the sin of Adam, emphasizing instead that each individual is responsible for their own actions.

[4] Authenticated as *hasan* by Ibn Mājah.

50

تُطْعِمُ الطَّعَامَ وَتَقْرَأُ السَّلَامَ عَلَى مَنْ عَرَفْتَ وَمَنْ لَمْ تَعْرِفْ

"Feeding and greeting those you know and those you do not know."[1]

51

مَنْ لَا يَشْكُرُ النَّاسَ لَا يَشْكُرُ اللَّهَ

"One who does not thank people, does not thank Allah."[2]

52

إِنَّ اللَّهَ لَيَرْضَى عَنِ الْعَبْدِ أَنْ يَأْكُلَ الْأَكْلَةَ فَيَحْمَدَهُ عَلَيْهَا أَوْ يَشْرَبَ الشَّرْبَةَ فَيَحْمَدَهُ عَلَيْهَا

"Allah is pleased with His servant who eats his meal and praises Him, or drinks his beverage and praises Him."[3]

53

لَا حَسَدَ إِلَّا فِي اثْنَتَيْنِ رَجُلٍ آتَاهُ اللَّهُ مَالًا فَسَلَّطَهُ عَلَى هَلَكَتِهِ فِي الْحَقِّ وَرَجُلٍ آتَاهُ اللَّهُ الْحِكْمَةَ فَهُوَ يَقْضِي بِهَا وَيعلمها

"There is no (permissible) envy except in two cases: A man whom Allah has granted wealth and he spends it in the right way, and a man whom Allah has granted wisdom and he makes decisions accordingly and teaches it to others."[4]

54

كُلُّ مَعْرُوفٍ صَدَقَةٌ

---

[1] Authenticated by al-Bukhārī. The Prophet gave this response when someone asked him, "What type of Islam is best?"

[2] Authenticated by al-Tirmidhī.

[3] Authenticated by Muslim.

[4] Authenticated by al-Bukhārī and Muslim.

"Everything good is charity."¹

55

وَالْكَلِمَةُ الطَّيِّبَةُ صَدَقَةٌ

"A good word is a charity."²

56

إِنَّكَ لَنْ تُنْفِقَ نَفَقَةً تَبْتَغِي بِهَا وَجْهَ اللَّهِ إِلَّا أُجِرْتَ عَلَيْهَا حَتَّى مَا تَجْعَلُ فِي فَمِ امْرَأَتِكَ

"You will not spend anything seeking the pleasure of Allah except that you will be rewarded for it, even the morsel of food you put in your wife's mouth."³

57

الْيَدُ الْعُلْيَا خَيْرٌ مِنَ الْيَدِ السُّفْلَى فَالْيَدُ الْعُلْيَا هِيَ الْمُنْفِقَةُ وَالسُّفْلَى هِيَ السَّائِلَةُ

"The upper hand is better than the lower hand; the upper hand is the one that gives and the lower hand is the one that asks (for help)."⁴

58

يَكْبَرُ ابْنُ آدَمَ وَيَكْبَرُ مَعَهُ اثْنَانِ حُبُّ الْمَالِ وَطُولُ الْعُمُرِ

"The son of Adam grows old, and so grows two things with him: Love of wealth and (desire for a) long life."⁵

59

لَوْ أَنَّ لِابْنِ آدَمَ وَادِياً مِنْ ذَهَبٍ أَحَبَّ أَنْ يَكُونَ لَهُ وَادِيَانِ ، وَلَنْ يَمْلَأَ فَاهُ إِلَّا التُّرَابُ

"If a son of Adam has one valley full of gold, he desires for two.

---

¹ Authenticated by al-Bukhārī.

² Authenticated by al-Bukhārī and Muslim.

³ Ibid.

⁴ Ibid.

⁵ Authenticated by al-Bukhārī.

Appendix I

Nothing satiates his mouth except the dirt (of the grave)."[1]

60

لَيْسَ الْغِنَى عَنْ كَثْرَةِ الْعَرَضِ وَلَـكِنَّ الْغِنَى غِنَى النَّفْسِ

"Being rich is not about having abundance of property; rather, being rich is about having contentment."[2]

61

أَعْطُوا الأَجِيرَ أَجْرَهُ قَبْلَ أَنْ يَجِفَّ عَرَقُهُ

"Give the worker his wages before his sweat dries."[3]

62

أَلاَ مَنْ ظَلَمَ مُعَاهِدًا أَوِ انْتَقَصَهُ أَوْ كَلَّفَهُ فَوْقَ طَاقَتِهِ أَوْ أَخَذَ مِنْهُ شَيْئًا بِغَيْرِ طِيبِ نَفْسٍ فَأَنَا حَجِيجُهُ يَوْمَ الْقِيَامَةِ

"Beware, if anyone wrongs a contracting man, or diminishes his right, or forces him to work beyond his capacity, or takes from him anything without his consent, I shall plead for him on the Day of Judgment."[4]

63

الْمُسْلِمُ أَخُو الْمُسْلِمِ وَلاَ يَحِلُّ لِمُسْلِمٍ بَاعَ مِنْ أَخِيهِ بَيْعًا فِيهِ عَيْبٌ إِلاَّ بَيَّنَهُ لَهُ

"A Muslim is a brother of another Muslim. It is not permissible for a Muslim to sell something to his brother in which there is a defect, without pointing that out to him."[5]

---

[1] Authenticated by al-Bukhārī and Muslim. Meaning, man's desire for more wealth comes to an end only in the grave.

[2] Authenticated by al-Bukhārī and Muslim.

[3] Authenticated by Ibn Mājah.

[4] Authenticated by Abū Dāwud.

[5] Authenticated by Ibn Mājah.

64

مَا أَكَلَ أَحَدٌ طَعَامًا قَطُّ خَيْرًا مِنْ أَنْ يَأْكُلَ مِنْ عَمَلِ يَدِهِ، وَإِنَّ نَبِيَّ اللَّهِ دَاوُدَ ـ عَلَيْهِ السَّلَامُ ـ كَانَ يَأْكُلُ مِنْ عَمَلِ يَدِهِ

"No one has ever eaten a better meal than that earned through working with one's own hands. David the Prophet of Allah, peace be on him, used to eat from working with his own hands."[1]

65

نِعْمَتَانِ مَغْبُونٌ فِيهِمَا كَثِيرٌ مِنَ النَّاسِ الصِّحَّةُ وَالْفَرَاغُ

"There are two blessings in which many people suffer loss: health and free time."[2]

66

مَا أَنْزَلَ اللَّهُ دَاءً إِلَّا أَنْزَلَ لَهُ شِفَاءً

"There is no disease that Allah has created, except that He has also provided its treatment."[3]

67

لِكُلِّ دَاءٍ دَوَاءٌ، فَإِذَا أُصِيبَ دَوَاءُ الدَّاءِ بَرَأَ بِإِذْنِ اللَّهِ عَزَّ وَجَلَّ

"There is a remedy for every malady, and when the remedy is applied to the disease it is cured with the permission of Allah, the Exalted and Glorious."[4]

68

مَنْ أَصْبَحَ مِنْكُمْ آمِنًا فِي سِرْبِهِ مُعَافًى فِي جَسَدِهِ عِنْدَهُ قُوتُ يَوْمِهِ فَكَأَنَّمَا حِيزَتْ لَهُ الدُّنْيَا

---

[1] Authenticated by al-Bukhārī.

[2] Ibid.

[3] Ibid.

[4] Authenticated by Muslim.

"Whoever among you wakes up in the morning feeling secured in his home, healthy in his body, and having enough food for the day, then it is as if the world has been bestowed to him."¹

69

إِذَا سَمِعْتُمْ بِالطَّاعُونِ بِأَرْضٍ فَلاَ تَدْخُلُوهَا ، وَإِذَا وَقَعَ بِأَرْضٍ وَأَنْتُمْ بِهَا فَلاَ تَخْرُجُوا مِنْهَا

"If you hear of an outbreak of plague in a land, do not enter it; and if the plague breaks out in a place you are in, do not leave that place."²

70

عَجَبًا لِأَمْرِ الْمُؤْمِنِ ، إِنَّ أَمْرَهُ كُلَّهُ خَيْرٌ وَلَيْسَ ذَاكَ لِأَحَدٍ إِلاَّ لِلْمُؤْمِنِ ، إِنْ أَصَابَتْهُ سَرَّاءُ شَكَرَ فَكَانَ خَيْرًا لَهُ ، وَإِنْ أَصَابَتْهُ ضَرَّاءُ صَبَرَ فَكَانَ خَيْرًا لَهُ

"Amazing are the affairs of a believer, for there is good for him in everything, and this does not apply to anyone but a believer. If something good befalls him, he is thankful (to Allah) and that is good for him. And if something bad befalls him, he is patient and that is [also] good for him."³

71

وَمَنْ يَسْتَعْفِفْ يُعِفَّهُ اللَّهُ ، وَمَنْ يَسْتَغْنِ يُغْنِهِ اللَّهُ ، وَمَنْ يَتَصَبَّرْ يُصَبِّرْهُ اللَّهُ ، وَمَا أُعْطِيَ أَحَدٌ عَطَاءً خَيْرًا وَأَوْسَعَ مِنَ الصَّبْرِ

"Whosoever would seek to be chaste and modest, Allah will keep him chaste and modest; and whosoever would seek self-sufficiency, Allah will make him self-sufficient; and whosoever would seek to be patient, Allah will grant him patience. No one has been granted a gift better and more comprehensive than patience."⁴

---

¹ Authenticated as *hasan* by al-Tirmidhī.

² Authenticated by al-Bukhārī.

³ Authenticated by Muslim.

⁴ Authenticated by al-Bukhārī and Muslim.

72

لَا تَتَمَنَّوْا لِقَاءَ الْعَدُوِّ فَإِذَا لَقِيتُمْ فَاصْبِرُوا

"Do not wish for an encounter with the enemy. [Instead] Pray to Allah to grant you safety; (but) if you encounter them, show patience."[1]

73

الْمُؤْمِنُ يَأْكُلُ فِي مِعًى وَاحِدٍ وَالْكَافِرُ يَأْكُلُ فِي سَبْعَةِ أَمْعَاءٍ

"A believer eats in one intestine, and an unbeliever eats in seven intestines."[2]

74

طَعَامُ الِاثْنَيْنِ كَافِي الثَّلَاثَةِ وَطَعَامُ الثَّلَاثَةِ كَافِي الْأَرْبَعَةِ

"Food for two suffices for three, and the food for three suffices for four."[3]

75

وَإِيَّاكُمْ وَالْغُلُوَّ فِي الدِّينِ، فَإِنَّمَا أَهْلَكَ مَنْ كَانَ قَبْلَكُمُ الْغُلُوُّ فِي الدِّينِ

"Beware of going to extremes in religion. Those who came before you were destroyed because of going to extremes in religion."[4]

76

إِنَّ الدِّينَ يُسْرٌ وَلَنْ يُشَادَّ الدِّينَ أَحَدٌ إِلَّا غَلَبَهُ فَسَدِّدُوا وَقَارِبُوا وَأَبْشِرُوا وَاسْتَعِينُوا بِالْغَدْوَةِ وَالرَّوْحَةِ وَشَيْءٍ مِنَ الدُّلْجَةِ

"Religion is easy. Whoever overburdens himself in his religion will not be able to continue in that way. So do not go to extremes, but try

---

[1] Ibid.

[2] Authenticated by al-Bukhārī. This saying of Prophet Muhammad means that a believer eats moderately, practicing self-restraint, while an unbeliever tends to overindulge in food or other consumables.

[3] Authenticated by al-Bukhārī and Muslim.

[4] Authenticated by al-Nasā'ī.

to be close to perfection and receive the good tidings (that you will be rewarded for your good efforts). And gain strength by worshipping in the mornings, in the afternoons, and during the last hours of the nights."[1]

77

مَهْ عَلَيْكُمْ مَا تُطِيقُونَ مِنَ الأَعْمَالِ فَإِنَّ اللَّهَ لاَ يَمَلُّ حَتَّى تَمَلُّوا

"Perform good (deeds) which is within your capacity, for Allah does not get tired but you will get tired."[2]

78

سَدِّدُوا وَقَارِبُوا وَأَبْشِرُوا فَإِنَّهُ لاَ يُدْخِلُ أَحَدًا الْجَنَّةَ عَمَلُهُ، قَالُوا وَلاَ أَنْتَ يَا رَسُولَ اللهِ؟ قَالَ وَلاَ أَنَا إِلاَّ أَنْ يَتَغَمَّدَنِي اللهُ بِمَغْفِرَةٍ وَرَحْمَةٍ

"Do good deeds properly, sincerely and moderately, and receive good news because one's good deeds will not make him enter Paradise." They asked, "Even you, O Allah's Messenger (ﷺ)?" He said, "Even I, unless Allah bestows His forgiveness and mercy on me."[3]

79

سِيرُوا وَلاَ تُعَسِّرُوا وَسَكِّنُوا وَلاَ تُنَفِّرُوا

"Make things easy and do not make things difficult. Calm people and do not scare them."[4]

80

النَّاسُ كُلُّهُمْ بَنُو آدَمَ وَآدَمُ خُلِقَ مِنْ تُرَابٍ

---

[1] Authenticated by al-Bukhārī.

[2] Ibid.

[3] Ibid. Even if one falls short in performing enough good deeds, he can still hold hope for Paradise; hence, the Prophet described it as "good news."

[4] Authenticated by al-Bukhārī and Muslim.

"All people are children of Adam, and Adam was created from dust."[1]

81

مَنْ قُتِلَ تَحْتَ رَايَةٍ عُمِّيَّةٍ يَدْعُو عَصَبِيَّةً أَوْ يَنْصُرُ عَصَبِيَّةً فَقِتْلَةٌ جَاهِلِيَّةٌ

"Whoever is killed under the leadership of a man who is blind (to a just cause), calling for tribalism,[2] or supporting his own tribe, dies the death of one belonging to the Days of Ignorance."[3]

82

اسْمَعُوا وَأَطِيعُوا وَإِنِ اسْتُعْمِلَ عَلَيْكُمْ عَبْدٌ حَبَشِيٌّ كَأَنَّ رَأْسَهُ زَبِيبَةٌ

"Listen to and obey, your ruler even if he is an Ethiopian slave whose head looks like a raisin."[4]

83

إِنَّ اللهَ كَتَبَ الْإِحْسَانَ عَلَى كُلِّ شَيْءٍ ، فَإِذَا قَتَلْتُمْ فَأَحْسِنُوا الْقِتْلَةَ وَإِذَا ذَبَحْتُمْ فَأَحْسِنُوا الذِّبْحَةَ ، وَلْيُحِدَّ أَحَدُكُمْ شَفْرَتَهُ وَلْيُرِحْ ذَبِيحَتَهُ

"Allah has decreed that everything be done in excellence. So if you kill, then kill well [minimizing pain], and if you slaughter, then slaughter well. Let each one of you sharpen his blade and spare suffering to the animal he slaughters."[5]

---

[1] Authenticated as *ḥasan* by al-Tirmidhī. This statement by the Prophet underscores the equality of all humanity since they share the same origin, and serves as a reminder that arrogance is unfitting for humans, given their humble creation from dust.

[2] In today's terms, "tribalism" can be understood as a form of racial/ethnic superiority.

[3] Authenticated by Muslim. The term "Days of Ignorance" refers to the pre-Islamic era characterized by lawlessness and moral decay.

[4] Authenticated by al-Bukhārī. In other words, no consideration should be given to a person's skin color, physical appearance, or past status as a slave.

[5] Authenticated by Muslim.

84

فِي كُلِّ كَبِدٍ رَطْبَةٍ أَجْرٌ

"There is reward for (showing kindness) to every living being."[1]

85

لَا تَتَّخِذُوا شَيْئًا فِيهِ الرُّوحُ غَرَضًا

"Do not use any living creature as a target."[2]

86

مَا مِنْ إِنْسَانٍ قَتَلَ عُصْفُورًا فَمَا فَوْقَهَا بِغَيْرِ حَقِّهَا إِلاَّ سَأَلَهُ اللَّهُ عَزَّ وَجَلَّ عَنْهَا

"No one kills a small bird or anything larger without a just reason except that Allah, the Mighty and Sublime, will ask him about it."[3]

87

إِنْ قَامَتِ السَّاعَةُ وَفِي يَدِ أَحَدِكُمْ فَسِيلَةٌ فَإِنِ اسْتَطَاعَ أَنْ لاَ تَقُومَ حَتَّى يَغْرِسَهَا فَلْيَغْرِسْهَا

"If the Final Hour[4] comes while you have a plant shoot in your hands, and it is possible to plant it before the Hour sets in, then you should [still] plant it."[5]

---

[1] Authenticated by al-Bukhārī and Muslim. The original Arabic word used here, *kabid*, literally translates to "everything with a moist liver," which essentially refers to anything that has life.

[2] Authenticated by Muslim.

[3] Authenticated as *ḥasan* by al-Nasā'ī.

[4] The "Final Hour" is a term from Islamic eschatology referring to the onset of the destruction of the present world, followed by the Day of Judgment. This saying of the Prophet emphasizes the importance of planting trees, even when it may seem there is no longer any practical benefit.

[5] Al-Bukhārī, *al-adab al-mufrad* (authenticated by al-Albānī).

88

مَا مِنْ مُسْلِمٍ غَرَسَ غَرْسًا فَأَكَلَ مِنْهُ إِنْسَانٌ أَوْ دَابَّةٌ إِلاَّ كَانَ لَهُ صَدَقَةً

"There is no Muslim who plants a tree and man or animal eats from it [it's fruits], except that it will be (recorded as) charity for him."[1]

---

[1] Authenticated by al-Bukhārī.

APPENDIX II: SUPPLICATIONS OF HUMILITY

The Prophet of Islam was known for his gentleness, but his humility before God was especially moving. His many roles as prophet, spiritual guide, prayer leader, head of state, teacher, judge, administrator, counselor, arbitrator, commander of the army, father, husband, and more must have kept him thoroughly occupied his wakeful time during the day, but that did not deter him from standing for long periods of time in prayers to God late in the night when every soul, including his own wives, was fast asleep—a practice that he almost never missed while he was alive.

Even with his impeccable character and moral excellence, the Prophet remained acutely aware of his human fallibility before God, Who knows the secrets of all hearts. Whether any inadvertent slip was known or unknown to him, or even whether such concerns ever materialized in action, his humility kept him perpetually mindful of his limitations as a human being. This deep awareness of his perceived vulnerability and God's overwhelming majesty left him in a constant state of awe and reverence before his Creator.

Below is a small sample of the many supplications the Prophet used to make to God. Given his spotless character and the fact that God had already forgiven his past and future shortcomings,[1] some Islamic scholars suggest that the Prophet offered these supplications to encourage his followers to adopt them. Whether this is true one cannot be sure, but there is little doubt—at least in the mind of this author—that the Prophet made these heartfelt supplications for himself first and foremost. These words of deep humility and devotion undoubtedly came from the very depths of his soul.

1

اللَّهُمَّ إِنِّي أَعُوذُ بِكَ مِنْ زَوَالِ نِعْمَتِكَ وَتَحَوُّلِ عَافِيَتِكَ وَفُجَاءَةِ نِقْمَتِكَ وَجَمِيعِ سَخَطِكَ

"O Allah! I seek refuge in You from the declining of Your favors, from the passing of Your safety, from the suddenness of Your

---

[1] Q. 48:2.

punishment, and from all that which displeases You."[1]

2

اللَّهُمَّ إِنِّي أَعُوذُ بِكَ مِنَ الْبُخْلِ ، وَأَعُوذُ بِكَ مِنَ الْجُبْنِ ، وَأَعُوذُ بِكَ مِنْ أَنْ نُرَدَّ إِلَى أَرْذَلِ الْعُمُرِ ، وَأَعُوذُ بِكَ مِنْ فِتْنَةِ الدُّنْيَا وَعَذَابِ الْقَبْرِ

"O Allah! I seek refuge in You from miserliness, and I seek refuge in You from cowardice, and I seek refuge in You from being reverted to the senility of old age, and I seek refuge in You from the afflictions of the temporal world and the punishment in the grave."[2]

3

اَللَّهُمَّ اغْفِرْ لِي خَطِيئَتِي وَجَهْلِي ، وَإِسْرَافِي فِي أَمْرِي ، وَمَا أَنْتَ أَعْلَمُ بِهِ مِنِّي ، اَللَّهُمَّ اغْفِرْ لِي جِدِّي وَهَزْلِي وَخَطَئِي وَعَمْدِي وَكُلُّ ذَلِكَ عِنْدِي ، اَللَّهُمَّ اغْفِرْ لِي مَا قَدَّمْتُ وَمَا أَخَّرْتُ وَمَا أَسْرَرْتُ وَمَا أَعْلَنْتُ وَمَا أَنْتَ أَعْلَمُ بِهِ مِنِّي ، أَنْتَ الْمُقَدِّمُ وَالْمُؤَخِّرُ وَأَنْتَ عَلَى كُلِّ شَيْءٍ قَدِيرٌ

"O Allah, forgive me for my faults, for my ignorance, and for lack of moderation in my affairs; You are better aware of them than myself. O Allah, forgive me (any faults I committed), whether seriously or otherwise, and whether inadvertently or deliberately. All these (failings) are mine (alone). O Allah, forgive me for all that has preceded from me and all that is to come, what I have done in privacy and what I have done in the open; You are better aware of them than myself. You are the First and the Last, and You are the Omnipotent over all things."[3]

4

اللَّهُمَّ إِنِّي أَعُوذُ بِكَ مِنْ شَرِّ مَا عَمِلْتُ وَمِنْ شَرِّ مَا لَمْ أَعْمَلْ

---

[1] Authenticated by Muslim.

[2] Authenticated by al-Bukhārī.

[3] Authenticated by al-Bukhārī and Muslim.

"O Allāh, I seek refuge in You from the evil of what I have done and from the evil of what I have not done."[1]

5

اللهمَّ باعِدْ بيني وبَيْنَ خَطايايَ كَما باعَدْتَ بينَ المَشرِقِ والمَغرِبِ ، اللهمَّ نَقِّني مِنَ الخَطايا كَما يُنَقَّى الثَّوْبُ الأبْيَضُ مِنَ الدَّنَسِ ، اللهمَّ اغْسِلْ خَطايايَ بِالمَاءِ والثَّلجِ وَالبَرَدِ

"O Allāh, distance between me and my failings as you have distanced between the east and the west. O Allāh, cleanse me of my failings as a white garment is cleaned of dirt. O Allāh, wash away my failings with water, ice, and snow."[2]

6

إنَّ صَلاتي ونُسُكي ومَحْيايَ ومَماتي لِلَّهِ رَبِّ العَالَمِينَ ، لا شَريكَ لَهُ وَبِذَلِكَ أُمِرْتُ وَأنا مِنَ المُسْلِمِينَ ، اللَّهمَّ اهْدِني لأحْسَنِ الأعْمَالِ وَأحْسَنِ الأخْلاقِ ، لا يَهْدِي لأحْسَنِهَا إلَّا أنتَ وَقِني سَيِّئَ الأعْمَالِ وَسَيِّئَ الأخْلاقِ لا يَقِي سَيِّئَهَا إلَّا أنتَ

"Verily, my prayer, my sacrifice, my living, and my dying are for Allāh, the Lord of the Worlds. He has no partner. And of this, I have been commanded, and I am one of those who submit. O Allāh, guide me to the best of deeds and the best of conduct, for no one can guide to the best of them but You. And protect me from bad deeds and bad manners, for no one can protect against them but You."[3]

7

اللَّهُمَّ لَكَ الحَمْدُ أَنْتَ نُورُ السَّمَاوَاتِ وَالأرْضِ ، وَلَكَ الحَمْدُ أَنْتَ قَيِّمُ السَّمَاوَاتِ وَالأرْضِ وَلَكَ الحَمْدُ أَنْتَ رَبُّ السَّمَاوَاتِ وَالأرْضِ وَمَن فِيهِنَّ ، أَنْتَ الحَقُّ وَوَعْدُكَ الحَقُّ وَقَوْلُكَ الحَقُّ وَلِقَاؤُكَ الحَقُّ وَالجَنَّةُ حَقٌّ وَالنَّارُ حَقٌّ وَالنَّبِيُّونَ حَقٌّ وَالسَّاعَةُ

---

[1] Authenticated by Muslim.

[2] Authenticated by al-Bukhārī.

[3] Authenticated by Nasā'ī.

The Most Praised Man

حَقٌّ ، اللَّهُمَّ لَكَ أَسْلَمْتُ وَبِكَ آمَنْتُ وَعَلَيْكَ تَوَكَّلْتُ وَإِلَيْكَ أَنَبْتُ وَبِكَ خَاصَمْتُ وَإِلَيْكَ حَاكَمْتُ ، فَاغْفِرْ لِي مَا قَدَّمْتُ وَمَا أَخَّرْتُ وَمَا أَسْرَرْتُ وَمَا أَعْلَنْتُ ، أَنْتَ إِلَهِي لَا إِلَهَ إِلَّا أَنْتَ

"O Allāh, to You belongs all the praise. You are the Light of the heavens and the earth. And to You belongs all the praise. You are the Sustainer of the heavens and the earth. You are the Lord of the heavens and the earth and all therein. You are the Truth, and Your Promise is the truth, and Your Speech is the truth, and the meeting with You is the truth, and Paradise is true, and Hell is true, and all the prophets are true, and the Hour is true. O Allāh, to You I submit, and in You I believe, and upon You I put my trust, and to You I repent, and for Your sake I dispute, and to You I leave my judgment. So forgive me all that has preceded from me and all that is to come, which I did in secret, or in the open. You are my object of worship; there is no deity worthy of worship but You."[1]

---

[1] Authenticated by al-Bukhārī.

APPENDIX III: ALLEGATIONS OF SENSUALITY

Scottish orientalist William Muir wrote the following about Prophet Muhammad in 1861:

> "As a husband his fondness and devotion were entire, bordering, however, at times, upon jealousy ... At the age of twenty five he married a widow forty years old; and for five and twenty years he was a faithful husband to her alone. Yet it is remarkable that during this period were composed most of those passages of the Coran in which the black-eyed Houris, reserved for believers in Paradise, are depicted in such glowing colours."[1]

Muir expresses surprise that Muhammad (ﷺ) "wrote" about the enticing damsels in Paradise—assuming, in his view, that the Prophet was the author of the Qur'an—and yet lived a contented life for two and a half decades with Khadīja, a widow significantly older than him. What is rather remarkable is Muir's opting to reduce this to a mere "remarkable" observation and then move on without giving it the serious consideration it warrants. Does this not strongly suggest that the Qur'an is authored by God, Who reveals His message independently of Muhammad's (ﷺ) personal thoughts, desires, or circumstances?

Western writers, including Muir, who hastily levy accusations of voluptuousness against Muhammad (ﷺ) due to his later multiple marriages, conveniently overlook a critical fact: for twenty-five years, he was faithfully married to a single woman, Khadīja, who was fifteen years his senior. As Stanley Lane-Poole observed, "During all those years there was never a breath of scandal," despite the fact that "Mohammad's life will bear microscopic scrutiny."[2] He further noted, "Never was [a] husband more tender or more obliging than he showed himself to Cadijah."[3] It was only after her passing at the age of about sixty-five, when the prime of his

---

[1] Muir, *The Life of Mahomet*, vol. iv, 309.

[2] Lane-Poole, *Studies In A Mosque*, 78-79.

[3] Stubbe, *An Account of the Rise and Progress of Mahometanism*, 227.

own youth had long since passed, that he entered into other marriages.

These marriages—all but one involving widows or divorcees and nearly all past their youth—served important purposes, such as forging political alliances with tribes and offering protection to women whose husbands had died or fallen in battles. "Each of these marriages had a social or a political reason," noted Vaglieri.[1] Margoliouth similarly observed, "Mohammed's numerous marriages after Khadijah's death have been attributed by many European writers to gross passion, but they would seem to have been mainly dictated by motives of a less coarse kind. Several of his alliances were political in character, the Prophet being anxious to bind his chief followers more and more closely to himself. This was doubtless his object in marrying the daughters of Abu Bakr and Omar; while a political motive of a different sort is to be found in his alliances with the daughters of political opponents or fallen enemies."[2] G. W. Leitner reminds his readers that "to the very great credit of Muhammad, in spite of many temptations, he preserved the utmost chastity in a state of society which did not practise that virtue. Living among heathen Arabs, he remained perfectly chaste till, at the age of twenty-five, he married a woman of forty," remaining married to her alone for two and a half decades. He then confronts the critiques, "Is it not fair to assume that in the case of a man who had shown such self-control till that age, there may be reasons other than those assigned by Christian writers for his many marriages?" To him, the answer was obvious: "I believe that the real cause of his many marriages at an old age was charity, and in order to protect the widows of his persecuted followers."[3] Pickthall echoed the same view in a more emphatic manner, stating that "his other marriages were acts of charity or State policy."[4]

The Prophet ensured scrupulous fairness and care for all his wives, regardless of their age, until his death. As Stanley Lane-Poole pointed out,

---

[1] Vaglieri, *An Interpretation Of Islam*, 67.

[2] Margoliouth, *Mohammed and the Rise of Islam*, 176-77.

[3] Leitner, "Religious Systems of the World."

[4] Pickthall, "The Prophet's Character."

he "never divorced one of his wives."[1] Lane-Poole also described it as "a melancholy spectacle" that some Western writers like to swallow baseless fables about the Prophet. Thomas Carlyle would exonerate the Prophet not just from sensuality, but even from simple enjoyments of life: "Mahomet himself, after all that can be said about him, was not a sensual man. We shall err widely if we consider this man as a common voluptuary, intent mainly on base enjoyments,—nay on enjoyments of any kind."[2]

Some orientalists argue that Muhammad (ﷺ) remained married to Khadīja out of consideration for her wealth. However, a little reflection reveals the superficiality of this claim. Wealth does not suppress passion; rather, passion often drives men to reckless behaviors, such as squandering fortunes or risking legal consequences. Lane-Poole provided a sufficient rebuttal to this argument, stating, "It is hardly necessary to point out that the fear of poverty—a matter of little consequence in Arabia and at that time—would not restrain a really sensual man for five-and-twenty years; especially when it is by no means certain that Khadija, who loved him with all her heart in a motherly sort of way, would have sought a divorce for any cause soever. And this explanation leaves Mohammad's loving remembrance of his old wife unaccounted for. If her money alone had curbed him for twenty-five years, one would expect him at her death to throw off the cloak, thank Heaven for the deliverance, and enter at once upon the rake's progress. He does none of those things." Lane-Poole, therefore, categorically rejected any accusation of sensuality against the Prophet: "to say that Mohammad was a voluptuary is false ... Mohammad was not the rapacious voluptuary some have taken him for."[3] Simon H. Leeder further condemned such mischaracterizations, describing the portrayal of the Prophet as a sensualist as "the cruelest libel of which Western judgment is guilty."[4] He attributed the Prophet's marriages to "tender

---

[1] Lane-Poole, *Studies In A Mosque*, 77.

[2] Carlyle, *On Heroes,* 79.

[3] Lane-Poole, *Studies In A Mosque*, 77, 79-80.

[4] Leeder, "The Tenderness of the Prophet."

compassion" for women in need, adding that these marriages saved some "from return to idolatry, others from poverty and neglect."[1]

As for the claim made by certain Western writers—whose scholarship often fails to delve beneath the surface—that Islam is a sensuous religion, citing the permission for a man to marry up to four wives, this notion is effectively refuted by the words of one of Europe's most prominent and influential Enlightenment philosophers. Writing in 1748, Voltaire sharply criticized the superficiality of these accusers:

> "I am telling you again, you ignorant imbeciles, whom other ignoramuses have persuaded that the Mahometan religion is sensuous and voluptuous, it is not true; you have been deceived on this matter as you have been on so many others. I ask you, you canons, monks, and prelates, if you had to obey the rule of neither eating nor drinking from four in the morning until ten at night when the fast falls in month of July; if you were forbidden from playing any game of chance under pain of damnation; if wine were banned for the same reason; if you had to go on pilgrimages in burning deserts; if you were enjoined to give at least two-and-a half percent of your income to the poor; if, having grown accustomed to enjoying eighteen women at a time, fourteen of them were suddenly removed; would you, in good faith, dare call this religion sensuous?"[2]

---

[1] Ibid.

[2] Voltaire, *Mahometans*, 20-21.

BIBLIOGRAPHY

Al-'Asqalānī, Ibn Ḥajar, *al-Iṣāba fī Tamyīz al-Ṣaḥabā*, vol. i, editor's introduction, in Ṣiddīqī, Muḥammad Zubayr, *Ḥadīth Literature: Its Origin, Development & Special Features* (Cambridge: Islamic Texts Society, 1993).

Al-Azami, M. M., *The History of the Qur'anic Text from Revelation to Compilation* (Leicester: UK Islamic Academy, 2003).

Andrae, Tor, *Mohammed: The Man and His Faith*, trans. from German by Theophil Menzel (London: George Allen & Unwin Ltd, 1932).

Arberry, Arthur J., *The Holy Koran: An Introduction with Selections* (New York: The MacMillan Company, 1953).

Archer, John Clark, *The Mystical Elements of Mohammed* (New Haven: Yale University Press, 1924).

Armstrong, Karen, *Muhammad: A Prophet for Our Time* (New York: HarperOne, 2007).

Arnold, Thomas W., *The Preaching of Islam*, (London: Constable & Company Ltd., 1913).

Bayle, Peter, *An Historical and Critical Dictionary*, vol. i (London: Hunt and Clarke, 1826).

Benson, A. C., and Tatham, H. F. W., *Men of Might* (London: Edward Arnold, 1921).

Besant, Annie, *The Life and Teachings of Muhammad* (Madras: Theosophical Publishing House, 1932).

Bodley, R. V. C., *The Messenger: The Life of Mohammed* (New York: Doubleday & Company, Inc., 1946).

Boulainvilliers, Henri de, *Life of Mohammed* (London: W. Hinchliffe, 1731).

Browne, Edward G., *A Literary History of Persia* (London: T. Fisher Unwin, 1909).

Chew, Samuel C., *The Crescent and the Rose* (Oxford: Oxford University Press, 1937).

Carlyle, Thomas, *On Heroes, Hero-Worship and the Heroic in History* (New York: Frederick A. Stokes Company, 1893).

Cole, Juan, *Napoleons's Egypt: Invading the Middle East* (New York: Palgrave MacMillan, 2007).

Davenport, John, *An Apology for Mohammed and the Koran* (London: J. Davy and Sons, 1869).

Dawud, 'Abdul-Ahad, *Muhammad in the Bible* (London: Al-Kitab Publications, 1991).

Dermenghem, Emile, *The Life of Mahomet*, trans. from French by Arabella Yorke (London: George Routledge & Sons, Ltd., 1930).

Deutsch, Emanuel, *Literary Remains* (New York: Henry Holt and Company, 1874).

Dibble, R. F., *Mohammed* (New York: The Viking Press, 1926).

Dods, Marcus, *Mohammed, Buddha, and Christ* (London: Hodder and Stoughton, 1887).

Draper, John William, *A History of the Intellectual Development of Europe*, vol. i (London: George Bell and Sons, 1875).

Draycott, Gladys M., *Mahomet: Founder of Islam* (New York: Dodd, Mead & Company, 1916).

Dupuis, Jacques, *Toward a Christian Theology of Religious Pluralism*, in John V. Tolan, *Faces of Muhammad: Western Perceptions of the Prophet of Islam from the Middle Ages to Today* (Princeton: Princeton University Press, 2019).

Elmarsafy, Ziad, *The Enlightenment Qur'an: The Politics of Translation and the Construction of Islam* (Oxford: Oneworld Publications, 2009).

Freeman, Edward, *History and Conquests of the Saracens* (London: MacMillan and Co., 1876).

Gabrieli, Francesco, *Muhammad and the Conquests of Islam* (New York: McGraw-Hill Book Company, 1968).

Gibb, H. A. R., *Mohammedanism: An Historical Survey* (New York: Oxford University Press, 1962).

Gibbon, Edward, *The History of the Decline and Fall of the Roman Empire*, vol. iv (Philadelphia: Claxton, Remsen & Haffelfinger, 1871).

———. *The History of the Decline and Fall of the Roman Empire*, vol. v (Philadelphia: Claxton, Remsen & Haffelfinger, 1873).

Goethe, *Poems of the West and the East*, in Tolan, *Faces of Muhammad: Western Perceptions of the Prophet of Islam from the Middle Ages to Today* (Princeton: Princeton University Press, 2019).

Goldziher, Ignac, *Tagebuch*, in John V. Tolan, *Faces of Muhammad: Western Perceptions of the Prophet of Islam from the Middle Ages to Today* (Princeton: Princeton University Press, 2019).

Guillaume, Alfred, *The Traditions of Islam* (Oxford: The Clarendon Press, Oxford, 1924).

Hallaq, Wael B., *The Impossible State: Islam, Politics, and Modernity's Predicament* (New York: Columbia University Press, 2013).

Haestens, Henrick van, *Apocalypsis or the Revelation of Notorious Advances of Heretic*, trans. from Latin by John Davies (London: John Saywell, 1658).

Hart, Michael H., *The 100: A Ranking of the Most Influential Persons in History* (New York: Citadel Press, 1989).

Headley, Rowland Allanson-Winn, *A Western Awakening to Islam* (London: J. S. Phillips, 1914).

———. "Self-Control", in *Islamic Review*, May, 1914.

———. "Simplicity of Faith", in *Islamic Review*, June, 1918.

———. "What Is Dogma", in *Islamic Review*, November, 1914.

Hitti, Phillip K., *Islam: A Way of Life* (Indiana: Renergy/Gateway, Inc., 1970).

———. *History of the Arabs* (London: MacMillan Education Ltd, 1970).

Hogarth, David Geroge, *Arabia* (Oxford: The Clarendon Press, 1922).

Hughes, Thomas Patrick, *Notes on Muhammadanism* (London: Wm. H. Allen & Co, 1877).

Hurgronje, C. Snouck, *Mohammedanism* (New York: G. P. Putna's Sons, 1916).

Irving, Washington, *Life of Mahomet* (London: George Bell & Sons, 1874).

Kremer, Alfred von, *Contributions to the History of Islamic Civilization*, trans. by S. Khuda Bukhsh (Calcutta: Thacker, Spink & Co, 1905).

_____. *The Orient under the Caliphs*, trans. by S. Khuda Bukhsh (Philadelphia: Porcupine Press, 1920).

Koelle, S. W., *Mohammed and Mohammedanism* (London: Rivingtons, 1889).

Lamartine, Alphonse de, *History of Turkey*, trans. from French by unnamed, vol. i (New York: D. Appleton & Company, 1855).

Lane-Poole, *Studies In A Mosque* (London: Eden, Remington & Co., 1893).

Laurens, Henri, *L'Exp´edition d'Egypte*, in John V. Tolan, *Faces of Muhammad: Western Perceptions of the Prophet of Islam from the Middle Ages to Today* (Princeton: Princeton University Press, 2019).

Leeder, Simon. H., "The Tenderness of the Prophet", in *Islamic Review*, January, 1917.

Lefroy, G. A., *Mankind and the Church* (London: Longmans, Green, and Company, 1907).

Leitner, Gottlieb W., "Religious Systems of the World", a delivered lecture that was published as "Muhammadnism" in *Islamic Review*, August, 1914.

Leon, Henry M., "Islam: A Rational Faith", in *Islamic Review*, January, 1915.

Leonard, Arthur Glyn, *Islam: Her Moral and Spiritual Value* (London: Luzac & Co., 1909).

Lings, Martin, *Muhammad: His Life Based on the Earliest Sources* (Vermont: Inner Traditions, 2006).

MacCambridge, Jeffrey, *Dante and Islam: A Study of the Eastern Influences in the Divine Comedy* (Indiana: Indiana University, 2016).

Margoliouth, Davis S., *Lectures on Arabic Historians* (Calcutta: University of Calcutta, 1930).

_____. *Mohammed and the Rise of Islam* (New York: The Knickerbocker Press, 1905).

Masserman, Jules, "Who Were History's Great Leaders?", *Time Magazine*, (July 15, 1974).

Massignon, Louis, *Essay on the Origins of the Technical Language of Islamic Mysticism*, trans. from French by Benjamin Clarke (Indiana: University of Notre Dame Press, 1997).

Maurice, Frederick, *Religions of the World* (Boston: Gould and Lincoln, 1854).

Michener, James A., "Islam: The Misunderstood Religion", in *Reader's Digest*, May 1955.

Michon, Jean Hippolyte, *Voyage religieux en Orient,* in Emile Dermenghem, *The Life of Mahomet,* trans. from French by Arabella Yorke (London: George Routledge & Sons, Ltd., 1930).

Miller, John C. (Ed.), *The Works of Henry Smith,* vol. ii (Edinburg: James Nichol, 1867).

Mills, Charles, *An History of Muhammedanism* (London: Black, Kingsbury, Parbury, and Allen, 1818).

Mommsen, Katharina, *Goethe and the Poets of Arabia*, trans. Michael Metzger (Rochester: Camden House, 2014) in John V. Tolan, *Faces of Muhammad: Western Perceptions of the Prophet of Islam from the Middle Ages to Today* (Princeton: Princeton University Press, 2019).

_____. "Goethe's Relationship to Islam" in *The Muslim*, vol. 4, no. 3, January, 1967.

Montgomery, James A., *Religions of the Past and Present* (Philadelphia: J. B. Lippincott Company, 1918).

Muir, William, *The Life of Mahomet and History of Islam*, vol. i (London: Smith, Elder & Co, 1857).

_____. *The Life of Mahomet and History of Islam*, vol. ii (London: Smith, Elder & Co, 1858).

_____. *The Life of Mahomet and History of Islam*, vol. vi (London: Smith, Elder & Co, 1861).

Noldeke, Theodor, *The History of the Qur'an*, trans. Wolfgang H. Behn (Leiden: BRILL, 2013).

Parkinson, John, "Muhammad As Social Reformer", in *Islamic Review*, January 1917.

Perceval, Armand-Pierre Caussin de, *Essai sur l'histoire des Arabes*, in Snouck Hurgronje, *Mohammedanism* (New York: G. P. Putna's Sons, 1916).

PEW, *The Future of World Religions: Population Growth Projections, 2010-2050* (Washington, DC: PEW Research Center, 2015).

Pickthall, Marmaduke, "A Sermon", in *Islamic Review*, February, 1920.

_____. "Address on the Prophet's Birthday", in *Islamic Review*, March, 1917.

_____. "Islam and Progress", in *Islamic Review*, August, 1917.

_____. "The Holly Prophet As An Example", in *Islamic Review*, December, 1917.

_____. "The Prophet's Character", in *Islamic Review*, December, 1918.

_____. "The Prophet's Gratitude", in *Islamic Review*, January, 1917.

Prideaux, Humphrey, *The True Nature of Imposture Fully Displayed in the Life of Mahomet* (London: E. Curll, J. Hooke, W. Mears and F. Clay, 1723).

Raleigh, Walter, *The History of the Worlds: The Second Part* (London: John Clark, 1753).

Rao, K. S. Ramakrishna, *Muhammad: the Prophet of Islam* (Riyadh: World Assembly of Muslim Youth, 1989).

Reade, Winwood, *Martyrdom of Man* (London: Trubner & Co, 1872).

Renan, Ernest, *Studies in Religious History* (London: Richard Bentley and Son, 1886).

Rodwell, John M., *The Koran Translated from the Arabic* (New York: J. M. Dend & Sons, 1909).

Rousseau, Jean-Jacques, *The Social Contract & Discourse*, trans. G. D. H. Cole (London: J. M. Dent & Sons, 1920).

Sale, George, *The Koran and Sales's Preliminary Discourse*, ed. Edward Ross (London: Frederick Warne and Co., c. 1877).

Say, Jean-Honoré Horace and Boissy, Louis Laus de, *Bonaparte au Caire*, in Juan Cole, *Napoleons's Egypt: Invading the Middle East* (New York: Palgrave MacMillan, 2007).

Schimmel, Annemarie, *And Muhammad Is His Messenger* (Lahore: Vanguard Books Ltd., 1987).

Semiond, Tristan, *Victor Hugo and his poetry against Islamophobia*, FUNCI, 2/17/2021, https://funci.org/victor-hugo-and-his-poetry-against-islamophobia/?lang=en, accessed 11/16/2024.

Ṣiddīqī, Muḥammad Zubayr, *Ḥadith Literature: Its Origin Development & Special Features* (Cambridge: Islamic Texts Society, 1993).

Smith, R. Bosworth, *Mohammed and Mohammedanism* (London: Smith, Elder & Company, 1874).

Stanley, Arthur Penrhyn, *Lectures on the History of the Eastern Church* (London: John Murray, 1862).

Stubbe, Henry and Shairani, Hafiz (Ed.), *An Account of the Rise and Progress of Mahometanism* (London: Luzac & Company, 1911).

Taylor, Isaac, "What Islam Can Do", in *Islamic Review*, June, 1915.

Tisdall, William St. Clair, *The Religion of the Crescent* (London: Society for Promoting Christian Knowledge, 1910).

Tolan, John V., *Faces of Muhammad: Western Perceptions of the Prophet of Islam from the Middle Ages to Today* (Princeton: Princeton University Press, 2019).

Toland, John, *Nazarenus, or Jewish, Gentile, and Mahometal Christianity* (London: J. Brotherton, J. Roberts, and A. Dodd, 1718).

Toynbee, Arnold J., *A Study of History*, vol. iii (London: Oxford University Press, 1935).

Vaglieri, Laura, *An Interpretation Of Islam* (Washington, DC: The American Fazl Mosque, 1958).

Voltaire, *An Essay on Universal History, the Manners, and Spirit of the Nations*, vol. 1, trans. Mr. Nugent (London: J. Nourse, 1759).

_____. *Essai sur les moeurs*, vol. i, in Ziad Elmarsafy, *The Enlightenment Qur'an: The Politics of Translation and the Construction of Islam*.

_____. *Mahometans*, in Ziyad Elmarsafy, *The Enlightenment Qur'an: The Politics of Translation and the Construction of Islam*.

Ward, Keith, "Blogging Theology at 200K - looking back over the past 2 years." *YouTube*, uploaded by Blogging Theology, 10/15/2023, www.youtube.com/watch?app=desktop&v=OZdXZzoh2nU.

Watt, W. Montgomery, *A Christian Faith for Today* (London: Routledge, 2002).

_____. *Muhammad At Mecca* (Oxford: Oxford University Press, 1960).

_____. *Muhammad At Medina* (Oxford: Oxford University Press, 1956).

Weil, Gustav, *A History of Islamic Peoples*, trans. from German by S. Khuda Bukhsh (Calcutta: The University of Calcutta, 1914).

_____. *Mohammed der Prophet, sein Leben und siene Lehre*, in Snouck Hurgronje, *Mohammedanism*, (New York: G. P. Putna's Sons, 1916).

White, Joseph, *Sermons Preached Before the University of Oxford* (Boston: William Greenough, 1793).

Whymant, Neville J., "The Philosophy of War in Comparative Religion," in *Islamic Review*, Nov, 1914.

Wright, Dudely, "Is Man Sinful By Nature?", in *Islamic Review*, December, 1916.

_____. "Islam: The Faith of Progress", in *Islamic Review*, June, 1919.

SUGGESTED RESOURCES

Muhammad: His Life Based on the Earliest Sources, by Martin Lings: Any divine message from God is invariably linked to the person who acted as its messenger, for he must be a role model for humanity with an impeccable character. This title by Martin Lings is based on authentic sources and the best biography of the Prophet of Islam in the English language. Lings was an expert in both English and Arabic—he taught English classics and Shakespeare—and thus was particularly adept for the task. The result is a biography of the Prophet in a masterfully eloquent narrative that almost brings him to life in the mind of the reader.

A Translation and Commentary of Riyadh as-Salihin: "God is compassionate and loves compassion," "The one who does not thank people, does not thank God," "Visit the sick, feed the hungry and free the captives," "Every act of goodness is charity," "The best among you is he who has the best manners." These are a sample from the words uttered by Prophet Muhammad (ﷺ) whose teachings and gentle manners transformed, in a mere 23 years, an utterly lawless people steeped in darkness into a most law-abiding and spiritual generation ever known in history. This book is an extraordinary collection of some of the sayings of the Prophet and a window into his mind about the kind of reform he initiated in people's characters and manners. It covers many aspects of life including obedience to God, compassion, empathy, care, justice, love, truthfulness, respect, brotherhood, etc. Originally compiled in the 13th century, this work has continued to illuminate the hearts and minds of millions in every generation across the globe. We recommend the edition by *Muslims at Work Publications* for quality of translation and format.

The Meaning of the Holy Qur'an, trans. and commentary by Abdullah Yusuf Ali: The majesty and eloquence of the original Arabic text can never be fully conveyed in another language. Nonetheless, even an English reader would feel the power of the divine revelation through this translation by Abdullah Yusuf Ali. Read, for example, sūrah *Yusuf* (Joseph) or sūrah *Maryam* (Mary). One might be surprised at discovering a type of literary work he/she has never known before. The heart might actually be shaken by the power of the divine speech, so characteristically distinct from human speech. There are many editions available of Ali's translation. We recommend the edition by Amana Publications for quality of format.

The Clear Quran With Arabic Text, trans. by Mustafa Khattab: If Yusuf Ali's translation comes across as too classy, then this translation is recommended as it is written in simpler English. It also provides commentary and context which is helpful for people not familiar with Islam and the relevant historical background.

Towards Understanding Islam, by Abul A'lā Mawdūdī, edited by Yahiya Emerick: This short book is a brief but comprehensive introduction to Islam. Well-written with a simple language, this popular book has been translated into over a dozen languages.

Islam and the Destiny of Man, by Gai Eaton: A classic work, and his best, by Gai Eaton, a British diplomat who discovered faith and spirituality in Islam around the middle of the last century. His expositions of Islamic tenants are profound that have attracted many Westerners over the last half a century to appreciate the beauty and spirituality of Islam.

www.ingramcontent.com/pod-product-compliance
Lightning Source LLC
Chambersburg PA
CBHW030511080526
44586CB00011B/149